Grotowski, Women, and Contemporary Performance

As the first examination of women's foremost contributions to Jerzy Grotowski's cross-cultural investigation of performance, this book complements and broadens existing literature by offering a more diverse and inclusive re-assessment of Grotowski's legacy, thereby probing its significance for contemporary performance practice and research. Although the particularly strenuous physical training emblematic of Grotowski's approach is not gender specific, it has historically been associated with a masculine conception of the performer incarnated by Ryszard Cieslak in The Constant Prince, thus overlooking the work of Rena Mirecka, Maja Komorowska, and Elizabeth Albahaca, to name only the leading women performers identified with the period of theatre productions. This book therefore redresses this imbalance by focusing on key women from different cultures and generations who share a direct connection to Grotowski's legacy while clearly asserting their artistic independence. These women actively participated in all phases of the Polish director's practical research, and continue to play a vital role in today's transnational community of artists whose work reflects Grotowski's enduring influence. Grounding her inquiry in her embodied research and on-going collaboration with these artists, Magnat explores the interrelation of creativity, embodiment, agency, and spirituality within their performing and teaching. Building on current debates in performance studies, experimental ethnography, Indigenous research, global gender studies, and ecocriticism, the author maps out interconnections between these women's distinct artistic practices across the boundaries that once delineated Grotowski's theatrical and post-theatrical experiments.

Virginie Magnat is Associate Professor of Performance in the Faculty of Creative and Critical Studies at the University of British Columbia, Canada.

Routledge Advances in Theatre and Performance Studies

1. **Theatre and Postcolonial Desires**
   Awam Amkpa

2. **Brecht and Critical Theory**
   Dialectics and Contemporary Aesthetics
   Sean Carney

3. **Science and the Stanislavsky Tradition of Acting**
   Jonathan Pitches

4. **Performance and Cognition**
   Theatre Studies and the Cognitive Turn
   Edited by Bruce McConachie and F. Elizabeth Hart

5. **Theatre and Performance in Digital Culture**
   From Simulation to Embeddedness
   Matthew Causey

6. **The Politics of New Media Theatre**
   Life®™
   Gabriella Giannachi

7. **Ritual and Event**
   Interdisciplinary Perspectives
   Edited by Mark Franko

8. **Memory, Allegory, and Testimony in South American Theater**
   Upstaging Dictatorship
   Ana Elena Puga

9. **Crossing Cultural Borders Through the Actor's Work**
   Foreign Bodies of Knowledge
   Cláudia Tatinge Nascimento

10. **Movement Training for the Modern Actor**
    Mark Evans

11. **The Politics of American Actor Training**
    Edited by Ellen Margolis and Lissa Tyler Renaud

12. **Performing Embodiment in Samuel Beckett's Drama**
    Anna McMullan

13. **The Provocation of the Senses in Contemporary Theatre**
    Stephen Di Benedetto

14. **Ecology and Environment in European Drama**
    Downing Cless

15. **Global Ibsen**
    Performing Multiple Modernities
    Edited by Erika Fischer-Lichte, Barbara Gronau, and Christel Weiler

16. **The Theatre of the Bauhaus**
    The Modern and Postmodern Stage of Oskar Schlemmer
    Melissa Trimingham

17. **Feminist Visions and Queer Futures in Postcolonial Drama**
    Community, Kinship, and Citizenship
    Kanika Batra

18. **Nineteenth-Century Theatre and the Imperial Encounter**
    Marty Gould

19 **The Theatre of Richard Maxwell and the New York City Players**
Sarah Gorman

20 **Shakespeare, Theatre and Time**
Matthew D. Wagner

21 **Political and Protest Theatre after 9/11**
Patriotic Dissent
Edited by Jenny Spencer

22 **Religion, Theatre, and Performance**
Acts of Faith
Edited by Lance Gharavi

23 **Adapting Chekhov**
The Text and its Mutations
Edited by J. Douglas Clayton and Yana Meerzon

24 **Performance and the Politics of Space**
Theatre and Topology
Edited by Erika Fischer-Lichte and Benjamin Wihstutz

25 **Music and Gender in English Renaissance Drama**
Katrine K. Wong

26 **The Unwritten Grotowski**
Theory and Practice of the Encounter
Kris Salata

27 **Dramas of the Past on the Twentieth-Century Stage**
In History's Wings
Alex Feldman

28 **Performance, Identity and the Neo-Political Subject**
Edited by Matthew Causey and Fintan Walsh

29 **Theatre Translation in Performance**
Edited by Silvia Bigliazzi, Peter Kofler, and Paola Ambrosi

30 **Translation and Adaptation in Theatre and Film**
Edited by Katja Krebs

31 **Grotowski, Women, and Contemporary Performance**
Meetings with Remarkable Women
Virginie Magnat

Figure 1.1 *Meetings with Remarkable Women* poster by Piotr Gardecki.

Grotowski, Women, and Contemporary Performance
Meetings with Remarkable Women

Virginie Magnat

NEW YORK LONDON

First published 2014
by Routledge
711 Third Avenue, New York, NY 10017

Simultaneously published in the UK
by Routledge
2 Park Square, Milton Park, Abingdon, Oxfordshire OX14 4RN

First issued in paperback 2014

*Routledge is an imprint of the Taylor and Francis Group,
an informa business*

© 2014 Taylor & Francis

The right of Virginie Magnat to be identified as author of this work has been asserted by her in accordance with sections 77 and 78 of the Copyright, Designs and Patents Act 1988.

All rights reserved. No part of this book may be reprinted or reproduced or utilised in any form or by any electronic, mechanical, or other means, now known or hereafter invented, including photocopying and recording, or in any information storage or retrieval system, without permission in writing from the publishers.

Trademark Notice: Product or corporate names may be trademarks or registered trademarks, and are used only for identification and explanation without intent to infringe.

Library of Congress Cataloging-in-Publication Data
Magnat, Virginie.
  Grotowski, women, and contemporary performance : meetings with remarkable women / by Virginie Magnat.
    pages cm. — (Routledge advances in theatre and performance studies ; 31)
  Includes bibliographical references and index.
  1. Women in the performing arts.   2. Feminism and theater.
3. Experimental theater.   4. Grotowski, Jerzy, 1933–1999—Criticism and interpretation.   I. Title.
  PN1590.W64.M2262 2013
  792.082—dc23
                                              2013006127

ISBN 978-0-415-81359-4 (hbk)
ISBN 978-1-138-92214-3 (pbk)
ISBN 978-0-203-06806-9 (ebk)

Typeset in Sabon
by IBT Global.

To remarkable women everywhere,
and to my partner, family, and friends
for their love, spirit, and unconditional support.

Contents

Figures xiii
Acknowledgments xv

1 Research Context, Interdisciplinary Methodology, Fieldwork Objectives 1

2 Practice: Mapping Out Interconnections 57

3 Towards an Ecology of the Body-in-Life 113

4 At the Crossroads of Theatre, Active Culture, and Ritual Arts 157

Afterword 207

Notes 211
References 213
Index 221

Figures

1.1	*Meetings with Remarkable Women* poster by Piotr Gardecki.	v
1.2	Ludwik Flaszen with the author at the Sorbonne, "L'Année Grotowski à Paris" conference, October 2009.	49
1.3	Group photo. *Meetings with Remarkable Women*, Grotowski Institute, Wroclaw, Poland, August 2009.	51
2.1	Rena Mirecka teaching the *plastiques*.	76
2.2	Maja Komorowska.	81
2.3	Elizabeth Albahaca.	88
2.4	Maria Fernanda Ferro in *The Night of Molly Bloom* directed by Elizabeth Albahaca.	92
2.5	Ewa Benesz in Sardinia.	96
2.6	Katharina Seyferth rehearsing her solo piece *Rooms* for the *Meetings with Remarkable Women* Festival.	100
2.7	Iben Nagel Rasmussen teaching the Wind Dance.	109
2.8	Iben Nagel Rasmussen rehearsing *Ester's Book* for the *Meetings with Remarkable Women* Festival.	111
3.1	Rena Mirecka in Brzezinka.	119
3.2	Ang Gey Pin rehearsing *Feast of You Shen* for the *Meetings with Remarkable Women* Festival.	140
3.3	Ang Gey Pin leading her work session.	142
3.4	Dora Arreola rehearsing *I, Rumores Silencio* for the *Meetings with Remarkable Women* Festival.	149
3.5	Dora Arreola leading her work session.	151
3.6	Forest of Brzezinka.	154
4.1	Ewa Benesz under *carrubo* tree.	175
4.2	Katharina Seyferth leading The Vigils.	179
4.3	Meeting in Sardinia. Italy, August 2010.	182

Acknowledgments

I am deeply grateful to the women who participated in my project: thank you for your trust, generosity, and energy; thank you for all that you have shared with me through your teaching, artistic work, and creative research; and thank you for challenging me to keep learning and growing. I am also thankful to my teachers Caroline (Boué) Erhardt and Bertrand Quoniam, and their teachers Ludwik Flaszen and Zygmunt Molik, as well as Jerzy Grotowski.

The fieldwork I conducted in Canada, Poland, Italy, France, and Denmark from 2008 to 2012 was supported by a Standard Research Grant and a Research/Creation in Fine Arts Grant from the Social Sciences and Humanities Research Council of Canada (SSHRC), and I would like to thank the selection committee members and anonymous reviewers who assessed my grant applications and decided that this project should be funded. Receiving such generous funding has enabled me to support the teaching and creative research of participating artists; hire professional photographers and videographers to document the work of these artists; invite three graduate and two undergraduate students to participate in, and contribute to, my fieldwork; provide two of my graduate students with year-long research assistantships; and travel to international conferences to discuss my project at different stages of its development. I would also like to thank Wisdom Tettey, the Dean of the Faculty of Creative and Critical Studies at the University of British Columbia's Okanagan Campus, for granting me a study leave to complete my manuscript and the companion documentary film series featured on the Routledge Performance Archive.

I am extremely grateful to all my research collaborators and would especially like to thank the Grotowski Institute in Wroclaw, Poland, including Grzegorz Ziolkowski, who supported my project at the critical time of its inception, as well as Jaroslaw Fret and Dariusz Kosinski. I received the invaluable assistance of Stefania Gardecka, who was the Laboratory Theatre's main administrator, and I greatly benefited from her expertise, dedication, and wisdom. I would also like to thank Justyna Rodzinska-Nair for her professionalism, enthusiasm, and resourcefulness, as well as

xvi *Acknowledgments*

her colleagues Monika Blige, Adela Karsznia, and Izabela Młynarz, who made me feel at home at the Grotowski Institute. In 2011–12, I discovered the hospitality of Eugenio Barba's Odin Teatret and am thankful for this experience.

I would like to acknowledge the curators of "2009, Year of Grotowski" who invited me to present my project at the international conferences they organized in Krakow, New York, Paris, and Canterbury, and would like to thank all my research allies within the academy in North America and Europe for their continued support and advice, from the grant-writing phase to the book-proposal phase: please know that your scholarship in the humanities, fine arts, and social sciences has been a great source of insight and inspiration.

I would like to thank my Routledge editors for all their support and guidance. I am also deeply grateful to Robert Ornellas for his collaboration throughout the editing, copy-editing, and proof-reading process. *Dziękuję* to the editors of *Didaskalia* for granting me the permission to refer to my series of articles on Grotowski's Collège de France lectures which they published in Polish between 2004 and 2007. I am also thankful to the editors of *Canadian Theatre Review*, Ashgate, and *Anthropologica*, for granting me the permission to refer to the interdisciplinary perspective on embodied research which I first discussed in the following articles: "Can Research Become Ceremony? Performance Ethnography and Indigenous Epistemologies" in *Canadian Theatre Review* (2012); the book chapter "Productive Disorientation, or the Ups and Downs of Embodied Research" in *Researching amongst Elites: Challenges and Opportunities in Studying Up* (Ashgate 2012); and "Conducting Embodied Research at the Intersection of Performance Studies, Experimental Ethnography, and Indigenous Methodologies" in *Anthropologica* (2011). Finally, I would like to extend a special *mahalo* to Manulani Aluli Meyer for generously sharing with me her text "The Context Within: My Journey into Research" prior to its publication in *Indigenous Pathways in Social Research* (Left Coast Press, 2013).

1 Research Context, Interdisciplinary Methodology, Fieldwork Objectives

Building upon her important re-evaluation of Konstantin Stanislavsky's System, Sharon Marie Carnicke provocatively posits actress and director Maria Knebel as the Russian director's true heir. Given that canonical theatre history has long upheld and at times revered Stanislavsky as the father of psychological realism, Carnicke's bold endorsement of Knebel interrupts patrilineal transmission processes that safeguard the legacies of great male pioneers. She provides solid evidence for her provocation by grounding it in Knebel's unique insight into the final period of Stanislavsky's work, in which she participated by serving as his assistant, and argues that although Knebel's interpretation of Stanislavsky's ultimate contribution to actor training was both more accurate and more sophisticated than that of her rival Mikhail Kedrov, the latter was nevertheless adopted as the official version that came to be known as the Method of Physical Actions. Carnicke historicizes the tension between Knebel and Kedrov over Stanislavsky's legacy by placing their divergent views in the political context of Stalinist Russia. Since both Knebel and Kedrov assisted Stanislavsky in the last phase of his research and drew from this experience to develop their respective directing careers, Carnicke remarks that "she, as easily as he, could have called herself Stanislavsky's heir" ("Stanislavsky and Politics: Active Analysis and the American Legacy of Soviet Oppression" 20).

However, Knebel did not share Kedrov's loyalty to Soviet cultural policies, and Carnicke suggests that by foregrounding physicality over psychology within Stanislavsky's final expression of his System, Kedrov's conception of the Method of Physical Actions expediently aligned Stanislavsky's approach with the Soviet regime's Marxist materialist expectations. In contrast, Knebel's understanding of what she named Active Analysis reflected "the full psychophysical range in the technique" (22) and engaged the actor's entire being—body, mind, and spirit. In "The Knebel Technique: Active Analysis in Practice," Carnicke observes: "Not only did this approach defy atheistic Marxist philosophy by embracing spiritual dimensions in art, but Knebel's term for the rehearsal process stressed the actor's holistic usage of body through 'action' and mind through 'analysis'" (104). As reported by Vasili Toporkov in *Stanislavsky in Rehearsal*, the Moscow Art Theatre director required from actors that they gain an understanding of the overall structure of a play by exploring on their feet, by means of improvisation, the actions and counteractions of dramatic conflict within each scene. Since Stalin's ruthless enforcement of Socialist Realism in the arts "had made conflict itself politically subversive" ("Stanislavsky and Politics" 22), Knebel's holistic approach and her view of Active Analysis as a "gymnastic for both body and soul" (23) became ideologically suspect and were superseded by Kedrov's more politically correct endorsement of the Method of Physical Actions.

In the post-Stalinist era, however, Knebel's importance as one of Stanislavsky's close collaborators and the significance of her artistic contribution became increasingly recognized by major Russian theatre practitioners. The prominent theatre director Anatoli Vassiliev, for example, claims both Knebel and Jerzy Grotowski as major influences, and has edited Knebel's writings in a book available in French under the title *L'Analyse-action*. Knebel nevertheless remains largely unknown in North America, and although she authored six books during her lifetime, Carnicke deplores the fact that none have appeared in English translation. This leads her to infer that the confusion around Stanislavsky's legacy "lies as much in gender politics as in Stalinist repression" ("Stanislavsky and Politics" 25). She concludes that, whereas literary critics have "sought to bring new visibility to female writers of the past" by questioning the process of canon formation that tends to privilege male authors in the academy, "a comparable process of selectivity" (25) continues to prevail in the theatrical canon, as evidenced by Knebel's conspicuous absence from official theatre history.

WOMEN AS ILLEGITIMATE DAUGHTERS: THE CONTESTED LEGACIES OF STANISLAVSKY AND GROTOWSKI

Carnicke's argument is particularly relevant to my research project for three main reasons. Firstly, Grotowski stated in several of his major talks, including his final Collège de France lectures, that he had always considered Stanislavsky to be his artistic ancestor, yet that it was only the final period of Stanislavsky's work which had deeply interested him and served as a foundation for his own approach. *Stanislavsky in Rehearsal*, the book in which Toporkov offers an account of his experience of Stanislavsky's last studio, was a key reference for Grotowski, and he strongly recommended this text to the MFA Acting and Directing students attending his Master Class at the University of California, Irvine, where he developed his Objective Drama Project in the 1980s.[1] Toporkov, as noted by Carnicke, referred to the Method of Physical Actions in his detailed description of Stanislavsky's experiments, and in his preface to *Stanislavsky in Rehearsal*, Jean Benedetti remarks that Toporkov's insights led Brecht himself to reconsider his harsh critique of Stanislavsky. Was Brecht's change of heart induced by the Marxist tenor of Toporkov's perspective, influenced as it may have been by Kedrov's authority as Stanislavsky's official heir? Or did Toporkov's description of

Stanislavsky's unprecedented experiments convince Brecht that the Russian director had undeniably touched upon something of substance, as later intuited by Grotowski? These are some of the questions I will address within the particular context of my reassessment of Grotowski's legacy in terms of its relevance for contemporary performance.

Secondly, Carnicke suggests that "in postmodern America, the historical paragon (still often taken for Stanislavsky the Seeker) seems a tarnished statue of a hero, whose thinking registers as too patriarchal for feminist actors and theorists, too essentialist for scholars of performance studies, and too absolute for contemporary theatre artists in a multi-cultural and unsure age" ("Stanislavsky and Politics" 25–26). Interestingly, these remarks are also applicable to the various academic constructions and deconstructions of the figure of Grotowski—which include but are not limited to Modernist Genius, Avant-Garde Elitist, Great Reformer, Trickster, and Charlatan—either corroborating or discounting the competing interpretations of the nature, function, and value of what Grotowski proposed in practice—a Polish version of Artaud's Theatre of Cruelty, a Western attempt at reinventing ritual and tradition, an outmoded counterculture movement, or even perhaps a dangerous sect.

Carnicke imbues the "tarnished statue of a hero" with new life through her documentation and analysis of the creative research which the founder of the Moscow Art Theatre pursued in spite of the oppressive regime's effort to control his work. Drawing from her detailed examination of Stanislavsky's interest in Yoga and Hinduism in *Stanislavsky in Focus*, Carnicke challenges us to reconsider his contribution to actor training in light of "his psychophysical experimentation with yoga and his interest in modern dance," which he pursued in his various studios; she asks that we take seriously his "probing of the actor's dual consciousness," which she suggests may be of particular interest to "those who try to capture the fragmented nature of the contemporary world"; and she points out that the important insights into "the cognitive processes of performance" which he gained from artistic practice are currently under investigation by cognitive scientists ("Stanislavsky and Politics" 26). Carnicke's refreshing investigation of Stanislavsky's lesser known yet arguably most fertile experiments makes it possible to perceive the latter as Stanislavsky's personal way of resisting Soviet oppression and testing the limits of his own approach. By choosing to work on *Tartuffe* with the actors of his last studio, Stanislavsky challenged them to cross the boundaries of psychological realism to explore a heightened reality which was more energetically demanding for the ensemble and resulted in a psychophysically charged sense of immediacy. In the last years of his life, Stanislavsky therefore seems to have taken a giant step into the future, anticipating what would later be known as improvisation techniques, physically-based performance, collaborative creation, and devising.

Given that Grotowski claims Stanislavsky as his ancestor, Carnicke's critical re-evaluation of Stanislavsky calls for an examination of Grotowski's own interpretation of Stanislavsky's experimental work identified by

4 *Grotowski, Women, and Contemporary Performance*

Knebel as Active Analysis and described by Toporkov in his book as the Method of Physical Actions. Since Grotowski considered that Stanislavsky's final experiments provided him with guiding principles for his own work, I will use the Stanislavsky-Grotowski lineage as an entry point into the work of Grotowski's collaborators, and examine how the artists involved in my project have integrated, adapted, and/or transformed such principles in their creative research and teaching.

Thirdly, and most importantly, Carnicke's argument is relevant to my research because women's participation in and contribution to Grotowski's cross-cultural investigation of performance has similarly been omitted from theatre history. In *The Grotowski Sourcebook*, Richard Schechner points to the small number of women among Grotowski's main representatives and their virtual absence among his official inheritors. Indeed, Grotowski's legacy seems so unquestionably linked to the men whom he designated as his heirs that my decision to focus exclusively on women may very well appear to theatre historians as radical as Carnicke's pledge to canonize Knebel, Stanislavsky's 'illegitimate' daughter. I must nevertheless stress one important distinction: I am not claiming that the women whose work I am exploring are Grotowski's 'true heirs.'

Instead, I question the necessity to legitimize the artistic achievements of women by tracing their lineage to an influential male innovator as the proof that they are worthy of being included in the canon. This is reflected in the title of my research project, *Meetings with Remarkable Women*, which appropriates and revises the title of Peter Brook's film *Meetings with Remarkable Men* based on the book by G.I. Gurdjieff, whose spiritual teachings influenced both Brook and Grotowski. My project subtitle *Tu es la fille de quelqu'un* (You Are Someone's Daughter) featured on the poster created by Polish visual artist Piotr Gardecki (Figure 1.1, page v) similarly reconfigures the title of Grotowski's 1985 talk "Tu es le fils de quelqu'un" ("You Are Someone's Son"). These appropriations and revisions have enabled me to challenge the latent assumption that the legacy of innovators such as Stanislavsky, Brook, Gurdjieff, and Grotowski must be channelled through highly selective patrilineal transmission processes to protect them from contamination by misguided applications and unwarranted interpretations.

It is important to note, however, that while such an assumption does appear to underscore dominant cultural constructions of intellectual and artistic lineage, its impact on such unconventional individuals remains debatable. Gurdjieff's decision to entrust Jeanne de Salzmann with the transmission of his research and the flourishing directorial career of Irina Brook are cases in point. As for Stanislavsky and Grotowski, the former chose a stage name derived from his admiration for the ballerina Stanislavskaia and was later influenced by the work of Isadora Duncan, while the latter's role model as a young director was Halina Gallowa, a key member of the Reduta Theatre who was Grotowski's teacher at the Krakow State Theatre Academy.

Moreover, Grotowski's collaborators always included women: as evidenced by on-going transmission processes, personal testimonies, and unpublished archival sources, as well as books, articles, and interviews unavailable in English, several generations of women from different cultures and traditions actively participated in all phases of Grotowski's practical research, and continue to play a vital role in today's transnational community of artists whose work reflects Grotowski's enduring influence. While they acknowledge and value this influence, these artists clearly assert their creative independence and define in their own ways their relationship to the Polish director's legacy. Consequently, their work often crosses and blurs boundaries which, in Grotowski's terminology, delineated the theatrical and post-theatrical periods, from "Art as presentation" to "Art as vehicle."

By focusing on key women from different generations who share a direct connection to Grotowski's work, I therefore propose a counter-perspective conducive to the type of re-evaluation advocated by Carnicke but not predicated on claims of faithfulness to a prestigious lineage. This is, of course, a delicate balancing act since the relevance of Grotowski's approach for contemporary performance practice cannot be underestimated and playing down the significance of his legacy can only be counterproductive. I am therefore grateful to the anonymous reviewers who argued on my behalf that while it was desirable that Grotowski's name be included in the title of this book, signaling that his approach served as a foundation, point of departure, and provocation for many of his collaborators, the main objective is to foreground the diversity of women's current artistic practices, the directions in which they have developed their creative research, and the modes of transmission through which they share their embodied knowledge.

Since my own Grotowski-based performance training is rooted in the transmission processes my project investigates, one of the ways of positioning myself within my research has been to reflect on the reasons why in my early twenties, after having studied acting in France for several years, I became interested in pursuing this type of training. I can now say retrospectively that I was searching for a performance practice that could provide women with creative agency beyond the limitations placed upon them by the conventions of psychological realism. In my Master's thesis, which focused on Sam Shepard and American experimental theatre, I discussed Shepard's collaboration with actor and director Joseph Chaikin and examined how Chaikin's work with the Open Theatre was a critique of and response to the dominance of psychological realism. In *The Presence of the Actor*, Chaikin refers to his experience as an actor initially trained to work in commercial theatre:

> My early training for the theatre taught me to represent other people by their stereotype—taught me, in fact, to become the stereotype. [. . .] In trade papers there are calls for ingenue, leading lady, character actress, male juvenile character, etc. The actor attunes himself to fit the type

for which he may be cast. He eventually comes to see people outside the theater as types, just as he does for actors within the theater. Finally, a set of stereotypes is represented to the audience. This in turn is a recommendation to the types within the audience as to how they should classify themselves. (12)

Feminist theorists who have scrutinized the assumptions underlying the conventions of psychological realism concur with Chaikin's analysis by arguing that realist theatre naturalizes the normative gender roles it reproduces on stage. However, whereas the feminist critique tends to focus on how realist plays and their staging affect audiences, Chaikin is concerned with the actor's positionality. He points out that actors working in realist theatre are typecast in accordance with the gender roles society expects them to play, and argues that by taking on these roles, actors become complicit with the naturalization process at work in psychological realism, while at the same time being deeply shaped by these representations. He concludes that actors who uncritically embody the role models prescribed by dominant culture inevitably contribute to sustain and promote what he calls "the big setup":

> Actors, through their acting, are validating a definition of identity and rendering other definitions invalid. Recommending a way to perform oneself is working to sell a mode of being. [For example,] there are people who indicate how we can suffer beautifully: if you can suffer the way Ingrid Bergman suffers, then it is not all that bad to suffer. These actors who become icon-star-favorites have a lot to do with our lives. [...] The more confused and chaotic the era is, the more these icon personalities are taken on as models. [...] They serve an extremely important function and sustain all kinds of misrepresentations, all of which help keep things going as they are. (69–70, 72–73)

In an attempt to break with psychological realism, Chaikin and the collective of the Open Theatre developed physically-based training that was influenced by their encounter with Grotowski. Chaikin's aim was to alter "the limitations of life as it is lived," for he was convinced that "when the theatre is limited to the socially possible, it is confined by the same forces that limit society" (22–23). Accordingly, my experience of Grotowski-based training is that it offers an alternative to psychological realism precisely because it challenges actual and perceived limitations, including social and cultural constructions of gender.

THIS LIFE IS NOT SUFFICIENT

Grotowski is commonly remembered by his collaborators as someone who entrusted them with doing the impossible, a recurring theme in the testimonies of the women and men who collaborated with the Polish director during the various phases of his practical research. The women involved in my project each attested in different ways to this propensity for the impossible, initially rooted in a defiance of the severe restrictions that characterized the oppressive socio-political system of Communist Poland.

For example, Rena Mirecka, a founding member of the Laboratory Theatre and the only woman to have performed in all its productions, asserts that the company's extremely exacting work ethic, which constantly required actors to go beyond what they already knew, gave her *the possibility to do*, and the freedom to explore what was missing in her personal life. Iben Nagel Rasmussen, a key member of Eugenio Barba's Odin Teatret, recounts that she derived from her experience of Grotowski's approach the need to forge her artistic independence as a creative artist by developing her own training and transmitting it to others. Maja Komorowska affirms that she gained from her foundational experience at the Laboratory Theatre the assiduity that enabled her to pursue a long and successful film and theatre career. Elizabeth Albahaca emphasizes that the Laboratory Theatre's final production, in which she performed within the context of occupied Poland, conveyed the power of the human spirit in the darkest of times. Czech theatre artist-scholar Jana Pilatova attests that when faced with the oppressive political situation in her own country, she drew strength, inspiration, and courage from the work she did and witnessed at the Laboratory Theatre. Katharina Seyferth, who was part of the core group of young people involved in the transitional period from paratheatre to the Theatre of Sources, explains that Grotowski urged his collaborators to search for something other than what was already familiar, obvious, or easy, a way of working which, as a young woman who struggled with social norms, she found particularly compelling. Stefania Gardecka, Grotowski's main administrator, relates how she managed to devise strategic and resourceful ways of dealing with particularly stringent material conditions in order to protect the integrity of the Laboratory Theatre, whose uncompromising stance became a defining feature of its artistic approach.

While inviting people to do the impossible may appear unduly demanding, it may also be interpreted as challenging them to find their own way. In "Réponse à Stanislavski" ("Reply to Stanislavsky"),[2] Grotowski suggests that the best way of responding to the perils of life is to tap into the sources of life, which he notes is only possible if one finds the direction leading to these sources. When assigning impossible tasks to his collaborators, he might thus have been relying on them to point him in the right direction. This quest for the impossible was addressed by the Polish director during his 1997–98 Collège de France lectures,[3] which I attended and documented in the Polish theatre journal *Didaskalia*.[4] Grotowski gave nine public lectures in French entitled "La 'lignée organique' au théâtre et dans le rituel" ("The 'Organic Lineage' in Theatre and in Ritual") in various theatres in Paris, with his inaugural lecture taking place at Peter Brook's

Théâtre des Bouffes du Nord. Each four-hour session was comprised of two parts: during the first, Grotowski spoke of his on-going research; he also presented and commented on documentary and archival film excerpts specifically selected for each session. The second part was entirely devoted to creating a dialogue with the audience through questions and answers. During his third Collège de France lecture, Grotowski touched on what he meant by the impossible when he stated that, for him, tradition did not only encompass theatre traditions, but also traditional practices in other fields, including both European and non-European ancient practices whose aim it was to search for *"ce que l'être humain peut faire avec soi-même"* ("what human beings can do/accomplish with their own self/being"), and evoked the *kōan*-like image of someone attempting to jump over their own head (*"sauter au-desssus de sa tête"*), which he said had been the object of his research all along.

Almost thirty years prior to this lecture, Grotowski gave an important talk known as "Holiday [*Swieto*], The Day That Is Holy" in which he stated that he would no longer create theatrical productions for an audience and explained that what mattered to him was not theatre but "a quest for what is the most essential in life." He declared: "No one who denies the quest will be happy. Many people do reject it; they feel obliged to smile, as if they were advertising toothpaste. But why are they so sad?" ("Holiday" 117). Around the same time, Chaikin indicted the model of the actor as salesman for similar reasons:

> An old idea of acting is that you make believe that you care about things which you don't care about. To the degree that you are convincing, you are a good actor. In New York, actors spend time making 'rounds' for plays they often don't care about. In between producers' offices actors go up for commercials. There the actor praises a product and testifies to the changes it has made in his life. In both cases the actor is a salesman. The salesman who sells vacuum cleaners is also an actor. Ideally, acting questions have to do with giving form to what one *does* care about. They renounce the setup which sees people as 'goods.' (*The Presence of the Actor* 10–11)

Over the course of the following four decades, actors would be increasingly pressured to put their embodied labor in the service of the commodification of social role models sanctioned by dominant culture and disseminated by global corporate networks.

Within this market-driven cultural economy, the female body has become a particularly effective marketing tool for the entertainment and advertising industries. British scholar Angela McRobbie examines in *The Aftermath of Feminism* the extent to which the globalization of what she identifies as the beauty-fashion industry complex is affecting women's lives across social and cultural divides in the so-called post-feminist era. In contrast, Grotowski's investigation of the human creative potential within the context of world performance traditions relying on embodied modes of transmission may be perceived not only to provide performers with concrete ways of resisting hegemonic modes of cultural production, but also to offer viable alternatives. I would suggest that women cast as illegitimate daughters might be uniquely positioned to resist social conformism and transnational homogeneity as they walk the less trodden paths on the periphery of official culture.

In "Tu es le fils de quelqu'un," Grotowski relates his experience as a Polish artist living in "an extremely rigid social system" (294) and associates creative practice with a form of resistance:

> The things which were forbidden before me should be permitted after me. The doors which were closed and double-locked should be open. I must resolve the problem of freedom and of tyranny through practical measures; that means that my activity should leave traces, examples *of freedom*. [...] It is necessary [...] never to give up, but always to go one step further, one step further. That's it—the question of social activity through culture. (294–95)

Such a conception of artistic work can be attributed at least in part to the tragic history of Grotowski's Poland and to his witnessing the ravages of fascism as a child[5] and of totalitarianism as an adult.

Accordingly, his close collaborator Ludwik Flaszen, who was the Laboratory Theatre's dramaturg, reflects:

> For most of our lives we were afraid that this totalitarian temptation in the human being, in nations, in the masses, in various civilizations, might prevail. [...] For us, fear and trembling and constant anxiety were not a picturesque fantasy, a philosophical concept, an exciting artistic dream, literature, or the play of the neurotic imagination... We had known the Apocalypse from our childhood. It was our direct generational experience starting with the outbreak of the war. From September 1939, when Poland was attacked by Nazi Germany and Soviet Russia, our biographies had been defined by events described in history books. (*Grotowski & Company* 220, 248–49)

Theatre can therefore be said to have represented for Grotowski a field of practical investigation in which he envisioned the performative as a privileged, intimate area of human experience within which life might manifest itself at its fullest, in sharp contrast to a social reality tightly controlled through propaganda, censorship, and repression.

It is within this specific context that Grotowski posits creative practice as a form of social activism, challenging us to consider art, culture, and spirituality as a means of resistance against the status-quo:

> All life is a complex phenomenon of counterpoise. It's not a matter of having a conceptual image of that, but of asking yourself the question: The life that you are living, is it enough? Is it giving you happiness? Are you satisfied with the life around you? Art or culture or religion (in the sense of living sources; not in the sense of churches, often quite the opposite), all of that is a way of not being satisfied. No, such a life is not sufficient. So one does something, one proposes something, one accomplishes something which is the response to this deficiency. It's not a question of what's missing in one's image of society, but what's missing in the way of living the life. Art is deeply rebellious. Bad artists *talk* about the rebellion, but true artists *do* the rebellion. They respond to the consecrated order by an act. (295)

Grotowski makes clear, however, that artists without competence who call themselves rebels are simply avoiding their responsibility as social actors by failing to develop and sustain the type of creative agency that would make them credible cultural activists:

> Here there is a most dangerous and important point. One can, in following this route, end up in a sort of rebellion [. . .] which is the refusal of our responsibilities. In the realm of art, this appears under the form of dilettantism: one is not credible in one's craft; one has no mastery; one has no capacities; one is truly a dilettante in the worst sense of the word—so one is rebelling. No, none of that. Art as rebellion is to create the *fait accompli* which pushes back the limits imposed by society or, in tyrannical systems, imposed by power. But you can't push back these limits if you are not credible. [You must] have created a *fait accompli* which is of such mastery that even your adversaries cannot deny it. If you don't have this attitude of competence at your disposal in your rebellion, you will lose everything in the battle. Even if you are sincere. (295–96)

Yet, the competence which Grotowski has in mind is not what actors usually regard as useful skills for their profession, nor does it have to do with the single-minded competitiveness necessary to achieve commercial success and celebrity.

Instead, for Grotowski, creative agency is paradoxically linked to the notion of *via negativa*, a process of stripping away which was central to his conception of Poor Theatre and also characterized his post-theatrical research:

> For years one works and wants to know more, to acquire more skill, but in the end one has to reject it all and not learn but unlearn, not to know how to do, but how not to do, and always facing doing; to risk total defeat; not a defeat in the eyes of others, which is less important, but a defeat of a missed gift, an unsuccessful meeting with someone, that is to say an unsuccessful meeting with oneself. ("Holiday" 118)

From this perspective, meeting the other entails disarming oneself, and creative agency arises from the action of entering a space in which one cannot choose not to respond to the other, yet which is not a space for confrontation. In this meeting, one does not refuse nor impose oneself, and one remains open to possibilities by refraining to push with one's presence: "It is as if one spoke with one's self: you are, so I am. And also: I am being born so that you are born, so that you become. And also: do not be afraid, I am going with you" ("Holiday" 119). I learned throughout my apprenticeship with artists from the Grotowski diaspora that the intrinsic value of this approach must be experienced through doing, which is why I conceived my multi-sited fieldwork as a series of meetings with women's embodied ways of knowing rooted in the very principles of the training itself and transmitted through the teaching of that training.

I would argue that the kind of creative resistance evoked by Grotowski takes place first and foremost at the micro-level of the training, where the notion of resistance translates into a constant play of opposing tensions within the performer's body, a process that Eugenio Barba relates to the Japanese principle of *jo-ha-kyu*, the cyclical ebb and flow of energetic forces moving all living things. In *The Paper Canoe*, Barba provides the example of precarious equilibrium or luxury balance, linked to the primary, visceral drama of pre-expressivity in which the pelvis and the spine, simultaneously pulling in opposite directions, towards the earth and towards the sky, towards the horizon and away from it, engage the entire organism in the fluid modulation of muscular tensions and oppositions. It is through this dynamic flesh-and-blood conflict of competing forces that the breathing, pulsating, dilated body sculpts energy in space and time. Honing this artisanal craft requires years of training, and it is this form of self-cultivation, as defined by Noh master Zeami, which enables the performer to turn the power of resistance into a flowing, vibrant, and infectious dance of energy.

In light of this particular conception of training, dilettantism, a term often used by Grotowski, is about taking shortcuts by choosing what's easy, banal, or cliché, which for Grotowski and his collaborators leads to imitation, illustration, and redundancy. The point of the training is to overcome all forms of obstacles, including lack of competence, confidence, and inspiration that they trace to a fear of what they call the unknown. Having the courage to enter into the unknown hence constitutes for them a necessary condition for engaging in creative work. However, it is important to note that while confidence and courage are linked to the notion of resistance, these defining features of the training should not be confused with or replaced by the raw force of muscular power, as specified by Ryszard Cieslak in the 1975 documentary film *The Body Speaks*, since the ultimate goal is, paradoxically, to enable the performer to relinquish control in order to experience the kind of freedom that comes from release through an active form of *lâcher-prise* (letting go). This might, in fact, be more of a challenge for men brought up in cultures that associate will, control, and physical power with masculinity, and where women are discouraged from being assertive, forceful, and decisive. Hence, it is ironic that Grotowski relied on very few women leaders in this training, given that women would seem to be *culturally predisposed* to disarmament, vulnerability, fluidity, and openness to change. It is precisely because these qualities are linked to principles that are central to both Stanislavsky's and Grotowski's respective conceptions of performance that it is possible to chart a tangible lineage between them and search for points of entry into the work of women who reclaim such principles in their creative research.

THE STANISLAVSKY-GROTOWSKI LINEAGE

In my discussion of the Stanislavsky-Grotowski lineage, I will first address Grotowski's understanding and interpretation of what he considered to be the culmination of Stanislavsky's System and the foundation of his own work. I will then examine what the implications of the ultimate and arguably most radical version of the System, developed during the last phase of Stanislavsky's research, might be for performance theory and the feminist critique of Stanislavsky-based performance practice. In the second chapter, I will focus on the ways in which the principles that are key to the Stanislavsky-Grotowski lineage have been integrated by women in their own work, in order to map out interconnections between their respective approaches.

During his Collège de France lectures, Grotowski discussed in great detail aspects of his research which he considered to be directly related to Stanislavsky's investigation of the actor's process. In his inaugural lecture held at the Théâtre des Bouffes du Nord, Grotowski acknowledged that Stanislavsky was very much part of the Russian tradition of realist theatre, whose actors sought how to behave 'naturally' according to a specific social code. He noted that the Moscow Art Theatre productions were so instrumental to the establishment of realist conventions, despite some notable exceptions such as the production of Gogol's *Dead Souls* adapted for the stage by Mikhail Bulgakov, that Stanislavsky's name had inevitably remained associated with the ascendancy of realist theatre. However, Grotowski stated he was convinced that Stanislavsky was actually looking for something else, and specified that he was fascinated by the wisdom developed by the Russian director at the end of his life, for he sensed that the last phase of Stanislavsky's research focused on human behavior beyond the conventional limitations of realism on stage. Grotowski explained that his interest in Stanislavsky's Method of Physical Actions came from his conviction that working on impulses that preceded small actions revealed the secret of the organic performer. I will return later to the key words "impulse" and "organicity" which, along with "personal associations," are central to Stanislavsky's and Grotowski's perspectives.

If Stanislavsky had chosen to focus on physical actions at the end of his life, Grotowski argued, it was not because he was no longer interested in emotions, but because the latter had been the main focus of his previous work and he now felt that he must discourage his actors from seeking emotions for emotions' sake. Grotowski specified that by physical actions, Stanislavsky also meant personal associations, memories, reactions of love, hatred, fascination, and so forth, yet, according to Grotowski, Stanislavsky had chosen to use the phrase "physical actions" in order to distinguish the new phase of his research from his earlier teachings. Building upon Stanislavsky's work with physical actions, Grotowski extended this research beyond the realm of psychological realism in which actors seek to behave as 'naturally' as people supposedly do in real life.

Grotowski remarked that what we usually consider to be 'natural' behavior is merely the type of behavior that is understandable according to certain social codes within a given time and place. He provided the following example: if during this lecture here in Paris he were to sit on the table in a lotus position, this would certainly not be considered natural behavior from the point of view of the dominant social code; on the other hand, if someone living in a hermitage in the Himalayas brought in a chair and sat on it as was customary in Western cultures, this behavior might strike others as odd and unnatural. Grotowski, well aware of the ambiguity of the term "natural," had therefore replaced it with the term "organic," which he borrowed from Stanislavsky.

Grotowski stressed that at the end of his life Stanislavsky renounced fifty years of research because the Russian director had come to the following conclusion: since emotions could not be controlled by will power in real life, and since life was the main focus of his research on the actor's process, it had become imperative to reconsider the way in which the actor could be fully alive while performing on stage. Grotowski declared that at this point in Stanislavsky's career, his research had taken a new direction, leading to the development of the Method of Physical Actions. He said that he had been inspired by some of its implications, which he noted might even be called intuitions. Hence, according to Grotowski, Stanislavsky derived from his previous work that it was impossible to directly summon emotions by hunting them down with the weapon of affective memory for they were like wild animals always escaping from the hunter. If actors were able to remember their bodily behavior at a given moment of their life, however, then the emotions associated with such a behavior would naturally follow. Grotowski stated that he himself had started his research where Stanislavsky's work with physical actions had ended. Instead of asking the actor "How did you feel when this happened to you?" which had been Stanislavsky's earlier strategy, Grotowski adopted his later tactic by asking "What did you do?"

Grotowski's interest in the final phase of Stanislavsky's work can be traced to his student years. From 1951 to 1955, Grotowski attended the

State Theatre School in Krakow, where he was dubbed "a fanatic disciple of Stanislavsky" (Osinski 17). He then received a scholarship to study at the Moscow State Institute of Theatre Arts (GITIS) from August 1955 to April 1956. While in Russia, Grotowski studied the techniques of Stanislavsky, Vakhtangov, Meyerhold, and Tairov, and also worked at the Moscow Art Theatre (Osinski 17). He managed to gain access to the highly protected GITIS archives in order to study Meyerhold's famous staging of Gogol's *The Government Inspector*, and familiarized himself with the work of Vakhtangov when studying under Yuri Alexandrovich Zavadsky, a directing instructor at GITIS who had worked with Vakhtangov.[6] It was during this time that Grotowski became interested in what Toporkov identifies in his book as the Method of Physical Actions. Convinced that this practical research would have led Stanislavsky to break new ground had he had more time, Grotowski chose to explore it further in his own work with actors.

In his second Collège de France lecture, Grotowski acknowledged that he had been influenced by what he had learned about Vakhtangov, whom he described as a disciple of Stanislavsky who followed in the latter's footsteps while being simultaneously fascinated by Meyerhold's exploration of non-realistic theatre. Grotowski felt that Vakhtangov had furthered Stanislavsky's and Meyerhold's own investigations of the Grotesque, as exemplified by his production of *Princess Turandot*. Grotowski remarked that after Vakhtangov's death, Stanislavsky invited his closest collaborators to join the small group of actors with whom he developed the Method of Physical Actions. Grotowski suggested that Stanislavsky had chosen to integrate Vakhtangov's actors into his last studio, thereby becoming the disciple of his disciple, because he wished to understand the secret of an approach that was not realistic in the usual sense of the term and yet that hinged upon a deep implication and engagement of the actor's inner life. Grotowski concluded from the testimonies offered by those who first worked with Vakhtangov and then with Stanislavsky during this final phase of his research that the founder of the Moscow Art Theatre had significantly reoriented his System and that he privileged the impulse-based process underlying his work with physical actions.

The most tangible traces of the Stanislavsky-Grotowski lineage can be found in the terminology employed by the two directors, as in the phrase "the work on oneself," which Stanislavsky used to refer to the life-long training he was convinced actor-creators must pursue, and which became part of Grotowski's own terminology, along with the key terms "organicity," "impulse," "associations," and "physical score." The connection between Stanislavsky's and Grotowski's work, however, remains mostly unexplored, if at all acknowledged by theatre scholars and practitioners. This is largely due to the fact that Stanislavsky and Grotowski are viewed as belonging to two radically opposite poles, namely, mainstream psychological realism and non-realistic, physically-based experimentation. Grotowski, of course, was drawn to an area well beyond the realistic context which had epitomized the Moscow Art Theatre's repertoire. However, Stanislavsky himself had searched for non-realistic means of staging the texts that had emerged from the Symbolist movement. In 1904, he commissioned Meyerhold to conduct research on new forms that he hoped could be employed at the Moscow Art Theatre. In 1908, his strained collaboration with Edward Gordon Craig on a production of *Hamlet* confirmed the limitations of his System, which convinced him that he needed to expand his perspective in order to encompass the irrational and the subconscious aspects of human experience. He wrote in his autobiography: "Time has come to stage the unreal. It is not life such as it is, such as it flows, that the stage must actually portray, but the life of which we confusedly have an intuition in our dreams, in our visions, in our moments of exaltation" (Stanislavsky, *Ma Vie* 357).

Grotowski specifically set out to explore such moments of exaltation, that is to say, extraordinarily intense experiences conducive to heightened perception and a sense of renewed awareness. In *Towards a Poor Theatre*, Grotowski remarks that in moments of extreme terror or tremendous joy, human beings do not behave in a daily manner but respond with "rhythmically articulated signs" and begin to dance, to sing. In his work with the Laboratory Theatre, Grotowski was therefore seeking a "distillation of signs by eliminating those elements of 'natural' behaviour which obscure pure impulses" and used the technique of "contradiction (between gesture and voice, voice and word, word and thought, will and action, etc.)" as a way of illuminating "the hidden structure of signs" (17–18). In the post-theatrical phases of his research, Grotowski continued to investigate non-daily forms of behavior, whether it be in his paratheatrical experiments—in which spectators, whom he had positioned as silent witnesses in his theatre productions, now took on the role of participants—or in the periods known as Theatre of Sources, Objective Drama, and Art as vehicle, during which he became increasingly interested in non-Western traditional cultural practices.

While Carnicke's reassessment of Stanislavsky's legacy makes it possible to identify specific points of contact between Grotowski and the Russian director whom he claimed as his predecessor, Grotowski's own remarks indicate that what made the last phase of Stanislavsky's research so compelling to him was that it breached the stylistic constraints of psychological realism by focusing on what Timothy Wiles names a primary reality, that of the living presence of the actor on stage. In *The Theater Event*, Wiles argues that Stanislavsky's insight, even if never fully explicit in his writings, precedes future analysis according to which the actor is defined as an "integral part of the theatrical artwork" and art is perceived to be "more a process than an object." Wiles infers that "Stanislavsky was the first to sense (although not to specify) that what is essentially 'real' about theatrical realism lies as much in the reality of the performance itself as in the true-to-life quality of the play's details" (14). The most salient aspect of Stanislavsky's approach hence lies in an abiding concern with the processual dimension of performance, a concern which is also central to Grotowski's work.

Victor Turner, who traces the etymology of the word 'performance' to the Old French *parfournir*, suggests that "performance does not necessarily have the structuralist implication of manifesting form, but rather the processual sense of 'bringing to completion' or 'accomplishing.' To perform is thus to complete a more or less involved process rather than to do a single deed or act" ("Dramatic Ritual/Ritual Drama" 101). Accordingly, performance vitally hinges upon embodiment, or the involvement of the whole being—body, mind, and heart—in the process of bringing meaningful actions to completion. This leads Turner to infer that performance can "[transcend] the opposition between spontaneous and self-conscious patterns of action," thereby affording an embodied reflexive standpoint where one is "at once one's own subject and direct object" (111). Turner's interest in performance is therefore linked to his conviction that the experiential dimension of performance processes is conducive to a particularly productive form of intersubjectivity, which may provide access to another way of knowing. Stanislavsky's own conception of performance as processual and experiential may thus be viewed through the lens of Turner's influential perspective.

D. Soyini Madison observes that such an articulation of the performance paradigm has been particularly instrumental to the critical investigation of "the meanings and effects of human behavior, consciousness, and culture" (*Critical Ethnography: Methods, Ethics, and Performance* 149). Referring to Turner's notion of "*homo performans*," Madison envisions human beings as a "performing species" and posits performance as "necessary to our survival" (150). Tracing such a conception of performance to Stanislavsky's most radical experiments therefore has significant implications for my discussion of the Stanislavsky-Grotowski lineage within the context of my project, since it enables me to address the critical stance taken by feminists towards Stanislavsky's System and the postmodern tendency to dismiss both Stanislavsky's and Grotowski's respective approaches as irredeemably universalist and essentialist.

Ellen Gainor and Rhonda Blair have each challenged feminists to reconsider their critique of Stanislavsky. In "Rethinking Feminism, Stanislavsky, and Performance," Gainor poses an important question: "Is Stanislavskian acting theory fundamentally at odds with feminist theatre practice, or is it evidence from the *application* of those techniques in key historical, creative contexts that is the real—even if not overtly acknowledged—object of feminist critique?" (165). Feminists are certainly justified in their suspicion of the System's early emphasis on psychology and emotions which, they argue, turns actors into accomplices of an insidious cultural process that naturalizes historically and culturally specific gender roles. Gainor objects, however, that when the transformation of the System into the Method is historicized, what becomes clear is that it is "in the enforced application of Stanislavskian-derived performance techniques to given plays and characters, as well as in certain kinds of directorial environments, [that] dynamics antithetical to feminism emerge" (165). Moreover, she remarks that "through such examination we can also trace the development of gendered conventions in acting instruction, theatrical direction, and playwriting emanating from locations strongly associated with the Method" (165). Warning against the "rhetorical collapsing together of [the System and the Method]," Gainor cites Carnicke's insightful encapsulation of the American version of the System: "By the 1950s, the Method mirrored America's obsession with the Freudian model of the mind by employing therapeutic techniques meant to free the inhibited actor from long-lived repressions; affective memory [...] had become its cornerstone" (170). Given the decisive influence of Freudian psychoanalytic theory on American culture, Gainor wonders whether feminists would envision the System in a different light if considered outside the American theatrical tradition. She also points out that the feminist critique of Stanislavsky tends to focus exclusively on audience reception, thereby neglecting to address the work of the actor. While she acknowledges the effectiveness of the tools honed by feminist scholars in the domain of dramatic criticism and reception, Gainor suggests that they need to "develop equally refined, informed, nuanced, powerful, and persuasive means to discuss the theories and mechanics of feminist creativity" (172).

Blair also addresses the shortcomings of the feminist critique of Stanislavsky in her article "Reconsidering Stanislavsky: Feeling, Feminism, and the Actor," where she interprets the suspicion of emotions by feminists as a reaction against the ideologically charged "affective memory" technique popularized by the Method. As with Gainor, Blair points out the important differences between Stanislavky's conception of actor training and its American variant. She goes on to argue that research in cognitive neuroscience and neurophysiology seems to corroborate Stanislavsky's intuitions about the nature and function of performance processes. She specifies that from the perspective of neuroscience, "feeling is emotion made conscious" (186), a view which challenges mind-body dualism, or what neuroscientist Antonio Damasio identifies as "Descartes' error," that is to say, the separation of intellectual processes and corporeal sensations. In *The Actor, Image, and Action; Acting and Cognitive Neuroscience*, Blair explains that Damasio presents "a way of picturing body, feeling, and intellect [...] as aspects of a single organic process," which leads her to observe that what is "particularly pertinent for the actor is Damasio's assertion that reason—in the fullest sense—grows out of and is permeated by emotion, and that emotion is consistently informed by our reason and conscious cognition" (22). Given Blair's suggestion that the notion of consciousness is pivotal to both Stanislavsky's and Damasio's respective understandings of embodiment, I would argue that Stanislavsky's concept of "conscious experience"— Martin Kurten's translation for the Russian word *perezhivanie*, a key term which recurs in Stanislavsky's writings throughout his career—provides further insights into Stanislavsky's intuitive understanding of the relationship between embodiment and consciousness, an understanding grounded in his practice-based research.

Kurten remarks that whereas *perezhivanie* is translated into Scandinavian languages as "affective, active awareness," in Elizabeth Reynolds Hapgood's English translation this word becomes "feeling" and is associated with the domain of the emotions. The word "feeling" is also used by Hapgood to translate *custvovat*, whose meaning in Russian oscillates between "to feel," "to perceive," "to notice," "to become conscious of," and "to see," in the sense of "to understand" (Kurten, "La Terminologie de Stanislavski" 67–68). Carnicke extends Kurten's analysis by observing that Stanislavsky's usage of *perezhivanie* is so idiosyncratic that Russian actors and scholars struggle with its possible signification, while in the American translation "the force and pervasiveness of Stanislavsky's central term gets entirely lost" (*Stanislavsky in Focus* 109). In light of all the attention that has been given to various catch phrases gleaned from the American translation, a terminology which is still the subject of passionate debate among theorists and practitioners, it seems ironic that a key term such as this one has fallen into oblivion.

Carnicke notes that the word *perezhivanie* is a derivation of the verb *zhit* (to live) and that the prefix "*pere-*" can serve the function of the English prefix "re-" to indicate that the action of the verb is repeated. This has led emigré teachers to speak of actors "re-living" their role on stage, a phrase that "entered into the Method's oral tradition" (110). She suggests, however, that many other possible nuances can be introduced by the Russian prefix "*pere-*." For instance, it can signify "through" and connote persistence, thus possibly describing "an actor's deep concentration on stage and absorption in the events of the play during performance" (110). Yet, according to Carnicke, these literal translations "do not capture the complexity with which Stanislavsky endows this vexed term" (110), and she traces the director's usage of the word to Tolstoy's 1897 text *What is Art?*, which equates artistic practice with the communication of experiencing rather than that of knowledge. She contends that Stanislavsky, inspired by Tolstoy's definition of art, was eager to challenge the prominent Russian author's disdain for theatre (111). Stanislavsky wanted to prove that theatre was a legitimate art form, yet had to confront a contradiction specific to the conditions of the actor's work: for unlike the novelist, the actor's medium is experience itself, embodied in the process of performance.

It is precisely the embodied nature of experience that cognitive neuroscience investigates, and by establishing a connection between Stanislavsky and Damasio, Blair makes it possible to compare Stanislavsky's insight into the actor's conscious experience with Damasio's own conception of embodied consciousness. Blair states: "Damasio argues that consciousness (which derives from the sense of [...] an aware and sentient self), attention, reason, behavior, emotion, and feeling are physically intertwined in our brains" ("Reconsidering Stanislavsky" 182). Looking at Stanislavsky's approach to performance through the lens of Damasio's theory, which posits that consciousness, emotion, and feeling "are all related to the organism sensing itself, i.e., as being a discrete body/entity either at risk or experiencing pleasure" (184), Blair concludes: "This makes the 'body-mind problem' not a problem at all, for mind—consciousness—is a process of the body" (184). If this is the case, the feminist critique of Stanislavsky might reconsider his ultimate and most radical insights into performance processes as providing an understanding of the creative potential of performance, foregrounded as a fundamental dimension of human cognitive processes by recent developments in neuroscience. Blair summarizes this understanding as follows: "In short, being aware of feelings allows us to be innovative and creative—conscious, not just automatic—in our responses to the thing causing emotion" (187). Blair infers from such a perspective that although "feelings, stories, and bodies can be messy, mysterious, and scary," we must nevertheless come to terms with our embodied condition since there is no denying that "we *are* bodies with feelings" (189).

Interestingly, cognitive neuroscience takes up questions about emotions and embodiment previously explored by American psychologist William James and his Russian counterparts Vladimir Bekhterev and Ivan Pavlov, whose research influenced both Meyerhold, as demonstrated by Mel Gordon's analysis of his Biomechanics, and Stanislavsky. In his seventh Collège de France lecture, Grotowski remarked that when researching emotional memory, Stanislavsky drew from the writings of French psychologist Théodule Ribot, yet when the Russian director came to the conclusion that emotions did not depend upon the will, he began to orient his work towards what he called physical actions and became much more interested in the type of research developed by Pavlov. It is therefore significant that when Blair applies the neuroscientific understanding of embodiment to acting, she envisions performance as "a kind of proto-narrative (i.e., sensing oneself in relationship to an object and sensing that one needs to *do* something about it, whether it be to eat it or run away from it)" (183).

Indeed, an early theory articulating how such a proto-narrative functions was proposed by James when he suggested that emotions corresponded to bodily reflexes through which human beings reacted to the stimuli of their environment. In "What is an Emotion?", James effectively dramatizes this theory by providing the example of seeing a bear, running, and feeling frightened. In his analysis of this scenario, James links the impulse to run to the perception of the bear, emotion to the physical action of running, and the experience of fear to the consciousness produced by the action. He writes:

> [T]*he bodily changes follow directly the* PERCEPTION *of the exciting fact [and] our feeling of the same changes as they occur* IS *the emotion*. Common sense says [. . .] we meet a bear, are frightened and run; [yet] this order of sequence is incorrect [. . .]. Without the bodily states

following on the perception, the latter would be purely cognitive in form, pale, colorless, destitute of emotional warmth. We might then see the bear, and judge it best to run, [...] but we could not actually *feel* afraid [...]. (189–90)

What is striking about James's theory is that it foreshadows the distinction now made by neurologists between emotions and feelings, two terms that were always conflated by Hapgood in her translations of Stanislavsky's writings. Blair hence states that in Damasio's view, "the brain creates strings of associations arising in the body first as an emotion (a term used by Damasio and other neuroscientists to describe a physiological state of the body), which is translated into a feeling (a "registration" of an emotional state), which then leads to behavior, which is a response to all of the preceding that may or may not be associated with reason or rational thought." Blair goes on to remark that "this sequence is not uncomplicated, since behavior often precedes awareness and direct feeling" (*The Actor, Image, and Action* 21–22), a perplexing quandary which has been at the heart of much Western acting theory.

I would suggest that what is unique about Stanislavsky's contribution to this on-going debate is that his understanding of performance practice was influenced by Hinduism and Yoga, which is the reason why he considered the body and mind to be inseparable, with no primacy of bodily or mental processes since, for him, they occurred simultaneously and interdependently. In *Stanislavsky in Focus*, Carnicke tracks the influence of Yoga throughout Stanislavsky's writings and buttresses her analysis with evidence found in Russian archival material never before examined by theatre scholars. She argues that, in contrast with the Freudian dimension of affective memory that has made Method Acting so popular in America, Stanislavsky's belief in the connection between body and mind was more holistic than psychological (140). Carnicke dates Stanislavsky's interest in Yoga back to 1906, a time at which he was struggling with the question of inspiration. She states: "His library contains several books on Hatha Yoga (the physical discipline) and Raja Yoga (mental training that teaches concentration and meditation), both of which approach spiritual understanding through biology, hence Stanislavsky's famous insistence on the 'organic' foundations of acting" (140). She remarks that Stanislavsky derived from Hatha Yoga "relaxation techniques and exercises in breathing and balance," and that he borrowed from Raja Yoga "techniques of observation, concentration, and communication" (141). She infers that, unlike Western philosophical systems, "Eastern thought undoubtedly offered him different and more satisfying models for the mind/body relationship. These he found not only theoretically but, more to the point, practically useful" (141). She notes that the Russian director's understanding of "superconscious," a notion found in Raja Yoga that cannot be conflated with the Freudian notion of subconscious, points to a definition of consciousness that no longer pertains to Western philosophy but instead begins "where the real ends"—and, for Carnicke, this is also the point at which the System itself begins (142). Her analysis of the influence of Yoga on Stanislavsky's work leads her to suggest that the director went far beyond "a standard conception of Realism in art" and that his entire System can be read through the prism of Yoga. She thus contends that Stanislavsky was "more in tune with Yoga than with psychology" (143). She remarks, however, that since the last five pages of the Russian text of *An Actor Works on Himself*, Part I, were edited out of the book *An Actor Prepares*, English-speaking readers (as well as the non-English speaking readers who often only have access to translations of Hapgood's translations, as in the French edition) have been deprived of Tortsov's conclusion, where he reminds his students that they have yet to acquire a holistic approach to acting that includes "the corporeal life of the actor" (143).

When examining the Stanislavsky-Grotowski lineage, accounting for the influence of Hinduism and Yoga upon the two directors is crucial. While this influence on Stanislavsky remained largely based on indirect knowledge derived from readings, Grotowski, who actively sought out books and public lectures on Indian culture and philosophy while still a student at the Krakow State Theatre School (Osinski 14), took his first trip to Central Asia in the summer of 1956. The following year, the twenty-four-year-old Grotowski, who by then worked as a director in Krakow and taught at the Theatre School, was giving a series of well-attended public lectures on Eastern philosophy.[7] Later, Grotowski's practical research at the Laboratory Theatre included travelling to India and working directly with Indian master practitioners, such as the Bauls from Bengal. The acting training he developed with his collaborators was deeply influenced by yoga practice and also included some exercises drawn from Kathakali. Stanislavsky and Grotowski's shared interest in non-Western conceptions of consciousness that foreground the relationship between mind and body can thus be said to have significantly informed their respective investigations of performance practice.

The implications of this conception of the interdependence of bodily and mental processes are particularly significant for acting theory and actor training, especially as regards reinterpretations of Stanislavsky's System, which has long been the dominant paradigm in North American and European acting schools and programs. One such reinterpretation has been developed by American director and acting specialist Robert Cohen, whose teaching is based on the final period of Stanislavsky's System. Cohen uses James's scenario of the bear in his influential book *Acting Power* to support what he defines as a cybernetic approach, that is to say, a future-oriented, non-deterministic perspective on performance. He argues that cybernetic thinking is particularly useful when investigating "living, ongoing systems that cannot be fixed and frozen for analysis (as on a psychiatrist's couch—or an autopsy table) without severe alteration" (31). Stressing that "a cybernetic approach focuses on feedback from the future rather than causes from the past" (32), he proceeds to demonstrate that James's theory offers an alternative to dominant American versions of Stanislavsky's System.

Cohen first proposes a deterministic interpretation of James's scenario in which "the bear is the cause and its effect is to make the man run away" (32). He contrasts what he notes is an outside observer's perspective of this event with the experience of the man running towards a cabin for shelter in order to escape from the bear. He remarks: "The man running [. . .] is totally concentrating on how he can save himself. [H]e is planning his future—the next few seconds of it—and making contingency plans [. . .] ('If the door is locked, I'll climb on the roof!')" (33). Cohen applies this interpretation of James's scenario to what is often called "motivation" or "objective" in Stanislavsky-based acting, and contends that when the actor is looking ahead, imagining possible and contingent futures, rather than "analyzing behavior in terms of the 'pushing' of past motivational causes," she is able to "focus every one of her powers on her goal"—which, for Cohen, is central to what he calls "acting power" (33–34). He thus outlines the three main principles of cybernetic thinking: actors should seek the purpose rather than the cause of their character's behavior; they should not ask "Why?" but "What for?"; and they should envision their character being "pulled" by the future, not "pushed" by the past (34).

Accounting for this strategic move from deterministic to cybernetic thinking is pertinent to the re-evaluation of both the feminist critique of Stanislavsky and the furthering of his work on physical actions by Grotowski and his collaborators. In the earlier version of the System adopted by the American proponents of Method Acting, Stanislavsky assumed that emotions stored in the memory could be isolated from their original causes in order to be 're-cycled', as it were, and transferred to the given circumstances of a role. However, as Schechner judiciously points out, dredging up emotions related to bygone events in order to 're-live' them on stage is the equivalent of creating "an effect without a cause" ("Exit 30's, Enter 60's" 7). Moreover, this "effect" can only be obtained through a self-introspective, result-oriented mental process, which puts on hold the actor's moment-to-moment experiencing of the given circumstances, unavoidably cutting her off from a more immediate and more dynamic inner life. It is in response to these shortcomings that Stanislavsky abandoned affective memory and developed the later phase of his research with the actors of his last studio. He thereby established that since performing was a psychophysical process, focusing on actions could enable performers to tap into memories and emotions while bypassing the rational and analytical mind which tended to interfere with associations of ideas and images that were vital to what he called the inner life. Stanislavsky thus became convinced that our human creative potential could only be apprehended indirectly through a thorough training of the body-mind that he identified as "the work on oneself":

As you are drawn to physical actions you are drawn away from the life of your subconscious. In that way you render it free to act and induce it to work creatively. This action of nature and its subconscious is so subtle and profound that the person who is doing the creating is unaware of it [...]. My method draws into action by normal and natural means the subtlest creative forces of nature which are not subject to calculation. (*Creating a Role* 240–41)

Calculation, premeditation, manipulation were precisely what Stanislavsky's Method of Physical Actions enabled actors to avoid by taking the focus away from emotion, mood, or feeling, as confirmed by Toporkov's testimony:

We know that throughout his career Stanislavsky investigated different key points in his system—rhythm, ideas, tasks, etc. By now his system was entirely based on physical action and he tried to eliminate anything that prevented actors understanding that clearly. When anyone reminded him of his earlier methods, he said he didn't understand what they were talking about. Once someone asked: "What is the mood in this scene?" Stanislavsky gave a look of surprise and asked: "'Mood.' And what's that? I've never heard of it." That wasn't true. It was an expression he himself had used. However, in the present case, it merely stood in the way, preventing from pointing us in the right direction. [...] When one of the actresses told him that she had kept detailed notes of all his rehearsals she'd had with him over a number of years and didn't know what to do with this treasure trove, Stanislavsky replied: "Burn them." (*Stanislavsky in Rehearsal* 111)

Conversely to Method Acting, Cohen's cybernetic approach to the System acknowledges this new development and builds upon it. Consequently, although Cohen is mostly concerned with the realm of realism, he shares the same connection to Stanislavsky as did Grotowski, whom he invited to develop the Objective Drama Project in his Theatre Department at the University of California, Irvine.

Following calls by Carnicke, Gainor, and Blair to revisit and possibly reclaim certain aspects of Stanislavsky's legacy, and in light of Cohen's reinterpretation of the System as it applies to actor training, I would contend that contemporary performance theories and practices must account not only for the last phase of Stanislavsky's research, but also for the work accomplished by subsequent theatre practitioners such as Grotowski and his collaborators, who take the culmination of Stanislavsky's System as a point of departure. For them, conscious experience is a form of embodied awareness that can instill performance with a renewed sense of aliveness, immediacy, and urgency. This awareness is linked to a visceral understanding of Heraclitus's theory of flux, according to which it is impossible to step twice in the same river. Schechner infers from this theory that whereas performing always entails recombining bits and pieces of restored behavior, each performance is unique because restored behavior is constantly recombined in new ways and the context in which performance is experienced always changes (*Performance Studies: An Introduction* 28–38). Such an understanding of performance challenges the notion that "'acting' implies make-believe, even lying," and Schechner points to a connection between Stanislavsky and Grotowski when observing that "the work of the great twentieth-century acting teachers from Stanislavsky through Grotowski has been to make acting more 'truthful'" (*Between Theater and Anthropology* 36, 96). Stanislavsky and Grotowski can thus be perceived to have both acknowledged and resisted the age-old anti-theatrical prejudice rooted in Plato's suspicion of performance, and in the course of his Collège de France lectures, Grotowski asserted on several occasions that acting implies "*really* doing, *now*, in the present time."

When discussing this particular conception of performance during his lectures, Grotowski evoked Cieslak's total act in *The Constant Prince* and defined it as a *don de soi* (gift of oneself) or sacrifice, thereby suggesting that this act necessarily engages the performer's whole being. Such considerations led me to ask Grotowski whether, when referring to Cieslak's *don de soi*, he was implying that this gift was addressed to someone or something. The Polish director was particularly animated when he announced from the stage of the Conservatoire National Supérieur d'Art Dramatique hosting his fifth lecture that this was a fundamental question. He proceeded to explain that although he had always stated that the Laboratory Theatre's work was not accomplished for the spectator, everyone had always insisted on understanding exactly the opposite, an attitude which he wryly described as driving him to despair since no matter how many times he told people they shouldn't forget that the actor's gift (*don*) was not addressed to the spectator, they continued to claim that it was. Having emphatically declared that he was baffled by the mechanical thought processes that generated such automatisms, he suddenly delivered a resounding "No!" that was unambiguously addressed to all those who still claimed that, in his theatre, the spectator was the intended recipient of the actor's *don de soi*. Yet Grotowski immediately qualified his declaration by posing the question that was on my mind: if this *don* was not addressed to the spectator, then to whom/what? Prefacing his response by pointing out that it was best not to formulate an elaborate answer to this particular question, he simply stated: to *something*.

Grotowski's remarks illuminate an important quandary: any attempt to articulate into words an artistic trajectory developed over decades of practical research is necessarily partial—a term which means both incomplete and subjective, as noted by James Clifford—even, or perhaps especially, when this attempt is made by artists addressing their own work. I would therefore like to preface my own attempt at articulating in writing what

I have learned about women's experiences and perspectives through my embodied research by acknowledging that my contribution is necessarily partial, in the double sense of subjective and incomplete. However, I also want to suggest, along with feminist and post-colonial scholars, that claims of impartiality based on scientific objectivity and neutrality can lead to a misrepresentation of the nature and function of research across the humanities, fine arts, and social sciences, a concern I will address when discussing my interdisciplinary methodology.

MEETINGS WITH REMARKABLE WOMEN—
TU ES LA FILLE DE QUELQU'UN

Although meeting remarkable women might sound like a straightforward thing to do, the artists whose work I set out to investigate are particularly wary of anyone purporting to be conducting research on performance. The main reason for their resistance is that they consider their own work to be a form of creative research whose meaning, purpose, and value can only be apprehended through practice by means of direct, embodied experience. Moreover, what makes their work particularly difficult to access is their high status linked to their level of expertise, so that the most prominent women in my project might, at first glance, be perceived to be the 'elite' members of an exclusive transnational intelligentsia of avant-garde theatre artists. However, the process-oriented, experimental nature of Grotowski's investigation of performance has meant that the kind of practice it supports remains marginal for the most part and drastically underfunded. Since women's contributions to this practice have been considered peripheral at best, my project attempts to redress this imbalance by foregrounding and promoting the vital transmission processes which characterize the artistic work of women in the Grotowski diaspora. My interdisciplinary methodology therefore addresses questions pertaining to: designing and conducting multi-sited fieldwork which entails participating in the work of experimental performance experts; becoming immersed in embodied research hinging upon trust and reciprocity; writing empathetically about artistic practice; and disseminating embodied knowledge respectfully.

My own Grotowski-based performance training is grounded in the transmission of embodied knowledge: I worked for four years in Paris with actors who were students of Ludwik Flaszen and Zygmunt Molik, two founding members of Grotowski's Laboratory Theatre. Later, I went on to work with Molik, the voice specialist of the company, as well as with Rena Mirecka, also a founding member. Several other encounters with women belonging to the Grotowski diaspora eventually led me to conceive of this project. While my Grotowski-based training endows me with the status of insider by giving me access to the artistic practice of the women who accepted to participate in my project, I did not work directly with Grotowski and therefore belong to what I would call the Grotowski diaspora's lost generation—a generation upon whom Grotowski's influence is, at best, invisible, as he noted during his Collège de France lectures.

The significance of the cross-cultural research conducted by Grotowski was recognized through his appointment, in 1997, to the "*Chaire d'Anthropologie Théâtrale*" created specifically for him at the Collège de France, and the enduring relevance of the Polish director's legacy was acknowledged by UNESCO on the tenth anniversary of his death through the designation of 2009 as the "Year of Grotowski." Although many theatre historians rank Grotowski, along with Stanislavsky and Brecht, as one of the most influential theatre innovators of the twentieth century, there is a comparative paucity of scholarly texts investigating all but the early stages of his life-long research. This is partly due to a dearth of primary sources, for the Polish director privileged the oral tradition and discussed his research publicly instead of writing about it. Grotowski's major public talks were later transcribed, translated, and published, and most of them are featured in *The Grotowski Sourcebook*, although his important 1982 Rome lectures and his final 1997–98 Collège de France lectures are not included in this anthology. Theatre scholars thus tend to focus exclusively on the theatre of productions period addressed in *Towards a Poor Theatre*, which remains the best-known primary source available in English.

Consequently, Grotowski's influence on contemporary performance is often reduced to that early phase of his work due to a lack of knowledge about the rarely documented post-theatrical phases of the research that he conducted from the 1970s to the late 1990s. Within this relatively limited extant literature, very little attention has been given to the work of women. In fact, although the particularly strenuous physical training emblematic of Grotowski's approach is not gender specific, it has historically been associated with a masculine conception of the performer incarnated by Ryszard Cieslak in *The Constant Prince* and disseminated through scarce yet iconic archival film footage and photographs. This virtually unchallenged conception, which overlooks leading women performers such as Rena Mirecka, Maja Komorowska, and Elizabeth Albahaca, to name only the main women identified with the period of theatre productions, points to a tendency among theatre critics, historians, and practitioners to assume that women's contributions to Grotowski's research are neither significant nor relevant to a thorough understanding and informed appreciation of his legacy.

Grotowski's uncompromising artistic research required from both his male and female collaborators unusually high levels of rigor and competence, sustained by their life-long commitment to a regime of extremely demanding physical and vocal training that set a benchmark in experimental performance practice. During his "Year of Grotowski" keynote address at the Théâtre des Bouffes du Nord on October 19, 2009, Brook suggested that, by setting the bar so high, Grotowski had challenged artists to constantly question their perceived personal limitations as well as the alleged limitations of their craft, so as to keep searching beyond what they already knew was possible. While the women involved in my project are independent artists, they acknowledge the lasting influence of Grotowski's research on their work and share his demand for rigor, competence, and commitment. From their perspective, my insider status is therefore all but relative since it necessarily ranks substantially lower than that of 'authentic' insiders who worked extensively with Grotowski. This is why I belong to a generation of theatre practitioners bound to remain almost but not quite Grotowskian.

I raised the question of Grotowski's indirect influence on my generation when I asked him, during his seventh Collège de France lecture, about the relationship between "Art as presentation" and "Art as vehicle." By way of introduction, I first thanked him for the 'invisible influence' his approach had had on those who, like myself, had not worked directly with him but trained with students of his collaborators. My usage of the phrase 'invisible influence' was an overt reference to Grotowski's text "From the Theatre Company to Art as Vehicle," in which he addresses the question of the influence that his research has had on theatre practitioners. He states about Art as presentation and Art as vehicle: "[A] passage between them should be possible: of the technical discoveries, of the artisanal consciousness [. . .] It is needed that all this can pass along, if we don't want to be completely cut off from the world. [In the history of art] there exist these anonymous influences. Both extremities of the chain (Art as presentation and Art as vehicle) should exist: one visible—public—and the other almost invisible. Why do I say 'almost'? Because if it were entirely hidden, it could not give life to the anonymous influences. For this, it should remain invisible, but *not entirely*" (134–35).

Grotowski responded to my remark by specifying that he did not mean to say that there was an invisible influence, but that *if there was an influence that worked, it was invisible*, and asked me whether I could sense the difference between these two statements. He stressed that if one searched for an influence, even an invisible one, it could very easily become illusory or turn into manipulation. He distinguished the notion of influence from that of direct lineage, which in his view entailed working under someone's guidance in a particular direction for many years, and explained that a real influence, if it existed, was akin to being receptive to something that was close to one's self, to one's heart and curiosity (*comme si quelqu'un capte quelque chose*), and that kept one going. He observed that, in this case, the influence probably existed but was invisible, and that it was thanks to its being so that it could be fruitful.

While I admittedly derive a certain sense of freedom and independence from not being a legitimate inheritor, from not having to 'defend' or 'preserve' Grotowski's legacy, I am also acutely aware that the feasibility of my project has vitally depended upon my ability to maintain my precarious insider status and to, somehow, become someone's daughter. Whereas my embodied knowledge of Grotowski-based training cannot entirely fulfill the expectations of the performance experts whose work I have been investigating, such knowledge not only constitutes my main point of entry into their creative research and teaching, but has also served to mitigate their extreme mistrust of my affiliation with the academy. Such mistrust is linked to Grotowski's own critical stance towards the production of abstract intellectual constructs that replace (and displace) performance practice as such. In his ninth Collège de France lecture, Grotowski hence stated that asking questions only with the mind (*questions mentales*) merely amounted to playing a game of ideas that was neither interesting nor true. Significantly, such a critical stance was constantly balanced by the exacting demand for rigor and consistency that characterized the Polish director's analysis of his own work.

Grotowski's perspicacity is shared by his collaborators, who staunchly resist academic forays into performance that colonize artistic practice to fit pre-established theoretical frameworks, thereby reducing such practice to lifeless formulas bound to fail to convey the kind of embodied knowledge that is gained through "doing." Moreover, they are equally weary of researchers who fall into the other extreme by mystifying artistic practice to liberate it from theory's grasp. For they consider that, in both cases, dominant academic research paradigms misrepresent, disrespect, marginalize, and delegitimize very sophisticated practice-based creative research endeavors hinging upon experiential modes of cognition.

The very title of my research project was initially challenged by several of the women who had otherwise agreed to participate because they resented the fact that it drew attention to their gender. Whenever I questioned them directly about their experience as women in the Grotowski diaspora I received a variety of responses, but what became clear to me was that most of them had very mixed feelings about being identified as "women artists" whereas their often more recognized male counterparts were simply referred to as "artists." My affiliation to the academy and the grants I was able to obtain as a university researcher further complicated the issue since, from their perspective, research endeavors supported by a large amount of institutional funding are often a sure sign that there must be a hidden agenda. And indeed, there always is, since the academy sets the criteria for successful research, such as dissemination by means of peer-reviewed scholarly publications addressed primarily to an academic audience, thereby excluding most practitioners from the debate even when claiming to support process-oriented and practice-based projects grounded in the notion of "performance as research" or "practice as research in performance."

In the field of performance studies, the gap that separates performance scholars from performance practitioners has been described by Dwight Conquergood as a counterproductive "academic apartheid" ("Performance Studies: Interventions and Radical Research" 153) and defined by Shannon Jackson as an insidious "division of labor" privileging those who think over those who do (*Professing Performance* 85, 111). This practice/theory divide often characteristic of performance research in the academy severely undermines practice-based research projects such as mine which require the building of relationships based on trust, respect, and reciprocity. Cree scholar Shawn Wilson points to a similar disjunction between Western and Indigenous scholars in his book *Research is Ceremony: Indigenous Research Methods*:

> As part of their white privilege, there is no requirement for [dominant system academics] to be able to see other ways of being and doing, or even to recognize that they exist. Oftentimes, then, ideas coming from a different worldview are outside their entire mindset and way of thinking. The ability to bridge this gap becomes important in order to ease the tension that it creates. (44)

Because of the complex negotiations in which I am engaged due to my positionality as a performance practitioner and scholar, I have witnessed and experienced tensions not unlike those described by Wilson as I straddle two worlds that often seem irreconcilable. While Indigenous research principles are designed by and for Indigenous scholars and activists working within their own communities, Wilson states: "So much the better if dominant universities and researchers adopt them as well" (59). I have found these principles to be more pertinent to my embodied research than the methodologies developed by those whom Wilson identifies as "dominant system academics."

WORKING AT THE INTERSECTION OF PERFORMANCE STUDIES, CULTURAL ANTHROPOLOGY, AND INDIGENOUS RESEARCH METHODOLOGIES

Respect, reciprocity, and relationality, which Wilson posits as the three R's of Indigenous methodologies, are particularly relevant to my project, and reading *Research is Ceremony* while conducting fieldwork was extremely helpful. Wilson specifies that "respect is more than just saying please and thank you, and reciprocity is more than giving a gift." Indigenous research principles are thus meant to ensure that the research conducted by Indigenous scholars "will be honoured and respected by their own people." Such research criteria are so fundamental to Indigenous communities that they "will not allow entry by researchers, Indigenous and non-Indigenous, until they have met the community's conditions" (59).

According to these principles, researchers must be willing and able to engage in a "deep listening and hearing with more than the ears" in order to develop a "reflective, non-judgmental consideration of what is being seen and heard" along with "an awareness and connection between logic of mind and the feelings of the heart"; finally, researchers bear the "responsibility to act with fidelity in relationship to what has been heard, observed, and learnt" (59). This engagement required from researchers is clearly embodied and empathetic, and, as such, it is especially well suited to Grotowski-based performance practice, which also requires a 'deep listening' engaging the whole being, that is to say, body, mind, and heart, as well as a suspension of judgment which can be understood as a form of 'fidelity' to the embodied knowledge accessed through the training. Working with the women involved in my project has therefore been more about doing than talking. Because intuition is inherent to creativity, a deep sense of trust is necessary, yet it takes time to achieve such trust. Investing oneself as fully as possible in this long-term process is an important way of demonstrating commitment, and as time passes trust increases along with the responsibility that comes with receiving someone's trust. Wilson suggests that, from an Indigenous perspective, research is ceremony because it is about making connections and strengthening them, a process which takes "a lot of work, dedication and time" (89–90). In the case of my project, the embodied research that was pivotal to the multi-sited fieldwork I conducted from 2008 to 2012 is predicated on establishing and sustaining the type of relationships that Wilson considers to be the necessary conditions for conducting research.

Embodiment, lived experience, and intersubjectivity are key to experimental approaches articulated at the intersection of performance and ethnography. Yet the slippery nature of the territories which this research proposes to investigate has often contributed to undermining its academic credibility. Since embodied experience eludes and possibly exceeds cognitive control, accounting for its destabilizing function within the research process potentially endangers conceptions of knowledge upon which the legitimacy of dominant academic discourses so crucially depends.

Within the discipline of anthropology, alternative ethnographic models that account for the lived experience of researchers and research participants have arguably been most compellingly articulated by Indigenous and feminist ethnographers. In the *Chicago Guide to Collaborative Ethnography*, Luke Eric Lassiter notes that American Indian scholars were among the first to produce a radical critique of ethnographic fieldwork and to "call for models that more assertively attend to community concerns, models that would finally put to rest the lingering reverberations of anthropology's colonial past" (6). Lassiter further remarks that feminist scholars, writing "as women whose knowledge is situated vis-à-vis their male counterparts (see Haraway 1988)" (59) are already positioned as Other. Indigenous and feminist anthropologists therefore raise related epistemological and methodological questions about ethnographic authority and the politics of representation because they share similar concerns about the ways in which conventional methodologies enable researchers working from within the academy to authoritatively speak for the Other (56, 59). Positioning themselves as members of the community they are studying and accounting for their own embodied participation in the culture of that community has led Indigenous and feminist researchers to develop alternative research methodologies which foreground embodiment, lived experience, and intersubjectivity, and which privilege collaboration and reciprocity.

While feminist ethnographers are committed to creating "more humane and dialogic accounts that would more fully and more collaboratively represent the diversity of women's experience" (56), for Indigenous ethnographers, consultation with community members is meant to ensure that the research they are conducting is mutually beneficial. In both cases, lived experience and accountability are linked, and the researcher bears a moral responsibility to the community. When reflecting on his ethnography of Kiowa songs, Lassiter acknowledges that what mattered most to the Kiowa community was the power his interpretation would have in "defining [this community] to the outside—and to future generations of Kiowas for that matter." The questions that emerged from the research process were therefore about "who has control and who has the last word" (11). What is ultimately relevant to the Kiowa people is the power of the songs, for it is the embodied experience of singing these songs which sustains the cultural continuity of the Kiowa community.

My research on women artists whose experiential approaches to performance crucially depend on embodiment similarly hinges upon questions of accountability, relevance, and reciprocity. For these women from different cultures and generations, who often work with traditional songs, it is the power of performance which gives meaning to their creative research and teaching. By focusing on women artists who do not readily align themselves or identify with post-structuralist feminist theory, however, my project confronts what Lassiter describes as "the gap between academically-positioned and community-positioned narratives," grounded in concerns about the politics of representation, that is to say, "about who has the right to represent whom and for what purposes, and about whose discourse will be privileged in the ethnographic text" (4). Addressing such concerns requires calling into question the legitimacy of theoretical claims that make use of artistic practice to demonstrate the validity of an argument underpinned by a particular analytical framework.

While extremely empowering for women scholars, the feminist critique of essentialist representations of gender is itself a construction informed by a particular way of positioning oneself, which contains its own limitations. It seems impossible, for instance, to argue against biological determinism while simultaneously being engaged in forms of practice-based research that foreground embodied experience and generate alternative conceptions of what constitutes knowledge. The women involved in this project have developed their own perspectives on these issues, and resolutely reject any kind of categorization which might limit, constrain, or stultify what they envision as the human creative potential. In my articulation of the project's objectives, it was therefore imperative to leave the term "woman" open-ended so as not to impose a pre-determined theoretical lens through which to view and interpret their work.

Furthermore, the women whose creative work I have been investigating often anchor their artistic research in cultural practices that can provide access to embodied experiences of spirituality. Such practices have existed around the world for thousands of years, yet their spiritual dimension is something which, when not simply dismissed as a form of false consciousness, is left entirely unexamined by post-structuralist analyses of cultural processes, and I have found in Indigenous research methodologies alternative theoretical frameworks that are inclusive of spirituality. Such inclusivity is especially critical to the analysis of Grotowski's post-theatrical work, in which several of these women actively participated. After having garnered international acclaim as the Laboratory Theatre's artistic director, Grotowski made the controversial decision to abandon theatre productions altogether in order to focus on practical research that ranged from one-time participatory experiments conducted in unusual indoor and outdoor settings, to the long-term investigation of ritual performance processes. From then on, Grotowski's research became increasingly focused on sources of embodied knowledge linked to traditional cultural practices.

Grotowski stressed that he did not address directly in his talks the spiritual aspect of his work so as not to encourage reductive generalizations based on a Eurocentric understanding of what may constitute spirituality. Yet, reconnecting with one's cultural ancestry was key to his post-theatrical research, especially in his practical investigation of ancient traditional songs. He states:

> As one says in a French expression, 'Tu es le fils de quelqu'un' [You are someone's son]. You are not a vagabond, you come from somewhere, from some country, from some place, from some landscape. [...] Because he who began to sing the first words was someone's son, from somewhere, from some place, so, if you refind this, you are someone's son. [If you don't,] you are cut off, sterile, barren.' ("Tu es le fils de quelqu'un" 304)

Although this statement seems to focus solely on sons and can appear to privilege the masculine gender, it is clear in the notes to the transcriptions and translations of his major public talks, usually given in French, that Grotowski was well aware of gender-based linguistic shortcomings and that he did not intend his discourse to apply exclusively to males. The subtitle of my research project, *Tu es la fille de quelqu'un*, nevertheless reclaims and reconfigures what is essentially a folk-saying borrowed by Grotowski from my native culture, which enables me to ask what it means for women to be someone's daughter—for, surely, they also experience the need to know where they come from.

Hawaiian scholar Manulani Aluli Meyer also links identity, lineage, and place when she writes: "You came from a place. You grew in a place and you had a relationship with that place. [. . .] Land is more than just a physical place. [. . .] It is the key that turns the doors inward to reflect on how space shapes us" ("Indigenous and Authentic" 219). Meyer goes on to cite the Hawaiian elder Halemakua, who states: "At one time, we all came from a place familiar with our evolution and storied with our experiences. At one time, we all had a rhythmic understanding of time and potent experiences of harmony in space." Meyer specifies that Halemakua believed it was possible to reconnect with this knowing in order to "engender, again, acts of care, compassion, and the right relationship with land, sky, water, and ocean—vital for these modern times" (231).

Meyer hence poses a question which I find particularly pertinent to my own research process when she asks: "Will your research bring forth solutions that strengthen relationships with others or will it damage future collaborations?"—to which she replies that "knowledge that does not heal, bring together, challenge, surprise, encourage, or expand our awareness is not part of the consciousness this world needs now. This is the function we as indigenous people posit." She therefore makes a direct appeal to researchers: "[S]ee your work as a taonga (sacred object) for your family, your community, your people," and suggests: "[Y]our relationship to your research topic is your own. It springs from a lifetime of distinctness and uniqueness only you have history with" (219–20). By stressing the necessity to clearly position oneself within the research process and to develop a personal relationship to one's research topic, Meyer evokes an empathetic form of relationality which is relevant to my project because of the solidarity I hope it can foster among women artists.

Meyer also insists that researchers should acknowledge that "objectivity is a subjective idea that cannot possibly describe the all of our experience" (226), and urges them to "expand [their] repertoire of writers and thinkers" in order to overcome "the limitations of predictable research methodologies." Finally, she challenges researchers to have the maturity to seek "what most scholars refuse to admit exists: *spirit*" (228). Having to admit the existence of 'spirit' is precisely what Lassiter was confronted with when conducting research on Kiowa songs. Kiowa people's lived experience of these songs is that of an encounter with *daw*, which he states translates into "power, or more precisely spirit" (7). For Kiowa people, "spirit is the deepest encounter with the song," and in the course of his research Lassiter came to understand that Kiowa people were "very conscious of how academics theorize this talk about song within their own academically positioned narratives, effectively dismissing or explaining spirit away in their texts." This led him to reflect upon his positionality and question his own disbelief. He writes:

> We may suggest, for example, that spirit doesn't exist as an empirical reality—that it exists because Kiowas believe it exists, that it is a product of culture. And because culture is very real, spirit is very real. Yet for [Kiowa people], spirit is not a concept. It is a very real and tangible

thing. An encounter with *daw* informs belief; not vice versa. We academics take a leap of faith—or one of disbelief [...] when we argue otherwise. And when we argue from our position of disbelief, however constructed, we argue from a political position of power, privileging our own voice in our literature. (7–8)

Valuing the lived experience of others in spite of one's personal convictions is, in this case, both an ethical and a methodological imperative since the purpose of the research is to investigate the power of Kiowa songs. Given the importance of spirituality for the artists involved in my project, the leap of faith I have taken is also linked to ethics and method since it has enabled me to curtail disbelief while learning from them about their work.

In her discussion of 'spirit', Meyer cautions her readers not to confuse the category of spirit with religion, since Hawaiian elders speak of spirit with regard to intelligence (218). Describing spirit as that which gives "a structure of rigor" to research, she specifies that it is about "moving towards usefulness, moving towards meaning and beauty. It is the contemplation part of your work that brings you to insight, steadiness, and interconnection. [...] In research, it is answers you will *remember* in your dreams. [...] It is understanding an unexpected experience that will heighten the clarity of your findings" (229). She is thereby pointing to an experiential form of knowledge in which "knowing is bound to how we develop a *relationship* with it," leading her to posit that "*knowing is embodied* and in union with cognition" (224), and that "*genuine knowledge must be experienced directly*" (224). This is also a fundamental aspect of Grotowski's conception of embodiment which his collaborators continue to uphold in their own creative research and their teaching, yet it is also what makes the investigation of their work particularly challenging for theatre and performance scholars.

The privileging of mind over body and spirit can be traced to the Enlightenment project of modernity, as argued by Conquergood when stating that "ways of knowing rooted in embodied experience, orality, and local contingencies," that is to say, epistemologies grounded in process, practice, and place, have been discredited through the systematic institutionalization of print-culture. He notes that in today's academy, "the class-based arrogance of scriptocentrism" once denounced by Raymond Williams continues to "assume that all the world is a text" and to construct non-literate cultures as the Other of this hegemonic economy of knowledge. Conquergood indicts what he defines as "an academically fashionable textual fundamentalism and fetish of the (verbal) archive," which he relates to "historical processes of political economic privilege and systematic exclusion" (147). Arguing not against text but against textocentrism, he calls into question the "world-as-text model in ethnography and cultural studies" and proposes "a riskier hermeneutics of experience, relocation, copresence, humility, and vulnerability" ("Performance Studies: Interventions and Radical Research" 146–51).

Scriptocentric constructions of the non- or pre-literate Other are also scrutinized by Diana Taylor, who posits that performance constitutes a repertoire of embodied knowledge, a learning in and through the body, as well as a means of creating, preserving, and transmitting knowledge. Taylor argues that Western culture, wedded to the word, whether written or spoken, enables language to usurp explanatory power, and goes on to suggest that performance studies asks us to take seriously other forms of cultural expression as both praxis and episteme (*The Archive and the Repertoire* 24–26). She points out that in Latin America, her area of specialization, "the legitimization of writing over other epistemic and mnemonic systems assured that [colonial power] could be developed and enforced without the input of the great majority of the population" (18). Stressing that forms of writing did exist prior to the conquest of Latin America but never as a form of knowing separate from oral traditions and other forms of embodied knowledge, she infers that the schism does not lie between the written and the spoken word but between discursive and performative systems, between literary and embodied cultural practices (19).

Dance studies scholars have perhaps most effectively unsettled this hierarchical configuration of knowledges within the academy by foregrounding the cultural specificity of mind-body dualism. In her article "Beyond 'Somatophobia': Phenomenology and Movement Research in Dance," Karen Barbour remarks: "Affected by dominant Western culture's denial and repression of the body, and of experience as a source of knowledge, lived movement experience has only recently been studied academically" (35). Within the field of theatre and performance studies, somatophobia casts a shadow of suspicion over the hybrid status of the artist-scholar and contributes to undermining practice-based research endeavors that require the building of mutually beneficial relationships with artists outside the academy. By foregrounding the embodied and performative dimensions of cultural processes, performance ethnography has significantly contributed to the bridging of creative and critical praxis by fully capitalizing on the "performance turn" in the humanities and social sciences.

PERFORMANCE ETHNOGRAPHY: FROM TURNER TO DENZIN

In Victor Turner's conception of performance ethnography, embodiment becomes an antidote to the visualist dimension of ethnography informed by the body-mind dichotomy inherited from the Enlightenment:

> Cartesian dualism has insisted on separating subject from object, us from them. It has, indeed, made voyeurs of Western man, exaggerating sight by macro- and micro-instrumentation, the better to learn the structures of the world with an "eye" to its exploitation. The deep bonds between body and mentality, unconscious and conscious thinking, species and

self have been treated without respect, as though irrelevant for analytical purposes. ("Dramatic Ritual/Ritual Drama" 111)

Dissatisfied with the fieldwork methodologies and writing conventions of mainstream anthropology, Turner rejects the positivist notion that the ethnographer must be detached and dispassionate, thereby anticipating the post-colonial critique by non-Western and Indigenous scholars who have demonstrated that voyeurism, exploitation, and lack of respect veiled by claims of scientific objectivity and impartiality constitute characteristic features of anthropology's colonial legacy.

Turner therefore articulates performance ethnography as both a critique of conventional research methodologies and an alternative providing researchers with a kinetic understanding of cultural processes. Advocating the performance of ethnographic texts in order to break away from the cognitive dominance of the written, Turner proposes to turn "ethnographic texts into playscripts, scripts into performance, and performance into meta-ethnography" (100), and to establish "a dialectic between performing and learning," so that "one learns through performing, then performs the understanding so gained" (104). Predicting the crisis of representation which, after his death in 1983, would shake the foundational principles of his profession, he writes:

> If anthropologists are ever to take ethnodramatics seriously, our discipline will have to become something more than a cognitive game played in our heads and inscribed in—let's face it—somewhat tedious journals. We will have to become performers ourselves, and bring to human, existential fulfillment what have hitherto been only mentalistic protocols. (111)

Accordingly, the next generation would foreground the performative and embodied dimensions of ethnography, thereby opening up new possibilities for performance-based research explored by scholars such as Conquergood in performance studies and Norman K. Denzin within qualitative inquiry across the social sciences.

Denzin builds upon Conquergood's contribution to develop qualitative inquiry strategies that are significantly informed by critical race theory, post-colonial studies, and arts-based research methodologies. This leads him to envision performance as "a form of kinesis, of motion, [...] an act of intervention, a method of resistance, a form of criticism, a way of revealing agency, [...] a way of bringing culture and the person into play" (*Performance Ethnography* 9–10). From such a perspective, "every performance, every identity [is] a new representation of meaning and experience, as well as a site of struggle, negotiation, and hope: a site where the performance of possibilities occurs" (328). The most provocative and productive dimension of Denzin's approach to performance ethnography is arguably its integration of the critique of Euro-American research by Indigenous scholars who also call for the legitimization, in the academy, of embodied knowledge as a counterhegemonic mode of inquiry. Denzin, writing in support of collaborations between Indigenous and non-Indigenous researchers, asserts that "Westerners have much to learn from Indigenous epistemologies and performance theories," and suggests that "the performance turn in Anglo-Saxon discourse can surely benefit from the criticisms and tenets offered by Maori and other Indigenous scholars" (108).

Nevertheless, while Denzin charts new directions for interdisciplinary and cross-cultural research, his own work draws extensively from Euro-American experimental theatre and arts-based research, combining surrealist montage techniques with text-based dramatic structures, and relies considerably on Paulo Freire's critical pedagogy and Augusto Boal's post-Brechtian Theatre of the Oppressed. In the preface to the *Handbook of Critical and Indigenous Methodologies*, Denzin and his co-editors state in a section titled "Limitations" that they were "unable to locate persons who could write chapters on [...] arts-based methodologies [...] and indigenous performance studies" (xii). Later in the introduction, Denzin and Yvonna S. Lincoln advocate what they describe as a "post-colonial, indigenous participatory theater, a form of critical pedagogical theater that draws its inspirations from Boal's major works: *Theatre of the Oppressed* (1974/1979), *The Rainbow of Desire* (1995), and *Legislative Theatre* (1998)" (7). A close examination of recent critical reassessments of the Marxist-inflected emancipatory discourses underpinning Boal's relationship to the work of Freire demonstrates, however, that the seemingly unilateral integration of the Boalian performance paradigm by social scientists is far from unproblematic, especially when applied to an Indigenous context. In the fourth chapter, I link the Indigenous critique of Boal to the environmentalist critique of Freire to address the dominance of this paradigm in the social sciences and consider para/post-theatrical alternatives.

PRODUCTIVE DISORIENTATION

Since the 'performance turn' in the academy often remains highly conceptual in spite of its claims to legitimize embodied ways of knowledge, I propose to counterbalance this tendency by turning to performance training and practice in order to provide an insight into the cognitive potential of performance. Barba, whose perspective is informed by his practice-based research on non-Western performance traditions, points out that alteration of balance is one of the techniques through which the performer experiences disorientation, the point being to destabilize the body-mind and alter the performer's perception of the world. Such disorientation techniques lead to a deconditioning designed to eliminate daily behavior, and eventually produce a reconditioning from which emerges the type of "extra-daily" behavior pertaining to highly stylized and codified forms of physically based performance traditions such as Japanese Noh, Chinese Opera, and Indian Kathakali.

I ground what I propose to name productive disorientation in Barba's notion of "thinking in motion," that is to say, an embodied way of knowing accessed through training by performance practitioners. Barba describes "thinking in motion" as an alternative to the type of thinking which is discursive and resorts to language, or "thinking in concepts." Barba contrasts "thinking in motion" with "thinking in concepts" by specifying that the former is linked to what he describes as "creative thought [. . .] which proceeds by leaps, by means of sudden disorientation which obliges it to reorganize itself in new ways" (*The Paper Canoe* 88). In *A Passage to Anthropology*, Danish anthropologist Kirsten Hastrup defines such disorientation as inherent to our embodied condition. An important contributor to Barba's International School of Theatre Anthropology, Hastrup establishes a relationship between performance processes and the ethnographer's fieldwork experience, and suggests that what Barba defines as the "body-in-life" becomes a pivotal concept whenever researchers attempt to account for embodied experience (82). She derives from her encounter with theatre the insight that "most cultural knowledge is stored in action rather than words," and specifies that such embodied knowledge is transmitted through psychophysical involvement in cultural processes (82). Situating flesh-and-blood human agents within a corporeal field "with which every individual is inextricably linked by way of the physical, sensing and moving body" (95), she infers from this embodied condition that "the point from which we experience the world is in constant motion [. . .] there is no seeing the world from above" (95). Hastrup hence provides an analysis of human agency which anchors the latter in the living body. This leads her to contend that the disorientation produced by "thinking in motion" is also inherent to the ethnographic process since fieldwork experience is always embodied, so that ethnographers, as with performers, are constantly responding and adjusting to what is occurring around and within them—a form of improvisation which engages their entire being: body, mind, and heart.

American anthropologist Sarah Pink concurs with Hastrup that disorientation is an unavoidable aspect of fieldwork experience. Whereas feeling disoriented and being taken by surprise are still often dismissed as lack of control in the social sciences, Pink objects that, no matter how prepared researchers may be, when opening themselves up to the new world in which they find themselves immersed during fieldwork, "[their] own sensory experience will most likely still surprise them, sometimes giving them access to a new form of knowing" (*Doing Sensory Ethnography* 45). It is precisely this new form of knowing produced by disorientation which I would like to foreground here, inasmuch as this kind of lived experience, which according to Pink can be simultaneously jolting and revelatory, relates to performance training as conceived by both Barba and Grotowski.

Engaging the entire organism in the research process is also critical to the notion of "sensuous scholarship" developed by Paul Stoller, who contends that ethnographers should become apprentices to those they are studying. Challenging the mind-body dualism which he argues still pervades Euro-American research paradigms, Stoller suggests that anthropologists who are searching for ways of accounting for embodiment must "eject the conceit of control in which mind and body, self and other are considered separate." The embodied research process he envisions values a "mixing of head and heart" and demands an involvement in the research process which I would submit is akin to performance training, namely, an "opening of one's being to the world—a welcoming," or an "embodied hospitality "which he argues is "the secret of the great scholars, painters, poets and filmmakers whose images and words resensualize us" (*Sensuous Scholarship* xvii–xviii).

Furthering Stoller's contribution to sensory ethnography, Pink asserts that the latter is about "learning to know as others know through embodied practice," which entails participating "in *their* worlds, on the terms of their embodied understandings" (*Doing Sensory Ethnography* 70–72). She relates the notion of "ethnography as a participatory practice" to conceptions of "learning as embodied, emplaced, sensorial and empathetic, rather than occurring simply through a mix of participation and observation." She emphasizes that this participatory practice is predicated upon a multisensorial, attentive engagement in which "visual observation is not necessarily privileged" (65). In light of Stoller's and Pink's alternative conceptions of ethnographic fieldwork, it becomes necessary to recalibrate methodologies in order to enable researchers to fully engage the dynamics of human interactions, and I am hence suggesting that what Pink refers to as the 'jolt' of fieldwork experience constitutes one of the most promising characteristics of embodied research. For the alteration of habitual behavioral and cognitive patterns produced by such disorientation is not only conducive to the mixing of head and heart evoked by Stoller, but can foster what Pink describes as a sensorial, empathetic way of knowing which is also pivotal to the Indigenous research principles I discussed.

THE INFLUENCE OF FLOYD FAVEL

In the early stages of the development of my project, Canadian theatre scholar Ric Knowles spoke to me about Cree director, performer, and writer Floyd Favel, whom he told me had worked with Grotowski. I met with Favel at the En'owkin Center in Penticton, British Columbia, where he often teaches, and invited him to perform, give talks, and teach workshops at my university. Favel stayed at my home during these visits and we had long conversations about his connection to Grotowski's work. I found out that he had encountered Rena Mirecka during his early apprenticeship in

40 *Grotowski, Women, and Contemporary Performance*

Europe and had worked very closely with her. When I later told Mirecka that I knew Favel, she enthusiastically acknowledged his influence, which had led her to integrate elements of North American Indigenous traditions into her teaching.

In January 2011, I conducted an informal interview with Favel and shared with him the documentary film on Mirecka created for my project. This dialogue with Favel has enabled me to gain an insight into the intercultural processes that have informed his relationship to Mirecka and Grotowski. Favel's perspective on Mirecka's teaching has also helped me to articulate my relationship to her within the context of my embodied research process, which entailed deeply engaging with women's work well beyond the conventional conception of the ethnographer's relationship to her fieldwork informants.

Mirecka, who was born in 1934, is an Elder in the Grotowski diaspora, that is to say, a very important knowledge keeper. After twenty-five years of collaboration with Grotowski, she went on to develop her own investigation of performance processes. In her teaching, she encourages each person to develop a psychophysical connection to human and non-human partners, including nature itself, whose organic qualities the training often seeks to emulate. Relationship to nature is central to her approach, and between 2007 and 2012 I worked with her in various natural sites, from the verdant campus grounds of the University of Kent in Canterbury to the Sardinian wilderness, as well as the forest of Brzezinka in Poland. While Mirecka's interest in ritual performance practices is wide-ranging, she came into contact with North American Indigenous traditions through her encounter with Favel, who took part in the last phase of Grotowski's practical research, known as Art as vehicle. She was later invited by a Native American woman to participate in an initiation ceremony. As far as I know, these are the only two direct forms of contact Mirecka has had with North American Indigenous cultural practices, and she has since honored in her teaching the four directions, colors, natural elements, and energies of the Medicine Wheel.

At the outset of my interview with Favel, he observed that he was probably "the only Indian" who had worked with Grotowski and his collaborators. When I spoke to him about Mirecka's integration of North American Indigenous cultural sources into her paratheatrical research, Favel explained that when he worked with her, these elements were not yet part of her approach, but noted that yoga was already integral to the training. I related to him that while staying in the house where Mirecka's work session participants reside when she teaches in Sardinia, I noticed many books dealing with traditional knowledge, ritual practices, and shamanism. I was surprised by the eclecticism of these books and perplexed by the questionable sources presented in some of them. For example, Mirecka seems to have been particularly influenced by Hyemeyohsts Storm's *Seven Arrows*. When I mentioned this to Favel, he observed that Grotowski himself had recommended to his collaborators the writings of Carlos Castaneda, especially *The Teachings of Don Juan: A Yaqui Way of Knowledge*. Favel specified that Storm and Castaneda had also been influential among Native American intellectuals even though their books were eventually discredited. He suggested that, while these books were misleading, they nevertheless served their time and place as "good fiction" that produced "good results" in the hands of highly competent artists such as Grotowski and his collaborators.

Favel recalled Mirecka as a particularly inspiring teacher and noted that her knowledge of techniques came from a wide range of sources. He told me that he had always fully participated in Mirecka's work and had had wonderful human experiences, which he said had been healing for him. This, he stated, was a very important aspect of any technique, for a technique was only useful and valuable if it made people feel better. He then asserted that no matter how much training one did and how many books one read, one's work would never reach its full potential if it wasn't a form of healing. He stressed that the main thing was "to be healthy and to feel good," and specified that this dimension is directly related to the actor's craft. He said that he hadn't been aware of that when he worked with Mirecka since he was very young at the time, but that as the years went by he had reflected upon his relationship to this work and realized that what he had experienced with her as well as with Grotowski was the best type of training for actors.

Favel added that Grotowski was a brilliant artist as well as a very decent and kind European man, whom he felt had saved his life because he might not have followed the path that led him to become an artist had it not been for Grotowski, and he explained that the Polish director had advised him to pursue artistic work that would connect him with his language and culture. Favel inferred that Grotowski was a good teacher, which he defined as someone who was sensitive to people's needs. He then suggested that Mirecka's integration of basic elements from North American Indigenous traditions was designed to assuage European people's fear of living, which he linked to the malaise of their civilization. He warned, however, that they shouldn't become focused on trying to obtain some kind of power or on having supernatural experiences, which he said was a trick and didn't mean anything.

For Favel, what distinguishes traditional practice from its New Age counterpart is that the former cannot be bought and sold: the reward of traditional healing practices is a form of blessing dependent upon the integrity of traditional knowledge. In his view, it can be productive for experienced artists such as Mirecka to draw from a wide range of sources as long as these artists are not attempting to "turn people into shamans" but are simply using basic elements from these traditions for healing purposes. Favel noted that it is what he tries to do in his work within his own culture. He believes that the best thing he can do with people from his community is to make them feel good enough that they can move, sing, succeed at something, rather than be bogged down in their failures, traumas, and dysfunctions. He remarked that, in light of what I told him about Mirecka's current work and the documentary film I shared with him, it was clear that she was trying to heal people from the harmful effects of modern society. He reiterated that the purpose of any technique should be to make people healthier and happier, and he observed that ceremonies in his culture served this very purpose. He specified that participating in ceremonies was linked to "being clean," and when I asked him what he meant by the term "clean," which happens to be recurrent in Grotowski's terminology (he employed the French word *propre*), Favel explained that, in his culture, being clean means that there are no obstacles between oneself and another person, oneself and the tree, oneself and the universe. To avoid mental or emotional obstacles, it is necessary to be in good relationship with the universe, which implies being in good relationship with oneself and others, including one's ancestors. Ceremonies are therefore an opportunity to put on a feast for the ancestors and to dance with them, which Favel associates with being healthy.

I asked Favel whether Grotowski and his collaborators might have felt constrained to resort to dubious sources and cultural inventions in their creative research precisely because they had no Elders from whom to learn about traditional practices. In response, Favel provided the example of walking in the woods at night, which had become an integral part of Grotowski's paratheatrical experiments and is still practiced today by those who worked with him. For example, both Katharina Seyferth and Ewa Benesz, two of the artists involved in my project, lead participants on such walks, although Benesz does so at sunrise whereas Seyferth leads nocturnal expeditions. As in all the other exercises where verbal communication is used neither by the leader nor by the participants, this walking always occurs in silence. Commenting on this kind of practice, Favel explained that in Northern Saskatchewan, he had come into contact with an elderly hunter-trapper medicine man who walked in the forest at night as if in daylight. This skill was linked to his intimate knowledge of the land, and Favel stressed that in this region hunters still walk at night in the forest and guide their boats through the water over vast areas that can span up to fifty square miles. He observed, however, that the difference between Northern Saskatchewan hunters and the guides who took participants in the forest at night during Grotowski's paratheatrical experiments was that the former had developed a "soft presence" that made them invisible, as if melting into their surroundings. The latter, on the other hand, were so focused on being present and aware that their walking could sometimes take on a dominating quality.

Favel emphasized that Grotowski and Mirecka were attempting to respond to a need in their society. He stated that Mirecka's use of basic elements from North American traditional practices such as the Medicine Wheel was clever and creative, and said that he had nothing against adapting a particular technique to specific needs as long as the teacher had the proper sensitivity to guide people through it. If it felt good for them to walk in the woods, for instance, then they should do so. He recalled that the healing process he had experienced when working with Mirecka had helped him when he was very young and very far from home, and he inferred from this personal experience that Mirecka, like Grotowski, was a good teacher.

This suggested to me that Mirecka's mastery comes from having walked the creative woods for a very long time, and often in the dark, given the impossibility for Poles of her generation to have direct access to non-Western traditional knowledge. Towards the end of our interview, I asked Favel if he realized that he had probably been her most direct connection to North American Indigenous cultural practices. He smiled and remarked that even though at the time he was unaware of the influence his encounter with Mirecka would have on both of them, he must have accomplished something worthwhile when he worked with her in Europe. He acknowledged Mirecka's approach, which had made him feel fulfilled, intrigued, deeply engaged, and said that he could have spent endless days working with her. He observed, however, that the privilege of learning from a master-teacher comes with the responsibility of searching for one's own way, pursuing one's own creative work, and transmitting it to others.

While my participation in Mirecka's creative research is necessarily enmeshed in the heritage of colonialism that Westerners have to confront in order to be clean, so to speak, Favel's perspective on her work has enabled me to see it more clearly for what he says it is, namely, a healing process in which relationality is paramount. According to Meyer, one's personal relationship to one's research topic informs the research process itself, and I am grateful for the ways in which Mirecka's teaching has helped me to be in good relation with her creative work, as well as the creative work of the other women involved in my project and, by extension, the work of Grotowski, an ancestor with whom we all continue to dance and feast, as we keep searching for our own way.

POSITIONALITY

Pursuing this project has led me to walk in the footsteps of feminist and Indigenous scholars, and I am inspired by the courageous ways in which they position themselves reflexively within their research process. Their double and often multiple consciousness provides insights into what is at stake in that process, and, following their lead, I will now foreground the various ways in which my own positionality has informed my embodied research.

I was born and raised in a French working-class family, and was fortunate to receive at the age of fifteen a two-year full scholarship to study at Lester B. Pearson College of the Pacific, a United World College located on the West Coast of Canada. United World Colleges are non-profit, non-denominational institutions promoting international understanding through education. My interest in world performance traditions and my commitment to developing interdisciplinary and cross-cultural research methodologies are rooted in this formative experience. I was the only student from France in this global village hosting two hundred young people from sixty-five countries in the coastal forest of Vancouver Island, and it was in the course of these two years that I became aware of the infinite potentialities that arise when people with different cultural legacies strive to achieve what phenomenologist J.N. Mohanty defines as "mutual communication."

In his essay "The Other Culture," Mohanty posits phenomenology as a philosophical attempt to "know knowing," or to "understand understanding," and goes on to ask how one can know another culture. He contends that no culture can be totally different from one's own since all human beings have a body. Indeed, we all apprehend the world through bodily, experiential processes, and while lived experience differs from one individual to the next, it is always embodied. Mohanty describes the foreign as that which is produced by the binary oppositions familiar/strange and sameness/different, and remarks that such binaries already exist within one's home-world. Subcultures, for example, are defined in opposition to dominant societal practices while belonging to the same larger cultural group, and members of a certain subculture might find the practices of another subculture 'strange' simply because they are unfamiliar. Therefore, the binaries familiar/strange and sameness/different cannot be said to exclusively define the foreign.

In order to bypass binary thinking, Mohanty proposes a dialogical model of cross-cultural research that hinges upon "mutual communication" between cultures. He states that if A, B, and C come from three different cultures, they will necessarily interpret one another's experiences in ways that will make notions of what is familiar relative. He observes that this complex triangular relationship "obliterates the priority accorded to one's home language (culture, world)" since it requires that A, B, and C engage in an on-going dialogical process in which no single perspective may be privileged. He concludes that "it is not simply one-sidedly knowing the other, but 'mutual' communication which removes 'strangeness.' The idea of one world for all is constituted through such communication and may serve as *a norm* for critiquing one's home-world" ("The Other Culture" 135–46).

At Pearson College, such a dialogical process not only enlivened classroom discussions but also fueled monthly village meetings, shaped personal relations, and underscored the live performance events through which students shared their cultural traditions by teaching them to each other. "How can there be peace without people understanding each other, and how can this be if they don't know each other?" asked Lester B. Pearson during his 1957 Nobel Peace Prize acceptance speech.[8] In this speech, Pearson refers to "cooperative coexistence," thereby suggesting that knowledge and understanding must be reciprocal. This sense of reciprocity significantly informed the curriculum at Pearson College, which combined the International Baccalaureate academic program with a wide range of social services and creative activities. The idea of "one world for all" hence became a very concrete reality for me at an early time of my life, and still deeply informs my work as a performance practitioner, researcher, and educator.

When I returned to France, I engaged in various forms of performance training while studying literature and theatre at university. I was then offered funding to pursue doctoral studies in theatre at the University of California, where I later held a post-doctoral faculty fellowship in anthropology. I went on to teach performance practice and theory at an English-speaking Canadian university, and have been directing a cross-cultural research project funded by the Canadian government. I am therefore always positioned as conducting research 'abroad', whether I am in Canada, the United States, Poland, or even France, since 'abroad' has paradoxically become what I now call 'home'. Due to my hybrid identity as an international artist-scholar, I am almost always simultaneously an insider and an outsider engaged in research processes where the distinction between practice and theory remains ambiguous, to say the least. This balancing act at the crossroads of disciplinary and professional affiliations constitutes my experience of precarious equilibrium, the phrase used by Barba to describe the organic tensions and oppositions cultivated in performance training to alter the balance of the performer's body-mind, thereby also altering the performer's perception or awareness of her relationship to her own self, others, and the world at large. It is this particular positionality that has led me to become interested in the implications, for performance studies, of the critique of dominant Euro-American models articulated by Indigenous researchers.

According to Indigenous research principles, positioning oneself within one's research and acknowledging where one comes from is paramount. In *Kaandossiwin: How We Come to Know*, Kathleen E. Absolon (Minogiizhigokwe) states: "Surviving the academy requires a vision beyond the academy, a sense of purpose, a grounding in identity [...] Internal fences keep us boxed into particular ways of thinking, being, and doing. [...] In order to survive we remember who we are and what we know. Our search for knowledge is ultimately connected to an emotional and personal search related to: Who am I? And where do I come from?" (108–09). Absolon explains that her mother showed her how to identify landmarks when walking in the bush: "She taught me to always turn around and to look at where I'd come from so I'd know how to get home and not get lost" (110). She links her experience of the bush to her experience of the academy: "In the academy, I think our research is about finding our way home. [...] Academic channels can become murky and muddy and can bog us down [...]. Obstacles do exist, but when we stop and open our minds up to the possibilities, we usually find another way of continuing on our journey" (110).

As the granddaughter of a coal miner who lost his life in a mining accident before I was born, and as the first person in my family to pursue post-secondary education, as well as someone living and working in a language which is not my mother tongue, my experience of the academy has often been one of having to 'pass' not in terms of race but of socio-economic as well as cultural background. This experience is further complicated by my being a junior female faculty member with unconventional research interests. Navigating choppy academic waters against the current is therefore an image that resonates for me, and heeding Absolon's mother's advice, I now turn back to look at where I've come from to avoid getting lost.

* * *

This is the last evening of my Pearson College thirty-year reunion, and I am sitting on a familiar bench outside the dorm-house where I once lived. Old friends have come from all over the world with their partners and children, but tonight almost everyone seems to have gathered at the other end of our small campus and everything is quiet. With none of my middle-aged peers in sight, I suddenly feel as if I had gone back in time to the two intense years I spent here, as if nothing within me or around me had changed. I remember how, at the time, I used to wonder what the future would hold, for I knew that once I left this place, which felt like home, and returned to the "real world," as we called it, there would be many challenges and uncertainties. Now, sitting on this bench again in August 2012, I ponder the extent to which my experience at Pearson has guided my journey up to this summer night. I think of all the students who have lived here before and after me, and of the new students who will arrive in the Fall. I think of the people on whose land the College was built, and I try to imagine their lives here before any of this existed. Looking at the tall cedar trees in the night sky, I wonder whether it is the spirit of all those who have lived here that gives this place its energy and power.

An impulse to get up and visit the Spiritual Center takes me on a dark and narrow path leading to a new building which stands on the edge of the campus and overlooks the bay. Two small candles and a few flowers have been placed on the floor of this open space fashioned from pine and cedar. The air is charged with the silent presence of a handful of Pearson graduates sitting in the semi-darkness, and this meditative mood reminds me of the years during which we learned to question everything. Tonight I ask myself: Why are we here? Who have we become? What is the purpose of coming back to this place? All this feels very familiar even though the Spiritual Center did not exist when I attended Pearson College. Perhaps it is because I recently participated in a paratheatrical retreat in the Polish forest, which also involved a small international group and took place in an open space with candles and flowers. But the route leading to Poland started here, and being back is a way of returning to the source of my desire to learn from world cultures and traditions. As I sit quietly, a rising tide of images, memories, and sensations floods in, reminding me how deeply my life has been anchored into my experience here, and it is as if all that had happened to me since Pearson somehow retrospectively made sense. As we sit together, ensconced in the stillness of this small wooden haven perched above the Pacific Ocean and surrounded by the darkness of the forest, I wonder whether others feel this sense of connection and belonging. Putting my trust in the visceral knowledge that my personal history is rooted to this place feels like a huge leap of faith, but doing so is clearly what has gotten me this far. So I give thanks for my on-going journey and ask for the strength and courage to face the new challenges and uncertainties awaiting me back in the "real world." And as my mind gently drifts between past and future and beyond national and cultural moorings, the people sitting close to me, the candlelight, the trees, the stars and the ocean remind me of who I am.

* * *

In my post-Pearson years, I became increasingly dissatisfied with French theatre which is, as my compatriot Antonin Artaud bemoaned before me, very much text-based. I was especially disappointed by the absence of rigorous training and particularly frustrated with the limitations of psychological realism. Searching for alternative forms of training, I fortunately came across a multidisciplinary performing arts program combining acting, improvisation, acrobatics, juggling, tightrope walking, opera, and traditional singing. I attended this program for two years for very little tuition because it was subsidized by the Communist municipality of Villeurbanne, just outside Lyon. I also enrolled in acting classes at the Comédie de Saint-Etienne, a nationally subsidized regional theatre with its own school. I eventually moved to Paris where my search for training resumed. Having ruled out exclusive private classes, workshops, and programs which I could not afford, I finally discovered in 1989 what I had unknowingly been longing for: Poor Theatre. No one had recommended this type of theatre to me, although I had come across the text *Towards a Poor Theatre*, which had made a strong impression on me. I was attracted to this way of working because I sensed that it was both unconventional and inclusive.

I was fortunate to be introduced to Grotowski-based work by Caroline Boué and Bertrand Quoniam,[9] who had both been members of a group led by Ludwik Flaszen, Grotowski's dramaturg, and had also trained extensively with Zygmunt Molik, the Laboratory Theatre voice specialist. Boué and Quoniam had gone on to create their own group, called *Présences en Regards*, and what was unique about the physical and vocal training they transmitted to the members of our group was that they led this training together, so that neither gender was privileged in the work, whose particular efficacy seemed to me to hinge upon this kind of energetic balance.

In my first year in the French capital, I met Robert Ornellas, an actor of Hawaiian and Portuguese ancestry who co-founded the American Theatre Group of Paris after graduating from the University of California, Irvine, where he was a Master of Fine Arts student when Grotowski launched his Objective Drama Project. Ornellas was in the first group of students selected by the Polish director at the outset of the Project and also attended his Master Class. During my conversations with Ornellas, he shared his experience with me and the notes he had taken during the Master Class, a year-long course in which students worked on Ibsen's *Peer Gynt*. Our shared interests led Ornellas and I to co-teach an English-speaking acting workshop in Paris while I pursued my training with *Présences en Regards*, and we have been life and work partners since that time.

During my four years of training with the group, I searched for books, articles, and film documentation about Grotowski's work, and the material that was available at the time invariably focused on men. The only woman's name mentioned in relation to Grotowski was that of Rena Mirecka, yet I was unaware that she had developed independent artistic research after the dissolution of the Laboratory Theatre, and the only trace of her contribution was her performance in the documentary film *The Constant Prince* which was available at my university theatre library. The other woman in the film is Maja Komorowska, who plays a male character and is unrecognizable since she was directed by Grotowski to brush her long hair forward so that it would hide her facial features throughout the piece.

At the time, I felt that my lifeline to Grotowski's work was Molik, whose teaching was the source of the body-voice training that was a major focus for *Présences en Regards*. Yet I was only able to work directly with the Laboratory Theatre's voice specialist years later when I received a University of California professional development grant to travel to Poland. This work session, which took place in Brzezinka in 2006, is documented in the film *Dyrygent* featured on the companion DVD to the book *Zygmunt Molik's Voice and Body Work: The Legacy of Jerzy Grotowski*. I worked with Molik again in 2007 and 2008, and was happily surprised, and admittedly relieved, to discover over the course of my experience with him that I had learned most of his exercises from his two students who had been my teachers. Of course, I was extremely grateful to gain access to the source of this work and encounter a master-teacher, but I also realized that my own teachers had been very good thieves, especially since they had told me that when they were members of Flaszen's group he had expressly forbidden them to teach what they had learned from him and Molik.

Flaszen resided in Paris during my formative years in the capital, and whenever I happened to see him, usually in a bookstore or theatre, I always made a point to salute him politely and introduce myself as a student of his students. Although his enigmatic gaze appeared slightly quizzical each time I performed this ritual action, Flaszen never once revealed his feelings about my flagrant illegitimacy. Many years later, I presented my research project to a very tepid academic audience in Krakow on a "2009, Year of Grotowski" panel chaired by Zbigniew Osinski, the preeminent Polish

Grotologist—to borrow Flaszen's playful neologism—and after my presentation, Flaszen himself, whom I knew had been sitting in the audience, suddenly walked towards me with his resolutely energetic stride. To my great surprise, he shook my hand and complimented me on having been "very concrete" in the discussion of my project. Six months later, Flaszen graciously approached me again at the end of another "Year of Grotowski" talk I gave at the Sorbonne and which was thankfully well-received. These experiences contributed to further bolster me in my determination to learn from the women who had dedicated their lives to the kind of creative research that had been transmitted to me.

Figure 1.2 Ludwik Flaszen with the author at the Sorbonne, "L'Année Grotowski à Paris" conference, October 2009—photo by Danièle Magnat.

EMBODIED RESEARCH IN ACTION

My fieldwork began during the month-long Laboratory of Creative Research that I organized in Poland from July 7 to August 5, 2009 in partnership with the Grotowski Institute for the "2009, Year of Grotowski" as designated by UNESCO. This Laboratory included five work sessions led by Rena Mirecka (Poland), Iben Nagel Rasmussen (Denmark), Katharina Seyferth (Germany), Ang Gey Pin (Singapore), and Dora Arreola (Mexico), a three-day theatre festival featuring the current creative work of these artists, as well as two days of meetings with other key women artists from the Grotowski diaspora such as Maja Komorowska and Ewa Benesz (Poland), Elizabeth Albahaca (Venezuela), and Marianne Ahrne (Sweden). These events took place at two historical sites: the performance space in Wroclaw where the Laboratory Theatre rehearsed and performed the landmark productions *The Constant Prince*, *Akropolis*, and *Apocalypsis cum figuris*, and the workspace located in the forest of Brzezinka, an hour and a half from Wroclaw, where Grotowski conducted his post-theatrical research.

I organized these meetings in Poland in collaboration with Stefania Gardecka, Grotowski's main administrator, and Justyna Rodzinska-Nair, who coordinates workshops and special events at the Grotowski Institute. Gardecka and Rodzinska-Nair belong to different generations of women who have been playing pivotal roles as administrators, coordinators, and facilitators—in fact, its directors notwithstanding, the Grotowski Institute is operated by a team of remarkable women from whose dedication, perseverance, and resourcefulness I benefited throughout the development of my project.

Participating in the five work sessions required "lending one's body to the world," as defined by Stoller, and constituted a form of apprenticeship through which one learns from others instead of studying them, as articulated by Pink. These sessions were led by artists who had themselves invested many years of their lives in a process of self-cultivation to which Stanislavsky and Grotowski both referred as the "work on oneself." This apprenticeship therefore provided participants with an experiential way of learning dependent upon the direct transmission of embodied knowledge. In the summer of 2010, I continued to develop this research process as I travelled to Italy, Poland, and France to meet individually with the artists, participate in workshops, and lead a group meeting that took place in Sardinia. In the winters of 2011 and 2012, I travelled to Denmark to document on film the work of Iben Nagel Rasmussen with her group The Bridge of Winds.

The collaborative documentation process I developed was designed to provide the artists with an opportunity to work closely with professional photographers and videographers to produce high-quality documentation which could then be used by the artists for their on-going research, personal archives, and the promotion of their work independently of this

Research Context 51

Figure 1.3 Group photo. *Meetings with Remarkable Women*, Grotowski Institute, Wroclaw, Poland, August 2009 (left to right: Stefania Gardecka, Maja Komorowska, Elizabeth Albahaca, Ewa Benesz, Rena Mirecka, Virginie Magnat, with translator Kasia Kazimierczuk)—photo by Francesco Galli.

project.[10] Such a collaborative approach to documentation ensures that the artists remain in control of the modes of production and the representational strategies throughout the creation of the audiovisual material, from the choice of medium (photos and/or video) to the selection and editing of that material, for respectful representation is critical if documentation is to be mutually beneficial. This resulted in a documentary film series created in close consultation with each artist and now featured online on the Routledge Performance Archive (http://www.routledgeperformancearchive.com).

Another mode of documentation employed throughout this project was a form of creative journaling which can provide artist-scholars with the means to account for their embodied research from a practitioner's perspective. Feminists conducting phenomenological research within dance studies argue that it is crucial to account for what Barbour identifies as "women's lived movement experiences" through the development of specific methodologies and alternative ways of writing. Barbour thus advocates first-person narratives privileging reflexivity, dialogism, intersubjectivity, and provides the example of creative writing that relies on the kinaesthetic properties of the "sensory-rich imagery" pertaining to stream-of-consciousness techniques and poetry. She points out that in this type of hybrid documentation "the researcher's voice, theoretical discussion and quotes from the dancers all mingle together in the research publication," and writing is often complemented with "'visual phenomenology' combining CD-Rom or video of dancing with text and voice-over" (39). She concludes that such methodological innovations can help to "avoid continuing the dominant Western practice of representing lived experiences as objective, 'real' knowledge that was discovered by a neutral researcher," and can "draw attention to the constructed nature of representation" as well as to the choice of specific representational devices, designed to "provide a framework which allows the readers the novel experience of positioning themselves within the richness of the lived experience" (43).

While Barbour's recommendations are particularly well suited to my research project, I must specify that although I hired a team of professional photographers and videographers to document these meetings, I am well aware that it is impossible to capture on film the most important dimensions of the performance processes I will later discuss, such as the personal associations that instill a physical score with visceral immediacy or the inner silence and stillness from which the vibratory qualities of movement and voice emerge, filling the workspace with energy and life. Whereas the pages of the participants' journals, mine included, overflow with words struggling to convey what can be learned from lived experience, they can only provide a partial perspective of how such an experience engages, affects, and possibly transforms performance practitioners.

For Grotowski and his collaborators, the performer's embodied experience is "a matter of doing," as in the performance of ritual actions: "Ritual is performance, an accomplished action, an act" ("Performer" 36). In his Collège de France lectures, Grotowski established a link between aesthetic and ritual performance, suggesting that theatre and ritual were related because of the live process they had in common and that may be described as a transformation of energy generating a different quality of perception—Grotowski employed the English term "awareness." Favel suggests in "Poetry, Remnants and Ruins: Aboriginal Theatre in Canada" that it is precisely this type of process which connects theatre, tradition, and ritual:

> Theatre and ritual traditions share the same characteristics: narrative, action, and the use of a specialized or sacred space. But theatre comes from across the Big Water and our traditions originate here. Both of these mediums have different objectives and goals. Where these two mediums connect is at the spiritual level. In the moment of performance, higher self is activated, and it is at this higher plane that theatre and tradition are connected and related. (33)

The women in my project have developed diverse perspectives which are often situated at the intersection of theatre, tradition, and ritual, and the heightened awareness evoked by Grotowski and Favel is also pivotal to their conception of performance practice. Moreover, spirituality in their work often entails a connection to nature, and their teaching promotes a search for balance between human and non-human life privileging experiential ways of knowing that I will relate in the third chapter to an ecology of the body-in-life grounded in the organic processes of the natural world.

Embodied experience, spirituality, and relationship to the natural world are also fundamental to Indigenous conceptions of knowledge, and for Indigenous scholars the purpose of research is "not the production of new knowledge per se" (Denzin et al., *Handbook* 14), but the development of pedagogical, artistic, political, and ethical perspectives guided by Indigenous principles and informed by the conviction that "the central tensions in the world today go beyond the crises in capitalism and neoliberalism's version of democracy" (*Handbook* 13). For according to Native Canadian, Hawaiian, Maori, and American Indian pedagogy, "the central crisis is spiritual, 'rooted in the increasingly virulent relationship between human beings and the rest of nature' (Grande, 2000, p.354)" (*Handbook* 13). In response to this crisis, Indigenous activists propose a "respectful performance pedagogy [that] works to construct a vision of the person, ecology, and environment" compatible with Indigenous worldviews (*Handbook* 13).

There are parallels between such a conception of pedagogy and the teachings of the women involved in my project, especially in terms of the centrality of experience as a way of knowing. Meyer states, for example, that from a Hawaiian perspective, experience lies at the core of cultural practice: " It is as most mentors reminded me: *practice* culture, *experience* culture, *live* culture. [. . .] It is a call to practice. It is a reminder of the most important aspect of a Hawaiian knowledge structure: experience" ("Our Own Liberation" 129). Meyer considers research itself to be necessarily experiential, yet conversely to the type of knowledge that is credited to individuals and protected by intellectual property rights, experiential knowledge acquired through traditional cultural practice is dependent upon the "maintenance of relationships, which takes conscious and deliberate thought and action" (134). She stresses that such knowledge is "the by-product of *dialogue*, or of something exchanged with others. Knowledge, for some mentors, is a gift that occurs when one is in balance with another." This implies that the person who receives such a gift also bears the responsibility of "continued rapport with those who 'keep' knowledge" for her (134–35). Being engaged in such an exchange therefore requires constantly striving for reciprocity to achieve what Mohanty defines as mutual communication.

Interestingly, Meyer defines the knowledge gained through this exchange as a *"practiced* knowing" which is relational and affects those involved in the research process. She points out that it is necessary to be changed by one's research in order to change the culture of research, and encourages researchers to reflect on the implications of research for their own lives, and to ask themselves: "Are the ideas learned by doing research something I *practiced* today? Truly, why do research if it doesn't guide us into enlightened action? Is the vision I hold in my heart something I extend in all directions?" ("The Context Within: My Journey into Research" 254).[11] For Meyer, research should not be conceived as a competition for knowledge between individuals striving for academic recognition, but as a relational process dependent on mutual trust, collaboration, and healing. Changing the culture of research thus entails resisting dominant theoretical frameworks that pre-determine research outcomes, acknowledging that each step of the research process is part of a larger journey whose meaning can only be learned through experience, and devising inclusive dissemination strategies that are mutually beneficial.

Since the call of Indigenous scholars to change research from within the academy can be perceived as an impossible task, it is helpful to be reminded by Bagele Chilisa that it is precisely because "all research is appropriation" that the way in which it is conducted always has consequences. She points out that when "benefits accrue to both the communities researched and the researcher," conducting research can be reconfigured as a two-way transformative process which she identifies as "reciprocal appropriation" (*Indigenous Research Methodologies* 22). Perhaps this is the kind of mutually transformative process Meyer has in mind when she asserts: "This is our time to find each other and to affirm the qualities inherent in earth, sky and water so we can once again regain a place of purpose and relationship with our natural world. [. . .] All relationships matter. Here is our work. Here are spaces for the practice of courage and consciousness" ("The Context Within" 259). It is also significant that Absolon chooses in *Kaandossiwin* to describe her research process by using "terms that reflect Indigenous ways of collecting and finding out [such as] searching, harvesting, picking, gathering, hunting and trapping" (21), thereby equating that process with travelling the land, gathering berries, and sorting them out to make jams, pies, and tarts, and sharing her harvest with others (10–11). Having travelled to meet and speak with Indigenous scholars about their respective methodologies, Absolon notes that once her "baskets of knowledge were full" she then proceeded to "make meaning of it all" in order to turn this harvest into an offering taking the form of a book (34).

During my conversation with Favel, he spoke of the warrior figure in reference to the Native American warrior ethic, which he explained has to do with taking care of others within a communal society. Accordingly, Absolon relates hunting for knowledge to ethics instilled in the land and transmitted across generations:

> We learned to give thanks and express our intentions, actions and feelings for what we needed and took from the earth. Indigenous ethics are implied in life itself and exercised through the teachings. If we needed bark from a tree, expressing thanks, intentions, and actions would precede the taking. Thus, the origins of any feast, basket, lodge or canoe would have been honoured and a consciousness of its Spirit respected. (25)

Whereas replacing the notions of fieldwork, informants, and data collection with the actions of travelling, meeting, and harvesting highlights the embodied dimension of the research process, envisioning data analysis as cooking and baking, scholarly interpretation as the production of culinary delights, and the dissemination of research outcomes as an offering foregrounds the researcher's responsibility for practicing her craft and developing her expertise ethically.

From this perspective, the researcher is cast in the role of the warrior figure as hunter, cook, and care-giver, which is inevitably more demanding than playing the stock character of the academic. For not only do her research outcomes have to be appetizing, flavorful, and nourishing, but they should also contain healing properties. In the preface to her book, Absolon thus declares: "This offering is to those who themselves are knowledge seekers and those who are searching for ways of knowing that wholistically include the spirit, heart, mind and body" (10). She specifies that she spells "holistic with a 'w' to denote whole versus hole or holy" (59) and ties the term "wholistic" to the importance of interconnectedness and relationality in Indigenous epistemologies. She also explains that she seeks "colorful ways to make the pages sing those songs that invoke Spirit and heart" and that she tries to "break the monotony of the written text by using voice, photography, poetry, stories, and visual aids" (20). In her book, for example, the different chapters outlining the various aspects of Indigenous research are all interconnected through her use of the central image of the flower: the roots of the flower correspond to paradigms, worldviews, and principles; the center flower to the self; the leaves to the methodological journey; the stem to the analytical backbone; and the petals to diverse methodologies.

She observes that "all these aspects are interrelated and interdependent," which is precisely what makes Indigenous methodologies "wholistic" (52).

Envisioning the research process as a form of cultivation and each project as organically blossoming from the seeds sown by others before us may be a productive way of thinking wholistically about the interrelatedness of the roots, stem, center, leaves, and petals of the flowers of research. It may also result in more fertile collaborations between Indigenous and non-Indigenous researchers and lead us to become ethical warriors who practice courage and consciousness and respectfully engage in reciprocal appropriation. It is therefore in the hope of contributing a few fresh petals and leaves to this worthwhile endeavor that I offer my harvest in the form of this book.

2 Practice: Mapping Out Interconnections

In the first chapter, I discussed what I identified as an artistic lineage connecting Stanislavsky's and Grotowski's respective conceptions of performance, and addressed the implications that acknowledging such a connection may have for contemporary performance practice and theory. I now turn to key principles within this lineage to provide the necessary context for my discussion of the creative practice of Rena Mirecka, Maja Komorowska, Elizabeth Albahaca, Ewa Benesz, Katharina Seyferth, and Iben Nagel Rasmussen. These artists constitute the first generation of women who share a direct connection to Grotowski's investigation of performance processes.

Mirecka, Komorowska, Albahaca, and Benesz worked at the Laboratory Theatre during the period of theatre productions: Mirecka is a founding member and the only woman to have worked at the Laboratory Theatre from 1959, when the company then based in Opole was named the Theatre of Thirteen Rows, until its official dissolution in Wroclaw in 1984; Komorowska joined the group in 1961 and apart from a short leave between 1962 and 1964 remained a core company member until 1968; Albahaca, an international intern at the Laboratory Theatre from 1965 to 1967, was then invited to join the company, performed in its final production, and actively participated in the paratheatrical period until 1980; Benesz worked at the Laboratory Theatre from 1966 to 1968, and returned to the company in the early 80s; Seyferth was involved in the paratheatrical and Theatre of Sources periods from 1977 to 1981 as a core member of the international group in charge of developing post-theatrical experiments in the forest base of Brzezinka; Rasmussen, who became a member of Eugenio Barba's Odin Teatret in 1966, was introduced to the Laboratory Theatre training during summer seminars led by Grotowski and Cieslak at the Odin in Denmark, an experience which significantly influenced her trajectory.

All first-generation women have gone on to work independently: Mirecka has developed her own approach to paratheatrical research which she has been transmitting internationally; Komorowska has pursued a prestigious film and theatre career in Poland and abroad; Albahaca has worked as an actress in Europe and North America and as a theatre director in Canada and Venezuela; Benesz has engaged in a wide range of performance experiments, including a sixteen-year collaboration with Mirecka; Seyferth has developed a hybrid approach combining stage acting with paratheatre and directs an artistic center dedicated to performance creation and transmission; and Rasmussen, while continuing to perform with the Odin Teatret, has also been working with The Bridge of Winds, an international group which she founded in 1989.

Prior to examining the most significant overlapping principles connecting the last phase of Stanislavsky's research to Grotowski's own investigation of performance processes—principles which will then serve as points of entry into these women's work—I must stress that, whereas much has been said and written about the System, the development of Stanislavsky's research during the last studio remains very little known since the only texts providing insights into this work are Toporkov's notes and some passages of Stanislavsky's own writings appearing in a compilation published posthumously under the title *Creating a Role*. However, based on the clues provided in these texts and in light of Grotowski's articulation of what he understood to be Stanislavsky's perspective, it is possible to identify specific elements which became foundational to Grotowski's theatrical and post-theatrical work and which continue to inform the transmission processes through which the Polish director's conception of performance has been circulating intergenerationally as well as transnationally.

IMPULSES

In the eighth chapter of *Creating a Role*, entitled "From Physical Action to Living Image," Tortsov, a stand-in for Stanislavsky, explains to fictional acting students how to work at the micro-level of impulses: "For the time being I shall limit myself to arousing inner impulses to action and shall fix them through repetition. As for the actions themselves, they will develop of their own accord" (226–27). Interestingly, repetition is used to fix impulse-based actions which nevertheless remain alive and unpredictable as they continue to develop. Grotowski describes a similar process when he suggests:

> 'In/pulse'—push from inside. Impulses precede physical actions, always. The impulses: it is as if the physical action, still almost invisible, was already born in the body. [...] If you know this, in preparing a role, you can work alone on physical actions. [...] You can train the physical actions, and try out a composition of physical actions, *staying at the level of impulses*. This means that the physical actions do not appear yet but are already in the body, because they are "in/pulse." [...] Before the physical action, there is the impulse, which pushes from inside the body, and we can work on this. ("From the Theatre Company to Art as Vehicle" 94–95)

The experiential observation that impulses generate physical actions and contribute to an inner creative dynamism is shared by Stanislavsky/Tortsov, who describes the process by which he begins to compose a repeatable physical score:

> I feel [. . .] that the individual, separate actions are shaping into larger periods, and that out of these periods a whole line of logical and consecutive actions is emerging. They are pushing forward, creating movement, and that movement is generating a true inner-life. [. . .] The more often I repeat the scene, the stronger the line becomes, the more powerful the movement, the life. (227)

Accordingly, repetition enables the actor to structure impulse-based actions into the physical score, and it is also through repetition that these actions become endowed with their own momentum. The connection between impulses and actions is foregrounded by Grotowski when he states that "impulses are the morphemes of acting [. . .]. The basic beats of acting are impulses prolonged into actions" (in Richards, *At Work with Grotowski on Physical Actions* 95). There are striking parallels between these two versions of the nature and function of impulses within the actor's process: for Stanislavsky, the actor must learn how to arouse inner impulses to action and to sustain the life of these actions by means of repetition; for Grotowski, impulses are already alive inside the body, pushing from within and creating a dynamic movement prolonged into actions. These actions remain deeply rooted in the flow of impulses and engage the performer's entire organism.

Perhaps most importantly, Grotowski extends Stanislavsky's conception of performance beyond the limits of psychological realism by relating impulse to intention, which may be understood as an embodied version of psychological motivation. Grotowski thus asserts that when one "intends to do something," one's action is primarily initiated and sustained by a physically-based motivation: "In/tension—intention. There is no intention if there is not a proper muscular mobilization. This is also part of the intention. The intention exists even at a muscular level in the body, and is linked to some objective outside you. [. . .] Intentions are related to physical memories, to associations, to wishes, to contact with others, but also to muscular in/tensions" (*At Work with Grotowski* 96). The embodied nature of impulses and intentions hence precludes an exclusively psychological conception of what constitutes motivation and points to the physical tension I have previously linked to the principle of *jo-ha-kyu*, which in the Japanese tradition is applicable to all forms of life. In his discussion of the physical/muscular basis for the relationship he establishes between impulse and intention, Grotowski specifies: "[T]he process of life is an alternation of contractions and decontractions. So the point is not only to contract and to decontract, but to find this river, this flow, in which what is needed is contracted, and what is not needed is relaxed" (*At Work with Grotowski* 97). In Grotowski's articulation of this process, recurring references to natural elements, which in this case is the flowing water of a river, further distinguish his understanding of impulse and intention from human psychology. One may also argue that the notion of muscular mobilization underlying the correlation between impulse and intention is reminiscent of the principles of Biomechanics developed by Meyerhold, who vehemently opposed psychological realism, since according to these principles the actor must focus on a "constantly changing arrangement of his musculature" (Gordon 78).

When Stanislavsky himself moved away from psychology and, like Meyerhold, became interested in reflexology, he stipulated that actors should concentrate not on emotions but on actions within the given circumstances of the play, since from "genuine, organic, productive, expedient action" everything else would follow (Toporkov 214–15). It is crucial to note, however, that it is the very notion of impulse that also distinguishes Stanislavsky's approach from Grotowski's. Thomas Richards, whom Grotowski designated as his official heir, reports that the Polish director identified "the fundamental difference [between] Stanislavsky's 'method of physical actions' and his own work" as originating from their respective conceptions of impulse. Richards states: "In Grotowski's version, the work on physical actions is only a door for entering the living stream of impulses, and not a simple reconstruction of daily life" (*At Work with Grotowski* 98, 104). Richards goes on to specify that, for Stanislavsky, impulses only manifested themselves within "the periphery of the body ('the eyes and the facial expression')" whereas in Grotowski's way of working "the actor looks for an essential current of life; the impulses are rooted profoundly 'inside' the body and then extend outward." Richards then points out that "this development of the work on impulse is logical if we keep in mind that Grotowski looks for the organic impulses in an unblocked body going toward a fullness which is not daily life" (95).

In his Collège de France lectures, Grotowski insisted that he was interested in an impulse-based process which applied to life's extra-quotidian dimensions, whereas for Stanislavsky impulses were connected to peripheral physical actions which conveyed a type of daily social behavior that pertained to a realistic context. Yet both directors highly valued organicity, a notion which Stanislavsky frequently associated in his writings and teachings with the life of the body. In his talk "Ce qui fut," Grotowski concurs when stating that "the body *is* our life," suggesting that when the body is searching for "that which is intimate [. . .] it is searching for an encounter and in the encounter it searches: I touch, my breathing stops, something stops within me—yes, yes, there is always an encounter in this, always the other . . . and then appears what we call the impulses" (58–59). Thus, in spite of their divergence insofar as the notion of impulse applies to their work, the two directors share the conviction that impulses are the source of physical actions, that both motivations and emotions have a physical basis, and that feelings, or emotions made conscious, emerge organically as a by-product of the embodied experience which they consider to be a fundamental aspect of performance.

ORGANICITY

Organicity is arguably the most important principle in the Stanislavsky-Grotowski lineage since for both directors it is linked to what they refer to as the life of the body. Grotowski establishes a connection between the human and the animal qualities of organicity and asserts that organicity implies, at a primal level, "living in accordance with the laws of nature," inferring from this definition that "a child is almost always organic." Grotowski links organicity to the impulse-based process which gives life to the performer's physical actions, stating that, when structuring these actions into a physical score, "the form should be preceded by what must precede it, that is, preceded by a process which leads to the form" ("C'était une sorte de volcan" 102). The primacy of organicity is reflected in the very title of the Collège de France lecture series ("La 'lignée organique' au théâtre et dans le rituel") and Grotowski explained during these talks that for him, two opposite but complementary poles were always present in the creative act: the pole of "organicity" and the pole of "artificiality," in the "noble sense" (first, second, and third Collège de France lectures). Organicity refers to the existence of the living process which, according to Grotowski, characterizes an "expression not elaborated in advance." During his inaugural Collège de France lecture, he provided the example of the movement of trees swaying in the wind, or the ebb and flow of the ocean on the shore. He remarked that the expressiveness that can be perceived in nature by the viewer appears without the purpose of illustrating, representing, or expressing anything. Without the presence of the viewer, these natural phenomena keep occurring and recurring, unnoticed.

"Artificiality," on the other hand, is characteristic of human efforts to shape, structure, and compose materials in order to represent something destined to be perceived. Grotowski stressed that all artworks were, by definition, art/ificial, and that both realistic and non-realistic means of creating theatre relied, at least partly, on artificiality. This is one of the main reasons why it is possible to speak of a Stanislavsky-Grotowski lineage in spite of important stylistic differences: Grotowski did not have to share Stanislavsky's concern with realism to share his interest in an organic performance process that was impulse-based. Although Stanislavsky investigated this process within the context of psychological realism, Grotowski continued this investigation in his own work outside that particular context. The notion of "montage," for instance, which is especially relevant to Grotowski's directorial work, belongs to the pole of artificiality, while the notion of impulse belongs to the pole of organicity.

While he clearly valued precision, technical competency, and artistic craftsmanship, Stanislavsky was always partial to the actor's inner life, and there are many clues in his writings of his allegiance to organicity. For example, he closes *Building a Character* with an homage to nature's mysterious creative powers and observes that it is impossible to "criticize lightning, a storm at sea, a squall, a tempest, dawn or sunset" (299). He compares these natural phenomena with inspirational peaks in an actor's interpretation of a role, and declares that although these rare, precious moments might sweep the actor away from the through-line of his role, such experiences always surpass achievements dependent upon technical perfection, no matter how masterfully executed and elaborate the technique might be. He concludes by confessing that the inner workings of creative nature remain secrets to him.

Throughout his various attempts to unleash the actor's creative power, Stanislavsky retained a balanced approach in which structure and organicity were complementary aspects of the actor's process. This is exemplified by the way in which he guided his actors when he told them: "I believe" or "I don't believe," and "I understand" or "I don't understand." As noted by Grotowski during his third Collège de France lecture, Stanislavsky linked 'understanding' to the clarity of composition because he was convinced that the audience must be able to perceive an inner logic dependent upon the coherence of the actor's work. However, he also maintained that understanding was not sufficient and needed to be accompanied by 'belief'—not in the sense of emotional identification but as the capacity to recognize the organicity of the actor's process. Belief is therefore related to and dependent upon the integrity of the impulse-based process I have identified as a fundamental aspect of the Stanislavsky-Grotowski lineage. Believing is closer to a bearing witness to what Grotowski envisioned as the actor's *don de soi* than it is to the mere attentiveness usually required from spectators attending a theatrical performance. Unlike the suspension of disbelief characteristic of theatrical realism, this capacity to believe which I am linking to organicity does not belong exclusively to the theatre event since it is also central to Grotowski's post-theatrical research. Flaszen hence notes in *Grotowski & Company*:

> Once, in our Genesis period, our intention was to eliminate the spectators by transforming them into *active participants* in a theatrical ritual. Then, the theatrical spectator was transformed into *a witness*: someone who does not collaborate with the actor actively, nor does he take part without taking action. A witness who is watching, for whom an actor-human sacrifices himself. [. . .] Then, the *elimination of the spectator-witness*: turning that *spectator in progress* into a participant in a paratheatrical ritual, introducing him into the uncommon dimension of existence, where theatrical acting—and also acting in the 'theatre of everyday life'—is stopped. (209–10)

Richards, who worked with Grotowski during the final phases of his research known as Objective Drama and Art as vehicle, reports that the Polish director still employed Stanislavsky's idiosyncratic terminology in the post-theatrical period: "Grotowski would often ask us two questions when analyzing the work of someone. First: what did you understand? [...] Second: Did you believe?" Richards specifies that when someone replied: "I did not understand, but I believed," then the work "could be said to be on the right track" (*At Work with Grotowski* 36–37). This indicates that Grotowski, like Stanislavsky, favored organicity over composition in the initial phase of the work, as Grotowski himself suggested during his Collège de France lectures. This is also confirmed by Grotowski's affinity with Vakhtangov, who successfully reconciled Stanislavsky's focus on the actor's inner process with Meyerhold's focus on theatrical stylization, thereby demonstrating that organicity could also prevail within non-realistic theatre seeking to convey a heightened sense of reality.

ASSOCIATIONS

Associations are an integral part of the actor's organic process for both Stanislavsky and Grotowski. Michael Chekhov provides an edifying example of Stanislavsky's work with associations in his book *On the Technique of Acting*. Chekhov explains that his term "psychological gesture," which is based on the connection he establishes between physical actions, images, and feelings, was inspired from his work on the character of Khlestakov for Stanislavsky's production of Gogol's *The Inspector General*:

> [W]hile giving me suggestions for the part of Khlestakov, [Stanislavsky] suddenly made a lightning-quick movement with his arms and hands, as if throwing them up and at the same time vibrating with his fingers, elbows, and even shoulders. "That is the whole psychology of Khlestakov," said he laughingly (his gesture was indeed humorous). I was charmed by Stanislavsky's action and [...] I could set the whole part [...] from the beginning to the end without difficulty. I knew how Khlestakov moved, spoke, felt, what he thought, how and what he desired, and so on. (89)

Chekhov's testimony reveals that what Stanislavsky meant by psychology was an impulse-based physical process vitally dependent on the interconnection of actions and associations. It is important to note, however, that the term "psychological gesture" itself, coined by Chekhov, appears to privilege through its focus on gestures the outer visible materialization of small impulses. Once these have passed what Grotowski calls "the barrier of the skin," they become visible in the form of quotidian gestures expressed by the extremities of the body: Chekhov refers to a gesture involving Stanislavsky's arms, hands, fingers, elbows, and shoulders. Grotowski's approach conversely relies on deeply rooted impulses that follow "the route of the spine," as he stated during his sixth Collège de France lecture, remarking that when we are cut off from impulses what dominates are gestures, the periphery of the body, that is to say, hands, arms, legs. In contrast, Grotowski always sought a process mobilizing the whole body and in which organic physical actions replaced daily, peripheral gestures. The associations connected to this process are therefore necessarily of a different nature than associations pertaining to psychological realism.

Stanislavsky's most notable reliance on associations can be found in his use of the Magic If. This clearly appears in Benedetti's translation of a passage of Stanislavsky's first volume, in which Tortsov tells his students that the secret of the Magic If lies in the fact that it does not refer to what is but points to what might be, which stimulates the actor's imagination not in the realm of abstraction but at the micro-level of physical impulses: "It arouses an artist's inward and outward dynamism but does so without forcing, through nature itself. The word 'if' is a spur, a stimulus to inner creative dynamism" ("The Actor: Work on Oneself" 41). For Stanislavsky, associations emerged from the given circumstances, which in his work were usually linked to a quotidian, conventional social context, and he used the Magic If to make these circumstances more compelling for the actor. Toporkov recounts that during their work on *Tartuffe*, when the actors of the last studio were struggling with a particularly demanding scene, Stanislavsky proposed what turned out to be a very effective Magic If: what if a madman with a knife had just broken into your house in search of a victim? (*Stanislavsky in Rehearsal* 124). Although this situation had little to do with Molière's play, it was summoned by Stanislavsky to trigger associations that incited the actors to action and led them to experience the kind of dynamism that was needed in this scene.

During his seventh Collège de France lecture, Grotowski remarked that organicity in and of itself was not necessarily a guarantee of creativity, and stated that a truly creative organic process was always connected to the flux of associations. He specified that he had not borrowed the term "association" from psychology, and insisted that, in his work, this term described a process that was very down-to-earth, which he summarized as follows: one does something and one has an association. Grotowski remarked that it was impossible to know in advance what that association was going to be. By way of example, he placed his right elbow on the table at which he was sitting, resting his head inside the fold of his right arm with his right hand on his left shoulder, close to his neck. He said that the association connected to this action might, for instance, remind him of a situation he had once experienced, and of his reaction to that situation. He remarked that, although this process could appear to be quasi-primitive, in the arts the ability to do (*capacité de faire*) was often something quite simple, so that the work with associations in itself was not psychologically or scientifically complex. Yet he stressed that in spite of this simplicity of means, a certain way of knowing, which he described as *souple* (flexible, supple), could be derived from such a process. Grotowski specified that associations could be linked to something that had happened to us in the past, or something that could have happened, or that we think should have happened: "something rooted in the personal life, for example a longing never nurtured." He linked this process to the notion of body memory (*corps-mémoire*), a phrase which he stated he did not employ to refer only to the body but to a larger territory, and which functioned *as if* the actor's body had memories *and* was the memory. He suggested, however, that a kind of mystery or non-verbalized secret inherent to the work should ultimately remain unspoken, and he evoked the image of a flowing river, whose shores and boundaries we may know, but which we should nonetheless allow to keep flowing freely.

Grotowski had previously defined the terms *corps-mémoire* and *le corps-vie* in his 1969 talk "Réponse à Stanislavski." In this talk, Grotowski makes clear that, unlike Stanislavsky, he never worked with actors on "affective memory," the "Magic If," or the "given circumstances." For the Polish director, acting is about mobilizing one's body memory or body-in-life, which simultaneously encompasses one's past and future, that is to say, one's lived experience and all of one's potentialities. Grotowski thus defines associations as actions that cling to one's life, experience, and potential, beyond the 're-living' of past events which have come to characterize psychological realism. Nor should associations be conflated with the character's 'subtext' since the former cannot be formulated or named and must be explored with the body memory, or body-in-life. Grotowski explains that impulses, which pertain to the pre-physical dimension of the actor's moment-to-moment experience, always occur in the presence of someone or something, so that physical actions are never a repetition of a 'real life' type of response that already occurred in the past, but constitute one's actual response to what is happening here and now. It is therefore impossible to predict how the interaction of impulses and associations will inform one's experience of the present moment, and it is the unpredictability of this organic process which keeps the actor's work alive.

According to both Stanislavsky and Grotowski, then, associations are connected to the flux of impulses, although for the former this flux tends to be limited to small, quotidian actions often confined to gestures, whereas for the latter, associations are more deeply rooted in the actor's organism and informed by a stream of impulses which engages the whole body in organic physical actions, beyond the conventions of the realistic reproduction of daily behavior on stage. These differences notwithstanding, Stanislavsky and Grotowski equally stress the importance of the work with associations.

PHYSICAL AND SPIRITUAL LINES

Another important point of convergence in the Stanislavsky-Grotowski lineage is the correlation between the physical and the spiritual. In *Creating a Role*, Tortsov calls the "unbroken line" of physical actions "the line of physical being." He goes on to explain that the "spiritual being" is linked to the "physical being": "It would seem that [the spiritual being] had begun to exist in me already, of its own accord and outside my will and consciousness. The proof of this lies in the fact that I [. . .] executed my physical actions just now not dryly, formally, lifelessly, but with liveliness and inner justification" (227). During his sixth Collège de France lecture, Grotowski also emphasized this dimension of performance when insisting that it was absurd to describe the Theatre Laboratory's work in terms of "physical theatre." He declared that this was an eternal legend mistakenly associated with his company since the body itself had never been its focus, and pointed out that the physical training he had developed with the Laboratory Theatre actors was designed to eliminate *blocages* (blockages) within the body in order to allow the flux of impulses to take place, unimpeded. He referred to the term *duchowe* to describe this process and specified that the literal translation for this Polish term was "a visible spiritual process" (*"un processus spirituel visible"*).

Stanislavsky seems to be envisioning a similar process when stating in Tortsov's words:

> The bond between the body and the soul is indivisible. The life of one engenders the life of the other, either way round. In every physical action, unless it is purely mechanical, there is concealed some inner action, some feelings. [. . .] While I am playing, I listen to myself and feel that, parallel with the unbroken line of my physical actions, runs another line, that of the spiritual life of my role. It is engendered by the physical and corresponds to it. [. . .] The more often I re-live the physical life the more definite and firm will the line of the spiritual become. (*Creating a Role* 228)

Tortsov describes the double task of "playing" and "listening" to himself in order to remain aware of the "merging" of the two lines, and a connection can be made with Grotowski's evocation, during the final phase of his research, of the "I-I," namely, a performative process which involves being simultaneously "passive in action and active in the seeing (reversing the habit)" ("Performer" 378). This implies that presence and perception are interrelated within the double task of the performer: "Passive: to be receptive. Active: to be present." Grotowski refers to an ancient parable expressing this interaction between receptive action and active receptivity:

> We are two. The bird who picks and the bird who looks on. The one will die, the one will live. [. . .] To feel looked upon by this other part

of yourself (the part which is as if outside time) gives another dimension. There is an I-I. The second I is quasi virtual; it is not—in you—the look of the others, nor any judgement; it's like an immobile look: a silent presence, like the sun which illuminates the things—and that's all. The process can be accomplished only in the context of this still presence. I-I: in experience, the couple doesn't appear as separate, but as full, unique. [...] I-I does not mean to be cut in two but to be double. [...] To nourish the life of the I-I, *Performer* must develop not an organism-mass, an organism of muscles, athletic, but an organism-channel through which the energies circulate, the energies transform, the subtle is touched. ("Performer" 378)

Grotowski conveys through the second "I," whose non-judgemental gaze illuminates the actions of the first "I," what he means by presence—a contested term in performance theory. He links this silent presence to a type of work on oneself which, although it is embodied, does not hinge upon the kind of muscular strength required from athletes, but on the ability to become a conduit—hence the importance of receptivity, which Grotowski posits as a fundamental aspect of action.

From such a perspective, the performer's presence may be understood as a form of embodied awareness. In his fifth Collège de France lecture, Grotowski employed the term *présence d'esprit*, which he defined as an awareness that entailed seeing and listening. He stressed that seeing signified really seeing (*voir*), not watching (*regarder*), that listening signified perceiving (*percevoir*) as well as hearing, and that this combination of really seeing and perceiving translated into a single word: presence (*la présence, tout court*). In "From the Theatre Company to Art as Vehicle," Grotowski similarly relates presence and awareness when he states: "*Awareness* means the consciousness which is not linked to language (the machine for thinking), but to Presence" (125). Grotowski referred to the parable of the two birds during his second Collège de France lecture and noted that the point of this ancient story, which appeared in several traditions, was that although these two birds existed at the same time we usually became engrossed with the bird that picked and consequently saw nothing. The Polish director suggested that when one looked on as one picked, it was as if a vast space suddenly opened up, and he associated this capacity to double up with master-performers in Asian performance traditions who are able to make small changes at the level of extremely minute details and observe these changes unfold, hence picking (performing an action) and looking on simultaneously.

Flaszen, whose function at the Laboratory Theatre included being the devil's advocate, seems to shed a different light on the same process when he declares: "The question is: how to be open when everything pushes us towards closure? How to be creative, when everything pushes us towards sterility? How to see, when we are blind? These are the problems. Or how to be, when there is no future? How to be wise, intelligent, when everything persuades us towards stupidity? How to be brave, when we are afraid?" (*Grotowski & Company* 163). One may further ask how such questions might be relevant to the principles I have identified as constitutive of the Stanislavsky-Grotowski lineage, hence to the work developed by Grotowski and his collaborators, and what the implications might be for women performers engaged in such work.

For example, how might physically-based training focused on impulses, organicity, and associations enable women to explore *what could have happened, what should have happened*, and what is rooted in their personal lives and linked to *a longing never nurtured*? Can alternative conceptions of presence and consciousness such as those advanced by Grotowski provide women with a form of embodied agency otherwise unavailable to them in more conventional forms of theatre practice and in the normative gender roles that society expects them to play in real life? Can the work on oneself, when envisioned as a form of self-cultivation leading to the self-knowledge of the I-I, help women (re)claim the power of performance and transmit it to others in order to change lives? These are some of the questions that have compelled me to seek out the teachings of women whose independent creative research has been significantly informed by their participation in and contribution to Grotowski's investigation of performance.

While the practices of these artists are very diverse, the transmission processes pertaining to their teaching are linked by common principles that are most clearly identifiable in the training. In my experience of the work sessions in which I participated, impulses, associations, and organicity thus constituted fundamental elements of the training and significantly structured the creative work, as demonstrated by the *plastique* exercises, which provide a salient example of the interrelation of these three key elements.

RENA MIRECKA

In his sixth Collège de France lecture, Grotowski recounted how Rena Mirecka became a specialist of these exercises, which can be said to represent a staple of the Laboratory Theatre actor training. The Polish director specified that the actors engaged in three types of exercises: vocal exercises, physical exercises, as well as what the group labeled *plastique* exercises. He noted that the development of this training was the product of a certain evolution that had not been planned from the outset. Having stressed that canonical traditional theatre hinged upon the rather banal image of the actor pronouncing words and making gestures, Grotowski asserted that although gestures did exist, they were only the end-point of organic impulses, as if the final articulation of something else. He stated that gestures were not the beginning of the process but its visible outcome, and, as a result, what the observer perceived appeared to be gestural, and he remarked that the question of gestures had emerged from the work of Mirecka.

He explained that Mirecka, whom he said went on to create remarkable roles in the company's theatrical productions, initially struggled with a kind of blockage (*blocage*) in her body and breathing when entering the creative process. As Grotowski observed her work, he sensed that this problem was linked to the rigidity of her spinal column, as well as to the marked narrowness of her chest. He added that this type of problem was common in performers whose chests tended to be narrower since this made abdominal breathing more difficult. To help her overcome this block, Grotowski had asked her to focus on the life and movement of her spine, as if it were a snake. However, he pointed out that this would have never worked if Mirecka had done so in a merely mechanical way and had tortured herself with pointless spinal movements. Grotowski therefore had to invent a kind of trick, and told Mirecka that the Laboratory Theatre actors needed to do "*plastique* exercises" and that she would be the group's instructor. He therefore asked Mirecka, the person in the group whom he felt had the most difficulty with letting life emerge out of the spinal column, to instruct others about an area of the work that was still unknown to them.

The Polish director was familiar with François Delsarte, whom he described as a kind of mad artist who, in the nineteenth century, had developed an outlandish study of the reactions of the human body and its gestures modeled after famous sculptures and artworks. Grotowski deemed the effects obtained by Delsarte quite banal and stereotypical, but decided that his investigation of human reactions could nevertheless become productive if one followed Delsarte's intuition that from such physical reactions something else could surface and come to life.

Grotowski explained that whereas he had asked Mirecka to use the rather suspect gestural work proposed by Delsarte as an entry point, he had warned that she must always be aware of how her exploration generated reactions in herself and others. Grotowski then told Mirecka that she needed to start teaching the other actors immediately. She had thus been compelled to focus on others as she experimented, which freed her from a type of self-observation that could have been paralyzing. He said that it worked very well and that, as she instructed others in the group, she developed a technical way of letting impulses emerge from inside the body, from the life of the spinal column and from the spine towards the outside. Thus, at a very basic level the group was working on the birth of impulses and on what it meant to react physically and concretely to external stimuli by engaging the spine. This, Grotowski concluded, was how the *plastique* exercises came to be.

Grotowski went on to remark that when other people tried to learn the training developed at the Laboratory Theatre, they often made two mistakes. The first mistake was to assume there was only one way to do things. He observed that he had used this particular aspect of Delsarte's work simply because he didn't know anything else that could have been helpful and sensed that he must start from something specific, which he had then transformed into what he needed for his own work. The other mistake, which he said was very dangerous to make, entailed focusing on the form resulting from this training, such as the final gestures, rather than the path (*la route*) that led from the spinal column towards something external, and from something external into the body. Grotowski inferred that whenever one merely imitated the form then everything was dead, a tendency which he felt was far too common. He stressed that the Laboratory Theatre actors had conducted research for many years to develop exercises such as the *plastiques*.

During a recorded informal interview with Mirecka that took place over a period of two afternoons in Sardinia in the summer of 2010, I mentioned Grotowski's discussion of the development of the *plastique* exercises at the Laboratory Theatre and his decision to give her this task in order to help her overcome physical limitations. Mirecka said that although this must have been his observation she hadn't been aware of it. However, she did remember that he had given her some material to learn about movement and that she went on to work on her body to create different structures with the elements from the *plastiques*, which she added were, to some extent, like the different cycles of a dance. A trace of this embodied knowledge developed over years of research was only captured on film on two occasions: the well-known film featuring Cieslak's training demonstration which involved two young Odin Teatret performers,[1] and a much lesser known film excerpt documenting Mirecka's specific approach to the *plastiques* which appears at the end of the film *Acting Therapy*.[2] This unique document is the only available film of the Laboratory Theatre training demonstrated by a woman. It begins at the forty-eight-minute-and forty-eight-second mark of *Acting Therapy* and lasts for ten minutes, featuring Mirecka alone in the main workspace of the Laboratory Theatre. When I asked Mirecka about the making of this film, she told me that the original footage featured a seventy-minute-long improvisation based on the different elements of the *plastiques*, and indicated that this film material had been edited down to this shorter version. I asked her whether the original footage still existed and she said that she did not know. She then told me that everyone at the Laboratory Theatre had begun to teach very early on, and that they taught not only each other within the company but also young people who came from all over the world to participate in work sessions. Mirecka taught the *plastique* exercises during these sessions as well as during the group's international travels. She stressed that for many years this work was very technical and every element had to be very precise and without motivation, without inner searching.

When I remarked that I thought that working only on the technical level was not sufficient when engaged in the training, Mirecka replied that in the beginning it was very important to attend to *blocages* (blockages) in many parts of the body, especially in the inner centers or chakras, because when energy could not flow the body had troubles and was in pain, which was why this technical work must be done. She added that they trained very, very hard because they realized that it was a way of lessening the presence of the mind, and because as the physical body became tired, the mind also became tired. Since the training was followed by creative research and rehearsals, it was a way of making it easier for actors to be open to possibilities when improvising. She noted that when the mind is very present, there is no truth. By observing the body it is possible to recognize when the mind is leading: the right side and the left side of the body move in the same way, the movements are sharp and all very similar. She explained that this is not a reaction, it is not movement, it is simply a gesture, for movement is rooted in impulses coming from inside the body and going towards the outside, and it is through this kind of embodied reaction that one begins to enter into a process in which one can be spontaneous. She stressed that to become spontaneous, the mind must be silent—and with a smile she added that the mind must be silent as much as possible but also present. She described this presence as a form of creative observation whereby the mind sustains a consciousness of the work, but she added that it is impossible to tell the extent to which the mind has to observe movement in order to know whether it is really organic, natural, authentic, or true. She said that it is only possible to know this through experience and years of work, and specified that, over time, she had gained a consciousness, an awareness enabling her to guide her own process without judging it or directing it.

Mirecka recounted that this attitude of exacting technical precision in the training was eventually followed by a creative time of exercises during which she opened up what she called her inner world so as to be present in the physical movement of every element of the *plastique* exercises and every part of the body. The film documenting Mirecka's improvisation based on the training she initiated hence provides an invaluable insight into the creative work that she accomplished as the specialist of the *plastiques*. She then remarked that in classical theatre, actors often focused on creating a character directly based on written words in a play, which she said often became an illustration of the text simply repeating what the playwright had created on the page. She observed that in such conventional acting the work was mostly physically external, technical, and a reiteration of what the author described in the play. Consequently, actions tended to be very close to daily forms of behavior because actors did not train their bodies to react differently from the ways in which they usually reacted in everyday life, even though in conventional theatre there were, of course, some exceptionally creative actors. The danger for these great actors, she said, was that in this kind of theatre directors expected them to do the same thing from one performance to the next, which imposed too great a limitation on actors, and was a way of using up their life, their energy, and this eventually became unsustainable.

Conversely, the Laboratory Theatre actors worked very hard to return to the kind of process that was needed to open up what was individual within each actor, as they searched for a flow of personal impulses and associations from which unusual actions could emerge, unexpectedly. Mirecka stated that the challenges of the training gradually led to a freedom which gave her joy as she acquired the ability to continue her own journey and which helped her to explore through her creative process the personal struggles, questions, dreams, and desires that were important to her. She noted that being able to achieve this through her work was a form of purification for her organism, and explained that this freedom gave her permission to create a life of her own within the work. She told me that this had enabled her to explore how to be present and authentic, aspects which she felt had been missing in her life, and these many years of very personal and very individual work had become the creative ground for her research—hence giving her *the possibility to do*, because, she emphasized, what was fantastic in this work was that it was possible to do everything.

Mirecka, whose approach is deeply influenced by Eastern philosophies and ritual practices as well as by aspects of North American Indigenous cultural traditions, frequently refers in her teaching to natural elements such as water, wind, sun, sky, and earth, whose organic qualities the training emulates. In her teaching, she introduces breathing exercises and the chanting of particular mantras practiced in the Indian and Tibetan traditions, and evokes the network of energetic centers in the human body identified as chakras in several Eastern traditions, suggesting that this circulation of energies within the human organism is reflected in the network of cosmic energies that structures the universe. Grotowski spoke about the chakras when discussing the complex notion of energy during his fifth Collège de France lecture, and also addressed various other ways of mapping out energetic centers within the human body, each center being conceived as a locus of forces.

The Polish director remarked that the perception of these centers of energy had been important in a number of cultures in different historical periods, and referred to the sketches by eighteenth-century German mystic Johann Georg Gichtel, which he said provided a map of the body's energetic centers from the most dense and most vital energies to the highest and most subtle. He pointed out that in India these areas within the human organism were delineated by the well-known system of the chakras, and that in China, for instance in Taoism, people worked on the body's energetic flow by focusing on these centers, although Grotowski noted that this was due, to a certain extent, to the influence of the Hindu tradition. He also referred to the little figurines of pre-Columbian art and stated that energetic centers had been inscribed upon these representations of the human body.

Grotowski indicated that from an experiential perspective, these centers of energy were perceived to be located simultaneously inside and outside the body. He added that researchers had made various speculations, including an attempt in Europe to link these centers to the different plexuses and endocrine glands, but said that he did not think that this kind of hypothesis could solve the problem at hand. He suggested that it might be more productive to use Stanislavsky's phrase "as if" to address this topic, so that one may state that it was "as if" there were different roots (*souches*) for our human capacities or resources, and "as if" these different centers were both inside and outside or around the body. Accordingly, Mirecka and Grotowski both relate energetic centers to organicity, while Stanislavsky, in his rehearsal notes, envisions organicity as the life force animating both human beings and nature. Indeed, as documented by Carnicke, Stanislavsky associates this life force with the Hindu concept of *prana*: "[Stanislavsky] accurately defines it as 'vital energy [...] which gives life to our body [...]. *Prana*—vital energy—is taken from breath, food, the sun, water, and human auras. [...] *Prana* moves, and is experienced like mercury, like a snake, from your hands to your fingertips, from your thighs to your toes [...]. The movement of *prana* creates, in my opinion, inner rhythm'" (*Stanislavsky in Focus* 141). Stanislavsky, Grotowski, and Mirecka thus consider that organicity instills the actor's work with vital energy and makes it kinesthetically compelling.

To provide an example, Grotowski referred to Cieslak's performance in *The Constant Prince*, which the actor himself compared to a lit candle in a glass: the subtle yet intense inner life which shone through his extremely precise physical score was like the flame of the candle forever changing within the glass. Grotowski suggested that accomplishing what he called the "total act" made the precarious flame of human life "sacred," in accordance with the etymological meaning of the word *sacrifice*. When I asked Mirecka about the notion of sacrifice, to which she also refers in her teaching, and whether it could be understood as a gift, she said that it was a total act of sincerity, which, for the Laboratory Theatre actors, entailed not behaving with each other nor with Grotowski as they did in daily situations. She described sincerity as the ability to speak non-verbally—with all her entity, through the body—and touch on the most intimate, hidden questions which she did not share with others in her everyday life. She explained that this would occur in the process of doing, and that it was not easy since this process could bring up troubling or painful aspects of existence that were very personal to each actor.

Mirecka asserted that this process was an immense way of knowing oneself, one's potential and lack thereof, a way of exploring what was possible in reality, in the imagination, as well as in between these two worlds, and a way of asking which one was real. Although such a process was sometimes very painful, it was necessary to give, to make a gift, and this constituted the sacrifice. This giving occurred within the group, and later it took place before the spectators, but it was initially facilitated by Grotowski, who worked individually with actors. She thus recalled that, in the course of a meeting with Grotowski, he asked her how she was doing in her personal life, and she told him about her problems. He prompted her to keep speaking about the difficulties she was experiencing, and when he finally asked her what she was going to do about it, her reaction was a particular expression of bewilderment which Grotowski immediately seized upon, encouraging her to explore this reaction for the facial mask she created in *Akropolis* as one of the concentration camp prisoners. As she related this story to me, a big intake of breath suddenly lifted the muscles of her face upward and the living mask resurfaced, conveying a striking expression of surprise which instantaneously caused me to react, as if producing a kind of reflex response in my body—perhaps this was what Delsarte had in mind in his study of human reactions. Mirecka inferred that all this demanded great discipline, a requirement she was able to accept because she loved the research process that had enabled her to work on a level that was unknown to her in her life outside the theatre.

Significantly, Mirecka continues to transmit the Laboratory Theatre training even though she has moved away from theatre per se to pursue her own paratheatrical research, and the *plastique* exercises have remained a key aspect of her teaching. From 2007 to 2012, I took part each summer in one of Mirecka's work sessions, and in 2009, the "Year of Grotowski," I organized a work session for her in Montreal as well as another in Brzezinka which was part of the Laboratory of Creative Research for my project, and participated in both. In each of these sessions, Mirecka taught the various elements of the *plastique* exercises as part of the training. My most recent experience of Mirecka's teaching was a two-week-long work session which took place in Brzezinka in the summer of 2012. At one point during the session, as we were lying on our backs with our eyes closed in the yoga pose known as *shavasana*, she stated: "Theatre is a pretext, a vehicle to know ourselves, to know what we love to do in this short life, and if this is what we love, then this is our destiny." She then spoke about the necessity of preparing the whole body because she said we could only begin to know through experience, yet she insisted that everything we tried to achieve was a pretext for the research on oneself which was the actual purpose of this work. As I lay down with my eyes closed and listened to the vibration of her voice filling the space, I was reminded of the conversation I had had with Mirecka three years earlier when we both stood by the lake at the threshold of the forest in Brzezinka shortly after the end of her 2009 work session. In my memory of that particular moment, she is telling me that Grotowski's work and legacy are like a tree with many branches and leaves, with everyone, including myself, somehow finding their place on the different branches, and fulfilling what they were born to do. Although I am still unsure whether I belong in this tree, the branch that makes me feel most connected to this legacy is that of the *plastiques*, which, along with the vocal work, gives me the sense of being rooted in a tradition.

While I was familiar with the film that features Cieslak demonstrating the *plastiques*, I had never practiced these exercises until I worked with Mirecka for the first time in 2007. This experience gave me the opportunity to compare Mirecka's *plastiques* with Molik's voice and body work initially transmitted to me by my teachers in Paris and later by Molik himself. As I grew more familiar with the *plastiques*, it became clear that the same key principles applied to both forms of training, which was what enabled Mirecka and Molik when they were colleagues at the Laboratory Theatre to co-lead work sessions such as the one documented in the film *Acting Therapy*. In *Zygmunt Molik's Voice and Body Work*, Molik explains that while daily physical training constitutes a necessary preparation, creativity requires one to go well beyond the repetition of exercises: "[T]he body must already be so well trained with those actions that we treat as training, that later, this training can and must be completely forgotten. The body remembers that it must be more alive than in everyday life, it must be something special, a different kind of life. [. . .] This is the reason why this process is done" (13–14). He stresses the importance of finding "the life" which exists beyond the training itself and remarks that, in his experience, it is about "not know[ing] in advance what you are searching for" (40). When speaking of how to physically and vocally explore what he calls the unknown, a term also used by Mirecka, Molik observes: "You never know how much you have to give. You must find the point where you are touching the impossible, and then give everything. I mean not by forcing the voice but by giving all of yourself. You have to be like this. All your heart must be in this" (65). Mirecka and Molik hence share the conviction that giving oneself entirely to this form of exploration without forcing and without anticipating enables one to tap into the sources of creative life.

When discussing the training developed at the Laboratory Theatre during his sixth Collège de France lecture, Grotowski insisted that it had immediately become clear to the group that exercises in themselves could not lead to the creative act. He noted that the members of alternative theatre groups who endlessly tortured themselves with exercises did not necessarily produce any creative work. He warned that doing exercises for the sake of exercises could become a self-satisfying activity that led to a loss of perspective, so that one forgot that the objective of the work was creativity, the construction of a role and of a composition within a specific network of associations, which he said was a very complex creative process. Grotowski nevertheless acknowledged the value of exercises that helped to counteract the type of corporeal inertia that increased with aging and that could also open certain technical possibilities.

Mirecka teaches the *plastiques* during her work sessions by demonstrating each of them in all their details, and participants follow the flow of her actions and sense the energy of her body in the workspace, a form of learning by induction which requires being entirely focused on the present moment. During this process, she simultaneously embodies these actions and observes participants around her, guiding them by bringing their attention to the principles that govern the training. She stresses that everything must start from the center: sacrum, pelvis, spine, the main areas of the body from which the performer draws her creative force. Some of the guiding principles for this work include staying in contact with the floor yet never being flat-footed, so that the feet, legs, pelvis, hips, and spine are always moving and alive; being aware of directions in the space and sustaining an embodied relationship to it; maintaining the precision of the details while using these exercises to react and respond with the whole body; remaining connected to personal associations which turn the *plastiques* into a form of creative practice.

76 *Grotowski, Women, and Contemporary Performance*

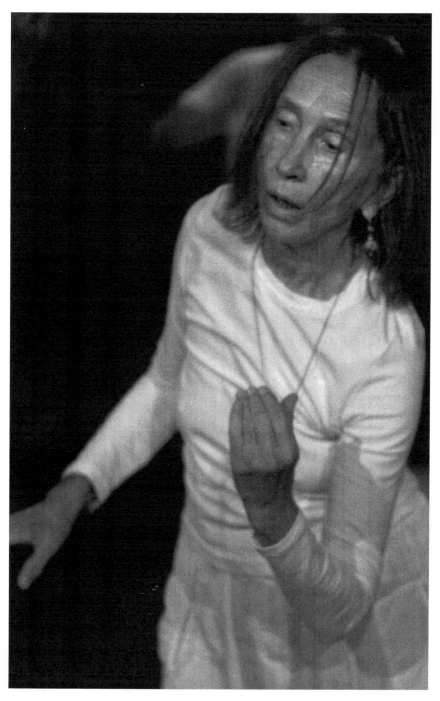

Figure 2.1 Rena Mirecka teaching the *plastiques*. *Meetings with Remarkable Women*, Grotowski Institute, Brzezinka, Poland, July 2009—photo by Maciej Stawinski.

Mirecka emphasizes that the performer's awareness of and relationship to the workspace ensures that the training does not become mechanical. She reminds participants not to look at what their hands and feet are doing but urges them instead to direct their energy outwards, towards the walls of the workspace, to really see the bricks, the ceiling, the trees outside the windows not only with their eyes but with their entire being, so as to be constantly in relation with something. She also stresses that each person's body is different and that each participant must keep searching for ways in which her/his body can become alive within the structure of the training. She often reminds participants that they should not act like dutiful students by doing the exercises for her, but should instead work for themselves. She cautions that when a personal commitment to challenge oneself is lacking, these exercises become lifeless and without purpose.

After working with Mirecka on the *plastiques*, participants usually engage in a group improvisation based on this training that leads to meetings between people allowing them to freely explore different ways of moving in the space they co-inhabit, yet Mirecka instructs participants to return to the *plastiques* whenever they feel that they are losing the life of the improvisation. Going back to the details of the physical training enables individuals to remain connected to their own process until the next creative encounter, or meeting with the unknown. At times, Mirecka makes specific comments about how particular individuals in the group approach the *plastiques* and the group improvisation, stressing that it is important to use the training to work on something very concrete so that the life of the improvisation can emerge.

Meeting the other is part of the performer's exploration of the unknown since, when working with someone else, it is impossible to predict what will happen. This unpredictability can sometimes lead to meetings between participants that involve very forceful physical movement, such as stomping on the floor or engaging in aggressive actions. Mirecka objects to such behavior by pointing out that it is merely the imitation of power. She makes clear that meeting the other is not about being overtly active, but about being open, and about seeing, hearing, sensing, and reacting. She reminds participants that a meeting is never a banal or stereotypical physical confrontation, for example, grabbing and holding onto someone, but an opportunity to find a different way to meet the other. She also notes that whereas the subtle power generated by a meeting between two people can sometimes be akin to erotic or sexual energy, something which is part of life, she does not provoke individuals to go towards this energy. Becoming aware of how energy shifts and transforms is an important part of this process, and when commenting on improvisations Mirecka often asks participants whether they noticed the moments during which they were really listening with the whole body, following and supporting the action that was unfolding, and searching together.

In my experience of the work on *plastique* exercises with Mirecka, for example, I recall a group improvisation during which we were given the task to use elements of the *plastiques* to explore a fantastical garden summoned by Mirecka through very specific yet non-realistic images. This was my third work session with her, and although practicing these exercises had admittedly become my favorite part of the training, using them within this group improvisation turned out to be quite challenging. Exploring the alluring images of the garden through the precision and rigor of the *plastiques* became an exacting search for the life of the garden, which was also the life of the body. Encountering others on the way and making contact with these partners, some of whom became the plants, animals, and spirits of the garden, added multiple layers to the journey. I felt particularly drained when this lengthy improvisation ended, and was huddled in a corner when I heard Mirecka's voice declaring that she had "believed" me, explaining that I had worked with everybody in the group using the *plastiques* as a base for these interactions within the imaginary world she had invited us to enter. Her comments took me by surprise as I felt that I had been struggling throughout this improvisation. What was it that had prompted Mirecka to "believe" in my encounter with this unknowable garden? I was unable to answer this question but was reminded of how, in his teaching, Molik succinctly conveyed what might be at stake in such meetings through the recurring injunction: "Never give up."

The following year, at the conclusion of a work session in Sardinia, I was sitting with some of the participants on the porch of the house when Mirecka joined us and began to speak about the creative research she had shared with us. She challenged us to recognize that this work was not about being ready to do, nor was it about doing something in a certain way for the sake of doing, for example repeating empty actions, and neither was it about the head or the emotions. Emphasizing that such misconceptions were misleading, she urged us to search for the most vital aspect of the work which she described as a sense of flow linked to what she called presence and which had to do with the capacity of being in the moment. Working with Mirecka has given me a renewed awareness that this is not only difficult to achieve but also particularly challenging to sustain, hence the need for on-going training and practice as the foundation for creative research.

Over the course of the seven work sessions in which I participated, I observed a tangible difference when Mirecka entered group improvisations, which would usually take place towards the end of each session. There are times when group improvisations can feel chaotic, ludicrous, and frustrating—which is an interesting experience in and of itself, creating a tension between the impulse to resist and the desire to yield, the law of contradictions that regulates life, if one agrees with Grotowski that life is, by nature, contradictory. When Mirecka participates in group improvisations, she seems to be following her inner process while effortlessly becoming the leader of the group, as if directing it from inside, drawing from everyone's energy and feeding it back into the group, modulating and sculpting this energy in time and space. In fact, it is usually when the group appears to have hopelessly lost its way that this journey into the unknown surprisingly turns into a ritualized action with a hidden purpose that we simultaneously create and discover together. An example of this group work can be seen in the film *The Dream* co-created by Maciej Stawinski and Mirecka to document her 2009 work session in Brzezinka, a film featured on the Routledge Performance Archive.

During my informal interview with Mirecka in Sardinia in the summer of 2010, we sat together under a magnificent old tree and as we spoke in the shade of its gnarly branches the bells of sheep were echoing down the valley. Mirecka confided that she had to accept that dedicating all her energy to the Laboratory Theatre was a sacrifice which entailed not partaking in what she called the *fiesta* of the world, and not being like other women, yet it also meant receiving something else from life, perhaps because of what she was born to accomplish. She told me that when the Laboratory Theatre officially closed in 1984, she did not suffer and felt free to do her own work. She recalled being the only one who tried to continue to train in the space where she had worked with her colleagues for twenty-five years. She kept going until one day, as she was entering more and more deeply into an improvisation, she suddenly stopped and looked around and saw only the naked walls. In that moment, she felt a great sense of danger which prompted her to work elsewhere and to use music so that she would not be alone as she continued her daily training. She said that she felt grateful for having had the strength not to stop. When I asked her if it had been difficult to continue alone, she replied that while working on one's own was challenging, it was also very creative. And although such practice came with a cost linked to having the discipline to *do*, it had also become a necessity and a source of life for her. She considered this ability to *keep doing* a great gift, and said she sometimes wondered how it was possible that this work could still give her such energy, which she acknowledged was incredible at her age.

What is perhaps most astonishing about Mirecka is the swiftness and fluidity with which her energy can change. Just when you think she is deeply irritated by your inability to precisely accomplish what you assume she is expecting from you, she bursts into laughter and you realize that you have been caught judging yourself. For she delights in shattering the reverence of would-be disciples eager to worship her as the great Grotowskian female guru. Although the inscrutable gravity of her face seems imbued with the wisdom of a Byzantine icon, she can, within the blink of an eye, shape-shift into a child-like being burning with desire and curiosity. A truly remarkable artist, Mirecka is a free-spirited master-teacher whose rigor and generosity, exigency and dedication, depth of insight and passion have been for me a constant source of inspiration.

MAJA KOMOROWSKA

Maja Komorowska was a guest artist during the 2009 Meetings with Remarkable Women in Poland, and the following year I was able to witness her work as an actress when the acclaimed Polish director Krystian Lupa kindly gave me his permission to attend and document on film the Warsaw rehearsals for a revival of his production of *Extinction* (*Auslöschung*) by Thomas Bernhard, first created in 2001, featuring Komorowska as the poetess Maria. Stefania Gardecka, who had helped me to organize the 2009 Meetings, and Celeste Taliani, a member of the project documentation team, accompanied me to Warsaw where we filmed Komorowska working on her scenes with Lupa over the course of a week. In spite of her extremely busy rehearsal schedule, Komorowska generously invited us to her home for an interview which was also filmed. Speaking with Komorowska and watching her work became for me an opportunity to gauge the enduring power of body memory, to which she dedicates an entire chapter in her book *Pejzaż* (*Landscape*) co-written with Barbara Osterloff.

In the course of the interview, Komorowska stressed that it was very difficult to write about her creative work and that she had therefore carefully weighed the words she employed in *Pejzaż*, to which she referred several times, pointing for example to the page on which she cites Grotowski's assertion, in *Towards a Poor Theatre*, that spontaneity and discipline "are mutually intensifying, they do not weaken each other" (*Pejzaż*, 32). Komorowska remarked that such a statement can only be experienced in practice. She explained that when she joined the Theatre of Thirteen Rows in Opole in 1961, three years after its creation and one year prior to its being renamed the Laboratory Theatre, she was already very fit: having gained stamina from practicing sports she could stand on her head and walk on her hands, and, consequently, the physicality of yoga-based exercises was not what she found the most challenging in the training. In *Pejzaż*, she recounts her experience in the chapter titled "At the Theatre of Jerzy Grotowski," and observes that, paradoxically, her physical ability meant that these exercises did not help her to search from inside the body, which was the point of the training. She states that she would simply stand on her head because her body was ready for it, hence she had no need to use her imagination in that situation. What the training eventually helped her to understand, however, was that when the body is truly involved in searching, it discovers by itself what the next step needs to be. She concludes: "Grotowski taught me diligence: if the body is to be a sensitive instrument—without which the actor's true creativity is impossible—one has to train, simply work" (30, 32).

Komorowska also referred to the chapter in *Pejzaż* titled "The Memory of the Body," in which she states that everything we go through leaves a mark in our memory, including the dreams we have, since they feed our memory and vice versa. For Komorowska, dreams, or unprocessed images,

Practice: Mapping Out Interconnections 81

Figure 2.2 Maja Komorowska. *Meetings with Remarkable Women*, Grotowski Institute, Wroclaw, Poland, August 2009—photo by Francesco Galli.

are part of who we are because they connect us with some of our most significant life experiences, including important relationships. During the interview, she explained that she often dreams of her mother, who passed away long ago but who remains present in her life through these recurring encounters. In "The Memory of the Body," Komorowska writes:

> Yes, dreams about my parents keep coming back to me. My father—when I'm holding him in my hands, he's always so small. And I also often dream about my mother. She comes to me. How? She is alive? But there was a funeral! Or maybe there wasn't. . . My God, Mother is alive, and I haven't visited her for so many years, haven't looked after her and she is so old. This dream really haunts me. (138)

She then shares a more joyful dream about her mother linked to the memory of her hair:

> Her hair was like that of a child. This is how I remembered my mother's hair. And I dreamed that Mother was lying on this catafalque in a long, black dress. I walked up to her and stood there. And—I started stroking her hair. I stroked and stroked and suddenly I saw that one hair turned into a feather, then another. . . more and more feathers. . . And then I suddenly saw that my mother had changed into a bird. A bird sitting on a catafalque. I woke up. And missed her. (138)

She spoke about this particular dream during the interview and suggested that such dreams come from our longing—that feeling which accompanies us throughout our life and influences what we do, what we search for. She observed that the further we advance in time, the longer the road, the more often we return to those years when everything was still possible and to our memories of people who are no longer among us. She thus states in her book: "The feeling that something has passed away—that *loss*—is important. One cannot deprive oneself of it. But one may try filling it. *Fill that loss*. Don't we create because of that?" (139).

Komorowska describes her dreams very precisely in *Pejzaż*, often connecting vivid images to embodied experience, almost as if trying to remember the details of a particular physical score linked to specific impulses and personal associations. In one of these descriptions, she employs the term "impulse" in relation to an image of the human body whose organic life seems to be reversed, beginning with death and ending with birth:

> I dreamt of a skeleton. It was all stiff. Lying down. And at a certain point—it lasted for quite a while (it would be easier to show this than to describe it)—an impulse came from the skeleton, a twitch somewhere in the pelvis. The skeleton started to move softly into a baby's position. Stiffness and then this soft movement. It gradually lifted its

knees up to its chin, and shifted onto its side, like a cat. The bones were not in the way. It shaped itself like an embryo and in the end it put its finger inside its mouth. It settled itself and rested. And I woke up. I was lying on my side with a finger next to my lips. Did I put myself into this position because I was dreaming it? Or did I perhaps dream it because I was already lying like this? (137–38)

The questions Komorowska asks of her dream evoke for me the performer's organic process whereby impulses and associations are deeply rooted in embodied lived experience. This moving (in the double sense of the term) image of a human skeleton gradually coming to life, as if in a second birth, may be related to her embodied memory of the Laboratory Theatre training, whose aim was to reconnect the body with its own energetic flow in order to enable the performer to be fully alive. In *Towards a Poor Theatre*, Grotowski describes the director-actor relationship as a phenomenon of "shared or double birth," and contends that "the actor is reborn—not only as an actor but as a man—and with him, I am reborn." Having acknowledged that such a statement is "a clumsy way of expressing it," he suggests that what is achieved in this collaborative creative process is "a total acceptance of one human being by another" (25). Grotowski also refers to birth in the chapter on Artaud where he declares: "When we propose to the actor that he should transform himself before the spectator's eyes using only his inner impulses, his body, when we state that the magic of the theatre consists in this transformation as it comes to birth, we once more raise the question: did Artaud ever suggest any other kind of magic?" (119). Grotowski often equates the organic creative process with birth, life, and rebirth, yet, unlike his male collaborators who fathered children, the women who chose to become mothers had to negotiate raising children while working at the Laboratory Theatre. In Komorowska's testimony, her lived experience as a daughter and a mother endows the images related to birth and death in her dreams with a poignancy that particularizes her perspective as a woman and creative artist.

In *Pejzaż*, she speaks openly of the challenges of being a mother at the Laboratory Theatre. She recalls that she was pregnant when working on *Akropolis* and that there were numerous sections of iron pipe on the stage as part of the stylized setting of the concentration camp, so that during the rehearsals she had to be very careful not to harm herself given her condition (26). She left the company in 1962, which was a very difficult decision for her, and moved to Warsaw where she gave birth to a son. There, she worked as a theatre actress until 1964 when she received a letter from Grotowski inviting her back. She accepted the offer and returned, yet she recounts that there were times during the training when she had nobody with whom to leave her baby and had to run out of the workspace during breaks to check on him. In addition, the group would often work all night with Grotowski, and while everyone else would get some rest during the day, she had to look after her child. She points out that she couldn't really leave her private life behind in order to focus solely on the work, and when the group relocated to Wroclaw she sent her son to stay with her sister-in-law who lived near Warsaw (26–27).

Komorowska acknowledges that she often asked herself whether an actress with a child really had a place in such a company, and she emphasizes that throughout her experience at the Laboratory Theatre, first in Opole and then in Wroclaw, she stubbornly tried to prove to herself and to Grotowski that being a mother was compatible with her commitment to the company, yet she admits that while she successfully dealt with this situation for many years, it became increasingly demanding (29–30, 33). Despite such challenges, Komorowska asserts that she was happy to have returned to the Laboratory Theatre because the work was even more intense and fruitful than previously (26–27). When she finally parted with the company in 1968, she went on to work with a wide range of prominent theatre and film directors both in Poland and abroad. During the interview, she remarked that although adapting to this new situation was difficult at first, her work with Grotowski had set her imagination in motion and the experience of daily training had increased her focus and perseverance, so much so that she is still drawing from this formative time.

Witnessing the rehearsals and public performance of Lupa's staging of *Extinction* provided me with concrete examples of the centrality of body memory in the work of Komorowska. In one scene, she turns into a shrieking bird through a striking physical action, and as I observed Komorowska during the rehearsals, I associated the energy of this action with an element of Mirecka's *plastiques* that is also part of Molik's Body Alphabet, and to which Molik refers in his book as "flying in the air" (56, 78). This action was first transmitted to me by my teachers in Paris, and it may be described as a soaring movement born from an impulse at the base of the spine, shooting energy from the pelvis to the top of the head and from the shoulder blades through the arms and wrists, opening the frontal part of the upper body in its flight towards the sky. This particular action has always seemed to me to be symbolic of the training developed by the actors of the Laboratory Theatre, and Cieslak demonstrates in the film documenting his work that fully engaging in the training can indeed become a way of flying. As emphasized by both Mirecka and Grotowski, however, training constitutes a preparation for the creative act, which must engage more than the physical body. Witnessing Komorowska's work in the rehearsals and public performance of *Extinction* gave me a renewed confidence in the evocative power that non-realistic physicality can convey on stage when deeply rooted in the actor's body memory.

During the interview, Komorowska explained that bird images recur both in her dreams and in her creative process. She provided the example of her work on the role of a Jewish woman named Rachela in the 1972 film *Wesele* (*The Wedding*) by Andrzej Wajda based on a play by Stanisław

Wyspiański, where she imagined that she was running towards the barbed wire in a concentration camp, an action linked to a personal association which she described as the image of a bird that is trying to take off but cannot lift its legs up from the ground, as when in a dream we attempt to fly. She stated that working on an animal image helps actors not to focus on themselves but imagine instead how to move as an animal. She then recalled that invoking the world of animals inspired her when working on the male character of Tarudante in *The Constant Prince*.

Grotowski referred to Komorowska's Tarudante during his third Collège de France lecture when speaking about the importance of personal associations in the creative process. He stated that when Komorowska developed this role in *The Constant Prince*, she walked with a military-like step, back bent, with her long hair covering her face, as if a kind of monster. At some point, this menacing, faceless creature performed a *Pieta* scene with Cieslak as she held his Christ-like body in her arms. For Grotowski, this mysterious figure was inspired by a close relative: one of his aunts, whom he described as possessing a form of utter contempt for all human beings, especially women. He explained that she would shut herself up in her room without letting anyone in, except for him, one of the rare persons she ever welcomed. He stressed that she was very intelligent and that, had she lived in a different era, she might have been a great scholar, but observed that the fate of women at that time was such that she did not have access to education. This self-taught recluse, whose misanthropic attitude somehow enabled her to analyze human beings with extraordinary insight, fascinated him. In the end, she committed suicide and became for him the model for the figure of Tarudante in *The Constant Prince*.

Komorowska, whom Grotowski had asked to search for her own personal associations for the creation of this character, states in her book that Tarudante reminded her of a rooster competing in a cockfight, and that each of Tarudante's movements in his heavy cloak and high boots, transformed by this association, became expressive. She remarks that it was quite a feat to perform bent in half without ever being able to straighten up, her hair obscuring her vision, and acknowledges that she had initially thought this might be an impossible task but had eventually found a way. She then foregrounds the highly productive contradiction that made her creation of Tarudante so alive: towards the end of the performance, a keening lullaby suddenly emerges out of the beast unveiling an extreme gentleness concealed within. Reflecting on her discovery of this revelatory moment, she suggests that the exacting nature of her efforts to fully embody the animality of this character had probably led to this song that she associated with the hardship of physical labor (*Pejzaż* 28).

In Lupa's *Extinction*, Komorowska's work with animal associations significantly informs the scene during which Maria transforms into a bird and summons its animal power to surprise, frighten, and chase away undesirable protagonists in the play. However, the scene most clearly rooted in Komorowska's body memory features Maria in a mid-length black dress, putting on heavy black shoes and performing an oddly rhythmical march. As I watched this action in the course of the rehearsals, it struck me as strangely familiar, as if echoing something else I had seen before. I recalled the film footage I had viewed at the Grotowski Institute, documenting a scene with Komorowska and Mirecka created for *Ewangelie (Gospels)*, a piece which would influence the development of *Apocalypsis cum figuris*, the final Theatre Laboratory production. I also made this connection because I remembered that, during his third Collège de France lecture, Grotowski explained that the scene developed by Komorowska and Mirecka came from an association that was very important to him, and added that he had worked on this scene for a very long time. This personal association was linked to his childhood during the war, when he lived with his mother and brother in a Polish village whose inhabitants only had what was strictly necessary to their survival. It was from his time in this village that he drew the most fruitful associations for his work as a director. For example, he used to watch the women walk to the church to attend the Catholic Mass. They usually went barefoot but he remembered a particular day on which they washed their feet and put on shoes, along with their best clothes, as well as long dark coats, and began marching together. There was a little path close to the house where Grotowski lived, and the women followed this path to get to the church. He drew from this memory to create the scene of the two women walking to the tomb of Christ. Grotowski observed that incorporating such associations in the composition of a piece always gave him a kind of joy, for it was as if his memories had been awakened and had become alive again.

When I asked Komorowska how she had developed the action with the shoes in *Extinction*, she pointed me to a passage in *Pejzaż* where she traces it to this particular scene with Mirecka and describes the two women washing their feet, dressing up with long black coats, and marching hurriedly towards the tomb, each wanting to get there first. She writes: "When I started walking in those shoes I remembered how I walked with Rena Mirecka to the tomb in the early version of Grotowski's *Apocalypsis cum figuris*" (80). She then acknowledges that working on this scene, created more than thirty years prior to Lupa's first staging of *Extinction*, was one of her most important experiences at the Laboratory Theatre.

During the interview, Komorowska reflected on the ways in which she has constantly defied expectations throughout her career as a film and theatre actress, and explained that she never had a stunt double in any of her film work, no matter how physically demanding her roles. On stage, Komorowska has received critical acclaim for her performance of two of Beckett's most challenging characters: the blind and tyrannical Hamm in a 1972 production of *Endgame* directed by Jerzy Krakowski, and Winnie, the unbearably garrulous optimist who is buried up to her waist in a mound of earth in *Happy Days*, directed by Antoniego Libery in 1995. As I watched Komorowska rehearse the precisely crafted physical score she had created for

Extinction, I became increasingly aware of the extent to which the energy and passion first ignited by her experience at the Laboratory Theatre at the very beginning of her artistic journey continues to inform her work. For in this piece Komorowska engages in bold physical actions not only in the two passages I described but throughout her other scenes as she dances across the stage, hops onto a table, leaps out of an upstage window, and is seen spinning around in a shower of snowflakes. Although she clearly relished her unconventional portrayal of the poetess Maria, Komorowska herself seemed surprised by the irrepressible energy of this character when, towards the end of our conversation, she spiritedly exclaimed: "I'm 72, and I jump through a window in *Extinction*—I should be walking around with a cane, I should be an old woman!"

ELIZABETH ALBAHACA

Elizabeth Albahaca was born in Venezuela and is of mixed cultural ancestry: her grandfather was from Syria but lived in Lebanon before emigrating to Venezuela, whereas relatives on the other side of her family were Spanish and lived in the Canary Islands. As a student, she was implicated in the left-wing movement in Venezuela and placed on a terrorist list by the government even though she did not participate in radical student activism. However, she was involved in the influential theatre movement of that time and travelled to Europe with her student theatre group. While she was away, government officials came looking for her at her parents' home, and she and her family decided it was not safe for her to return. In Europe, she encountered the work of Grotowski and became the first non-Polish member in the core group of actors at the Laboratory Theatre.

I met Albahaca for the first time when she attended the 2009 *Meetings with Remarkable Women* events as a special guest and contributed to the Festival a one-woman piece titled *The Night of Molly Bloom* in which she directed Maria Fernanda Ferro, a member of the Venezuelan theatre group with whose actors she works. This piece is an adaptation by José Sanchis Sinisterra of Molly Bloom's soliloquy in the final chapter of James Joyce's *Ulysses*, a stream-of-consciousness experiment which presents particular challenges for the creation of a solo performance. In Albahaca's direction of *The Night of Molly Bloom*, the endless flow of words is contained and intensified by her choice to stage the entire piece on Molly's conjugal bed, with a black hat symbolizing her husband. In the striking closing tableau, Molly's body is seen lying silently on the white sheets as if finally drained from the excesses of language, while the bed, soaring above the earth, flies over the hustle and bustle of a restless world glimpsed in a video projection which creates a powerful dream-like montage effect.

In the course of my three other meetings with Albahaca in her home in Montreal in 2010 and 2011, I was struck by the passion and enthusiasm

88 *Grotowski, Women, and Contemporary Performance*

Figure 2.3 Elizabeth Albahaca. *Meetings with Remarkable Women*, Grotowski Institute, Wroclaw, Poland, August 2009—photo by Francesco Galli.

with which she recalled her fifteen-year experience as a member of the Laboratory Theatre, and I could sense the energy that animated her as she sat on the edge of her seat, her eyes sparkling with the vivid intensity of her memories. She said that she had always loved to move, which had led her to pursue dance training both in Venezuela and in Europe, where she had also studied with Jacques Lecoq and Etienne Decroux's son, and had discovered a completely different approach to performance in Grotowski's work. She was especially interested in the organic dimension of this work, and in the way imagination was combined with an exigency for precision, which she experienced in the physical training led by Cieslak and the vocal work taught by Molik, as well as in the image and theme-based improvisations which became the basis of *études* the actors developed over long periods of time under Grotowski's guidance.

Albahaca, who participated in both the theatrical and paratheatrical periods of Grotowski's research, remarked that what was common to all the phases of his work, including the final period known as Art as vehicle, was the intensity and rigor of the training. She stated that it was almost like natural selection: those who were able to keep up with the training stayed, while others gave up and left. She first was an international *stagiaire*, the temporary status of the young people who came to Wroclaw from around the world to pursue an apprenticeship at the Laboratory Theatre. She was then invited to stay by Grotowski, who obtained for her a small scholarship from the Polish government. When Albahaca became an official member of the Laboratory Theatre, she was one of three women in the core group of actors, the other two being Mirecka and Komorowska. She worked extensively with both of them on *études* in the course of which they developed some of the material that constituted the basis for the creative work that eventually led to *Apocalypsis cum figuris*, the company's ultimate theatre production. Albahaca emphasized that the entire work process was at once intensely demanding and immensely fulfilling. She specified that Grotowski worked very closely and carefully with actors to help them to grow and that although he had high expectations from his collaborators he never exploited them as was often the case in commercial theatre.

Albahaca explained that there were three different versions of *Apocalypsis cum figuris*, a piece that was preceded by the work on *Ewangelie (Gospels)* in which the role of Mary Magdalene was played by Komorowska. The first version of *Apocalypsis*, presented publicly only once in 1968, featured elements of the *études* that had been developed for *Ewangelie* yet the figure of Mary Magdalene did not appear and the two female characters in this piece were performed by Albahaca and Mirecka. Albahaca created the role of Mary Magdalene for the second version and performed it from 1969 to 1972. With Grotowski's support Albahaca continued to work until the fifth month of her pregnancy and then took some time off. Meanwhile, a third incarnation of *Apocalypsis* was created with Mirecka as Mary Magdalene, a role she then performed in alternance with Albahaca from 1974 until the closing of the piece in 1980.

Embodying Mary Magdalene is a challenging task, as I discovered when working on Michel de Ghelderode's play *Les Femmes au tombeau* (*The Women at the Tomb*) as a member of *Présences en Regards*. In the Gospels, the figure of Mary Magdalene witnesses the crucifixion, discovers that the tomb in which Jesus was buried is empty, and witnesses his resurrection. Whereas apocryphal texts and early Gnostic writings uphold Mary Magdalene as a visionary and a leading disciple favored by Jesus, and the Eastern Orthodox tradition considers her to be a particularly important biblical figure equal to the Apostles, such a view is challenged by the traditional Roman Catholic conception of Mary Magdalene as a reformed prostitute and devout penitent. This less favorable interpretation has been widely disseminated by Western Christian iconography, Donatello's harrowing sculpture being a case in point. Art historian Martha Levine Dunkelman argues that Donatello's harsh materialization of Mary Magdalene "illustrate[s] not only the frequently emphasized pain and suffering but also a great deal of strength and endurance [and] can be read as a representation of continuing physical and emotional tenacity in the face of adversity—her suffering having increased her power" ("Donatello's Mary Magdalen: A Model of Courage and Survival" 10). However, the agency Dunkelman attempts to locate within Donatello's rendering of Mary Magdalene's ravaged body is predicated upon her ability to withstand suffering linked to guilt and shame and her willingness to transform her sinful life into one of repentance.

In Maurizio Buscarino's striking performance photos of *Apocalypsis cum figuris*, Albahaca's Mary Magdalene certainly does not appear to be repenting: she has lush black hair, wears a short dress revealing powerful legs firmly planted in the ground, and her energy leaps out of the frame. When I asked her about the experience of creating and performing the role of Mary Magdalene, Albahaca told me that she felt a connection to the themes that were at the core of the piece, and that investing this biblical figure with her own energy and her own life was very fulfilling work because it enabled her to create a multidimensional being who accepted herself entirely as a woman, beyond the prejudices through which this archetypal character has often been perceived.

In his book, Molik recalls Albahaca as follows: "[W]hen she came, she was like from Amazonia, directly imported from Amazonia. She came from Brasilia, I guess, so she was a very strange person. Nobody knew what language she was speaking, because sometimes she spoke

Polish, but it wasn't really Polish. Sometimes she spoke Spanish, but it wasn't really Spanish. Sometimes she spoke Portuguese, but it wasn't really Portuguese. However, she was a great person" (Campo and Molik 150). Given that Molik seemed to have perceived his colleague as radically different, I am compelled to wonder how Polish audiences viewed this particular Mary Magdalene. When I asked Albahaca whether she felt that cultural difference might have informed the way in which her interpretation of this archetypal character was received by spectators within the context of Catholic Poland, she replied that this was something which was difficult to assess. She recalled that she was fascinated by Polish people and that, in her experience, cultural difference had often led to encounters that could be quite rich when fueled by mutual interest. She also emphasized that she sensed a positive force within the darkness of *Apocalypsis* where, as in *The Constant Prince*, the human spirit was like a flame that kept on burning through a raging storm.

Albahaca asserted that what distinguished *Apocalypsis* from previous productions was that it was envisioned by Grotowski both as a culmination of his directorial work with the Laboratory Theatre and as a transition from theatre to paratheatre. She stated that it was during the creation process of *Apocalypsis* that Grotowski told the Laboratory Theatre actors he had decided to abandon theatre. He explained to them that in this final production, he did not want to resort to the theatrical means he had previously used in his mises-en-scène. This transition from theatre to paratheatre was gradual, however, since Albahaca observed that the early phase of paratheatre was still marked by theatrical elements, so that Holiday and Special Project were precisely structured performances but were closer to ritual and celebration than to theatre per se. She added that there was a great sense of joy in these early experiments, with some quasi-miraculous work taking place in Brzezinka, and observed that everyone was still working as hard as previously, if not harder, and that in spite of the experimental nature of paratheatre, the level of commitment remained extremely high. In her view, this was a particularly fruitful and important period of Grotowski's research, which she said was as enriching for her as the work she did in *Apocalypsis*. I asked Albahaca whether she felt that her involvement in paratheatre while performing in *Apocalypsis* had influenced her work as an actress, and she replied that since the piece had kept evolving it was possible that the changes that had occurred over time were due in part to the fact that the performances overlapped with the paratheatrical experiments in which several members from the core group of the Laboratory Theatre were fully engaged.

Albahaca told me that her experience at the Laboratory Theatre had been the best of schools for her, since she had learned to train, carry out artistic research, develop work towards the creation of a performance, collaborate with highly experienced colleagues who had also been her mentors, and even teach, since transmission was an important part of the work that Grotowski required everyone to do. She remarked that as far as training was concerned, she was convinced that it always had to be developed to fulfill very specific needs, which, in the case of the Laboratory Theatre, included solving the technical problems that prevented actors from rising to the level of competence that Grotowski deemed necessary to accomplish the goals the group had set out to achieve. For Albahaca, who had a dance background and was interested in movement-based performance, the Laboratory Theatre training was what she needed at the time. She had loved learning the physical training from Cieslak, who she said was an extraordinary guide and teacher who was acutely perceptive and knew what would be beneficial to each person, thereby ensuring that the training could be useful to everyone in a different way. She added that when the Laboratory Theatre closed, the question of what to do next became a huge challenge since it was unthinkable for some of the actors to return to conventional theatre after having worked at such a high level, yet she felt that it was very important for her to continue to act and to remain open to possibilities. She went on to perform various roles in Poland, Italy, and Montreal, and began working as a director in 1988 when she was invited to stage a theatre piece in Venezuela.

Figure 2.4 Maria Fernanda Ferro in *The Night of Molly Bloom* directed by Elizabeth Albahaca. *Meetings with Remarkable Women* Festival, Grotowski Institute, Wroclaw, Poland, August 2009—photo by Francesco Galli.

During our conversation, Albahaca expressed a keen interest in Art as vehicle, the final period of Grotowski's research on vibratory chants that Thomas Richards and Mario Biagini, the Polish director's designated heirs, have continued to carry out at his Workcenter in Italy. She nevertheless suggested that their way is not the only way, and that while it is important to preserve the integrity of Grotowski's work, he must have been aware that after his death his approach would inspire new research in unforeseeable directions through different modes of transmission. She said that she had heard that Biagini's group members are now singing songs from the counterculture era and working on texts by Allen Ginsberg, and noted that it is probably good that things are changing. She also referred to the groups in Poland who work with traditional songs and music, and conjectured that these are perhaps necessary phases for something else to emerge. Albahaca hence wholeheartedly expressed her support for those who explore new directions, break the rules, and shatter models, so long as the next generation acknowledges the achievements of its predecessors.

EWA BENESZ

Ewa Benesz was a guest artist during the 2009 Meetings, and the following summer I met with her in Sardinia and attended one of her work sessions. During my interview with her in August 2010, she explained that she was a member of the Laboratory Theatre throughout the development of *Ewangelie* and said that these two years of creative work were particularly challenging, and that when Grotowski ceased working on the structure of *Ewangelie* and began to develop *Apocalypsis*, she left the group. After an enriching experience in a Yiddish Theatre in Warsaw, she went on to co-found her own company with two young colleagues in the provincial town of Puławy where they created a number of successful productions from 1970 to 1973, at which time their artistic activities were deemed subversive by the authorities, who abruptly closed down the company in spite of Grotowski's support, which Benesz specified he expressed publicly. The group continued to work clandestinely until it became impossible to carry on within these circumstances. Benesz then embarked upon an independent project: having memorized half of the epic poem *Pan Tadeusz* by Polish Romantic author Adam Mickiewicz, which she said took six to seven hours to read aloud, she decided to walk along the Eastern border of Poland from village to village and to perform this text on her way. The provocative idea behind this unusual undertaking was that, since *Pan Tadeusz* was beloved by the Polish people and considered to be a national epic, it was the nation itself that should be its director. She explained that as an itinerant story-teller, she experimented with various ways of engaging the people she met. Her long-term goal had been to create a travelling literary theatre born from *Pan Tadeusz*, but after receiving renewed threats from the authorities she had to develop other strategies to continue her creative work.

Benesz went on to collaborate with visual artists in Wroclaw and devised durational solo performances that were based on Rainer Maria Rilke's poetry and took place in the city's public spaces. She told me that she wanted to infuse people's lives with poetry by creating surreal images in the midst of everyday reality, and remarked that Polish social reality had been a good school for this kind of work. Grotowski, whom she said feared for her safety, invited her to return to the Laboratory Theatre where she worked with Mirecka and Molik until martial law was declared. Benesz recounted that during this troubled time she and Mirecka engaged in very intense training, leading to a sixteen-year collaboration focused on paratheatrical research in which relationship to nature was central. Benesz has since been conducting independent creative work, which she stressed significantly diverges from paratheatre in that it focuses on the ancient roots of theatre and is based on simple actions connected to nature and grounded in her research on the sources of European culture as well as her interest in other cultural traditions.

In August of 2010, I participated in a work session led by Benesz in a rural area of southern Sardinia which had been home to the research she and Mirecka had conducted together and where Mirecka still teaches regularly. I had heard of their Sardinian house, known as Casa Blanca, from a variety of people in the Grotowski diaspora who had explained to me that it had neither electricity nor hot water. I first worked there with Mirecka in July of that same year, and by the time I took part in Benesz's session I had become quite familiar with the family of wild cats and somnolent donkeys sharing the sun-battered courtyard, and, of course, the *carrubo* tree outside the house under whose protective branches numerous activities and meetings took place. While my experience of Benesz's teaching is limited to my participation in a single six-day work session, which I will address in greater detail in the fourth chapter, my sense is that her creative research operates on two interrelated planes: a relationship to place, in the here and now, embodied by the participants through their engagement in very specific material practices related to the seasonal cycles of nature; and a relationship to cultural memory, experienced by the participants through their exposure to Judeo-Christian archetypes and myths activated by the ritual dimension of such practices.

On the first day, Benesz outlined what she called the principles of the work, asking participants not to speak with each other about what would happen during the work, which she explained was fragile because it was about what we didn't know—she stressed that even she didn't know—so that it was important to protect what would occur. She explained that each person's song, text, or action should be about who this person was at this point of their life, and remarked that accomplishing this was not easy—she described it as honest work, something growing from the heart. She also emphasized that it was only possible to be creative when working with others, and stressed that our meeting should be focused on serving each other.

Every morning of this work session we woke up before sunrise, met under the *carrubo*, and walked off into the countryside in a long line led by Benesz, returning an hour later. This way of walking in line required that everyone start on the same foot, moving as one, maintaining silence, and keeping the same rhythm for the entire walk. It took quite a bit of concentration to keep the walking precise and Benesz instructed us to always look forward as if through a single collective eye. Keeping the rhythm was everyone's responsibility, and when someone lost the group's rhythmic pattern it immediately impacted the person following and everyone behind. The sense of interconnection and interdependence created by this communal walk was a very concrete way of experiencing the necessity of serving others in the work.

Although I found that there certainly were some overlaps between Benesz's and Mirecka's approaches, one major difference is that, in my experience of Benesz's teaching, yoga is the main physical practice and she does not lead exercises pertaining to the training from the theatrical period. As with Mirecka, however, music and singing are integrated into much of the group work, and while participants are invited to contribute songs, Benesz and her collaborators also lead chants from the Indian, Tibetan, and Jewish traditions, some of which I recognized, having previously encountered them in Mirecka's teaching. During a conversation I had with Benesz after the work session had ended, she told me that her teaching was about subtracting rather than adding, her goal being to eliminate tensions. She specified that it was something that she sensed and said that it wasn't possible for her to formulate what she meant more specifically, although it involved attending to physical tensions in the eyes, the throat, the hands, and the musculature of the body. Working with natural elements, she remarked, was an effective way of subtracting tensions, for example when working with the element of water. One of the activities had entailed walking to a river and bringing with us a gift—a poem, a song, or an offering crafted with natural materials such as leaves, bark, plants, or flowers, a practice which is also an integral part of Mirecka's teaching. When making their offering to the river, some participants touched the water, dipped their feet in it, or immersed themselves entirely. Benesz stated that this can help to release tensions because when the body is surrounded by water it is possible to feel one's own skin, a sensation linked to the experience of being born.

Benesz explained to me that she worked with seasonal plants, herbs, flowers, and fruits, from which the local people used to make wine, medicinal infusions, and oil to light lamps. She said that medicinal plants and herbs were connected to specific seasons as well as to mythical stories and ancient

Figure 2.5 Ewa Benesz in Sardinia—photo by Celeste Taliani.

rites. For instance, in the region of Umbria, people used to celebrate the day of San Giovanni by harvesting flower petals at sunset on a specific day at the end of June, just before the summer solstice. The petals were soaked in water overnight and the next morning both men and women cleansed their faces with the solution. Benesz suggested that performing this ritual action had a double function: honoring flowers and appropriating their beauty, which she remarked was a way of making natural things meaningful so that their existence mattered. She drew a parallel with our daily walk at sunrise by pointing out that if we don't endow the dawn with significance through our actions, then it is as if the dawn did not exist for us.

When I asked Benesz about the sources of her work, she stated that she had always been interested in the roots of European culture, especially Mediterranean traditional practices. She provided the example of simple ritual chants and dances, which she said were very useful to foster alertness and connection not only with others but also with the earth and sky. Many of these cultural practices were related to nature or natural elements such as Greek songs linked to the sun, and she recalled that a sun dance had also been transmitted to her by a young man from Canada who had worked with her and Mirecka in the mid-eighties. I asked Benesz what his name was and she replied: Floyd Favel. I said that I knew Favel and that he had told me that Grotowski had encouraged him to return home to work within his own tradition. She observed that she had also been focusing on her own tradition and that her work was very Polish. Reflecting on her particular trajectory, she explained that at one point in her life she felt she had to decide whether to work toward perfectionism as the main focus or whether to seek what was most simple. She had chosen the path of simplicity, which she said also applied to the way she lived, as reflected by the rusticity of Casa Blanca. She concluded that going towards the most simple had been good for her and that she now experiences simplicity as a form of well-being.

KATHARINA SEYFERTH

Katharina Seyferth is the youngest among first-generation women: after working with Ryszard Cieslak in New York in the context of André Gregory's Manhattan Theater Project, she travelled to Poland in 1977 to participate in the Mountain Project, followed by The Vigils, two of the Laboratory Theatre's major paratheatrical activities, and went on to contribute to Grotowski's research project known as the Theatre of Sources. Seyferth's approach blurs the distinction between the theatrical and post-theatrical periods of Grotowski's work: in her teaching, she combines elements of the training such as the *plastique* exercises developed during the theatrical period, with post-theatrical elements, drawing from her experience as a core member of the group of young people upon whom Grotowski relied during this phase of his research. Seyferth, originally from Germany, is the founder of the International Centre for Theatrical Research and Training of Las Teouleres, located near Bordeaux, France, where she conducts creative research, teaches, and hosts workshops led by international artists. She continues to work as a performer, and her solo piece *Rooms*, which she conceived and directed, and which is based on her adaptation of Gertrude Stein's *Tender Buttons: Objects, Food, Rooms*, was featured at the 2009 *Meetings with Remarkable Women* Festival. This performance was documented on video by Celeste Taliani and is featured as a full-length film on the Routledge Performance Archive, along with two other films documenting Seyferth's 2009 work session in Brzezinka with commentary by the artist and introducing the forest base where Grotowski and his collaborators worked extensively during the Paratheatre and Theatre of Sources periods.

While my objective is not to draw direct parallels between the distinct approaches developed by Mirecka and Seyferth, whose perspectives are informed by very different personal histories and professional experiences, I would like to focus on several aspects of Seyferth's teaching and creative research which are closely related to some of the key principles that are also central to Mirecka's work. Indeed, both Mirecka and Seyferth chose to lead their 2009 work sessions in Brzezinka rather than at the Grotowski Institute

98   *Grotowski, Women, and Contemporary Performance*

in the city of Wroclaw and, in their teaching, both artists combine training that includes the *plastiques* with paratheatrical work exploring the relationship between human beings and nature, an important aspect which I will further discuss in the third chapter. The most significant interconnection between Mirecka's and Seyferth's teaching is their focus on organicity.

For Mirecka and Seyferth, organic engagement in the various elements of the training is the necessary condition for something unexpected to take place, enabling the performer to encounter what they refer to as the unknown. In their teaching, they make clear that although the training they transmit is physically demanding, the point is not to be exhausted but to find an organic way of working that energizes the body-mind. I learned early on from my teachers who studied with Flaszen and Molik that it is necessary in the training to go beyond tiredness in order to discover another quality of energy which turns mere exercises into creative exploration. In the course of her 2009 work session in Brzezinka, Seyferth gave a talk addressed to the participants in which she spoke about this seemingly paradoxical aspect of the work, stating that the less one does, the less one interferes in the process, the more one has a chance to find something, although it does not mean that one should not do anything. She noted that this is a very fine line, because to some extent, one has to do a lot but in a certain way. She stressed that the question was how much energy or how much effort one has to make, and in which direction one should take the work, so that something will emerge from what one does. She specified that all of this is precise and tangible but that it takes a lot of time to discover. If one is constantly making too much effort, then one might never find anything. On the other hand, if one does not make any effort, if one does not do anything, then nothing will happen. She observed that once one finds the right balance between doing and not doing, there is no longer any need to make efforts. Yet, before one is able to reach this point, one must first discover how to get there, and she stressed that there are no recipes, only what might be called hints about the direction in which to take the work, and every person needs to find their own way.

Seyferth's attempt to articulate this delicate balance is reminiscent of Grotowski's evocation, in *Towards a Poor Theatre*, of "a state in which one does not '**want to do that**' but rather '**resigns from not doing it**'" (17). Interestingly, in the French version of the same text, this statement reads: "*un état dans lequel on 'ne veut pas faire cela,' mais plutôt on 'se résigne à ne pas le faire'*"[3] (15), which may be translated as: "a state in which one 'does not want to do that' but, instead, one 'resigns from doing it'." When comparing these two statements, it becomes clear that they contradict one another: in French, "one resigns from doing," and in English, "one resigns from not doing." I am indebted to Michel Masłowski, the Sorbonne professor who, in 2009, organized the conference "L'Année Grotowski à Paris" in partnership with the Grotowski Institute, for sharing with me an alternate French version of this statement based on the original Polish text published in *Odra* in 1965 and reprinted by the Grotowski Institute in 2007.[4] The corrected statement reads "*un état dans lequel non pas on veut* 'faire cela', *mais plutôt on* 'renonce à ne pas le faire'"[5] which may be translated as: "a state in which one does not 'want to do that,' but, instead, one 'renounces not doing it'." Evidently, the original Polish meaning is more accurately translated in *Towards a Poor Theatre* than it is in *Vers un théâtre pauvre*, which means that Francophone theatre scholars, students, and practitioners have all been misled into thinking that Grotowski was prescribing a "not doing" when, in fact, he meant "a doing which is not willful," or what Seyferth describes as something that could never take place if one were to do nothing at all, and yet which one *cannot make happen*, since it can only take place when there is *almost nothing that needs to be done*.

This was corroborated by Grotowski during his third Collège de France lecture when he declared that the organic actor did not need to *do* anything, and did not *show* that he was present, that is to say, did not concern himself with making his presence visible to the audience, and yet was unquestionably present. This actor was never empty since he was like an open channel through which forces and energies were constantly flowing, and he simply allowed the latter to flow through him, without showing that this was taking place because there was no need to do so. This, Grotowski remarked, was something that had been extremely important to his life-long research. He further observed in his seventh lecture that when we willed our mind to direct, to find out how to achieve something, then it couldn't possibly work. Whenever doing so we committed the perpetual error that epitomized a manipulative culture: wanting to know first and then applying that knowledge. He explained this didn't work because, in the arts, one must take another route where doing is knowing (*faire c'est savoir*), instead of knowing and then doing. Grotowski noted that this other route was akin to *wu wei*, the Taoist notion of non-doing, where one lets the doing happen, *as if*—and he insisted that his recurrent use of the phrase "as if" was significant—*as if* the doing occurred in and of itself (*ça se fait*) and one let it happen. He pointed out that it was about not hindering this process and simply letting the doing occur. He emphasized that *wu wei* did not signify "not doing anything" but rather allowing what can be accomplished to occur. He said that the best example he could provide was that of the arrow that shot forward by itself, not in relation to the point on the target the archer wanted to hit, but because something within the archer, not the archer himself, allowed the shooting to occur. Grotowski acknowledged, however, that when working with actors it wasn't possible to ask them directly to apply the notion of non-doing to their work because they would simply end up doing nothing at all.

In light of such considerations, I would suggest that Seyferth's solo piece *Rooms* subtly conveys the organic unfolding of the performance process defined by Grotowski. Seyferth performed this piece in 2009 in the Laboratory Theatre's main space known as the "*Apocalypsis* Room." Standing in the dark corridor leading to the entrance, she opened the door to the workspace and stepped into the unknown, which we entered with her as we became witnesses to her precarious balancing act between doing and not doing, being and not being, knowing and not knowing. Through her *resignation from not performing* Stein's proliferating minimalism masquerading as a seemingly random arrangement of words, Seyferth miraculously resurrected the existential

Figure 2.6 Katharina Seyferth rehearsing her solo piece *Rooms* for the *Meetings with Remarkable Women* Festival. Grotowski Institute, Wroclaw, Poland, August 2009—photo by Francesco Galli.

tremor and metaphysical malaise underlying *Tender Buttons*. In the spirit of Poor Theatre, she reminded us all on that day that when it comes to organic presence, less is not more—it is simply sufficient.

Eirini Kartsaki, a Greek artist-scholar whose research focuses on performance and repetition, participated in the 2009 *Meetings with Remarkable Women* work sessions and attended Seyferth's solo piece during the Festival that concluded these meetings. In her doctoral dissertation titled "Repeat Repeat: Returns of Performance," Kartsaki discusses her experience of Seyferth's performance:

> Seyferth performs [Stein's text] in such a way that convinces us that she knows exactly what she is talking about. And I believe her. I believe that there is sense in what she is saying, but not 'getting it' is not important. The rhythm of the speech and its intonation capture my attention at each separate moment. I experience the intensity of performance throughout its duration, [. . .] I participate in it through something close to [Bergson's notion of] direct perception. [S]he spins around at times, she walks, she hides like a child, she lifts the chair, she jumps, runs, spreads the pieces of white paper [across] the floor [. . .] The Steinian language succeeds in making time matter with an emphasis upon each moment. [. . .] In Stein's words, 'it is when it is and in being when it is being there is no beginning and no ending.'[6] (111–12)

In her dissertation, Kartsaki remarks that Stein's experimental approach to writing can be traced to her involvement in the research laboratory directed by William James at Radcliffe. In "Gertrude Stein in the Psychology Laboratory," Michael J. Hoffman explains that Stein, who at the time was an undergraduate student, participated in projects titled "The Place of Repetition in Memory" as well as "Fluctuations of the Attention" and "The Saturation of Colors." Kartsaki links Stein's research on automatic, habitual, repetitive actions to a conception of conscious awareness which, for Stein, was linked to a sense of immediacy, or what she called a consciousness without memory. She specifies that Stein eventually became interested in "combining two elements: production ('motor automatism') and watchful 'knowing' or attentive inattentiveness in which 'memory plays no part' and which [Wendy Steiner defines as] continuous present" (97). Citing Stein's claim that if anything is alive there is no such thing as repetition, Kartsaki argues that what we refer to as the 'liveness' of performance may be understood as a form of attentive consciousness in the moment-to-moment process of performing and watching.

The notions of conscious awareness, watchful knowing, and moment-to-moment attentiveness within a continuous present, which emerged from Stein's work in James's experimental psychology lab, resonate with his conception of embodied experience and Stanislavsky's notion of "conscious experience" (*perezhivanie*) which both foreshadowed and, to some extent, anticipated, the neuroscientific investigation of embodiment and consciousness. In light of Kartsaki's testimony as a spectator, Seyferth's embodiment of Stein's writing experiment may be considered to be an exploration of conscious experience as a moment-to-moment affective, active awareness (Martin Kurten's suggested translation for *perezhivanie*) that can be traced to Seyferth's unique positionality at the crossroads of theatre and paratheatre, which overlap and inform each other in her work.

During my 2010 interview with Seyferth, I asked her whether she felt that her experience of paratheatre had influenced her creation of *Rooms*, and specified that I was curious about the connection between the more technical aspects of the training that takes place in the rehearsal studio and the paratheatrical work that takes place in nature. For although these two dimensions of Grotowski's research belong to different periods of his work and therefore do not seem to be connected, Seyferth consistently interrelates them in her teaching. In her 2009 work session, she combined indoor physical training that included the *plastique* exercises with outdoor paratheatrical work. Every evening at sunset, for example, we would walk to a forest clearing and perform the original version of the "Motions"—precise patterns of movement performed collectively in the four cardinal directions. Albahaca told me that the Motions had been devised by Teo Spychalski, a Polish collaborator of Grotowski who was in charge of training the young international interns; a later version of the Motions was practiced during the Objective Drama Project at the University of California, Irvine, as well as at Grotowski's Italian Workcenter.

At night, Seyferth would lead us on silent expeditions into the heart of the forest of Brzezinka. We followed in her brisk footsteps in a long line, trusting that the alertness of our bodies developed during the training would help us to avoid ditches, puddles, and stinging nettles. At times we would run in her stride through the darkness of the forest, or, still following her lead, we would lie down on the earth and listen to the nocturnal life of the forest. Seyferth also invited each of us to explore the forest on our own by daylight and choose a particular place with which we were to build a relationship by developing a site-specific individual action that would eventually be shared with others.

Seyferth replied to my inquiry about the connection between theatre and paratheatre by explaining that, in her own experience, while the training constituted a very effective foundation for the work of the actor, so did paratheatrical actions created in nature, even though they seemed to be unrelated to theatrical work. She stressed that it was very beneficial for people to experience paratheatre because it was linked to a kind of personal authenticity and, by extension, was also very useful to actors. Referring to our nocturnal expeditions, she pointed out that the body reacts differently when in darkness because sensations become particularly vivid. She specified that it was necessary to engage in this kind of activity for quite a long time in order to notice these changes, which could alter the perception of one's environment. She remarked that it was very simple and that simplicity was what she found important in this type of experience. She insisted that what was so effective about paratheatrical practices was precisely that they entailed doing very simple things.

Relating her experience of paratheatre to her work as a performer in her solo piece, Seyferth stated that what matters is always to get to the point where one is no longer doing but serving something. She referred to Grotowski's text "Performer" and drew a parallel between the process she was describing and Grotowski's assertion that "Performer knows how to link body impulsion to sonority (the stream of life should be articulated in forms). The witnesses then enter into intense states because, as they say, they have felt a presence. And this is owing to the Performer, who is a bridge between the witness and something. In this sense Performer is *pontifex*, a maker of bridges" (37). Seyferth stressed that it was important not to work from a concept because it was only through *doing* that the performer could structure her work and find the life of the structure.

When I asked Seyferth how the training from the theatrical period could serve as a preparation when working across the theatre/paratheatre delineation, she replied that she continued to be convinced that exercises such as the *plastiques* that had produced outstanding results at the Laboratory Theatre could still be extremely useful today, which is why they had remained part of her teaching. I pointed to Kartsaki's research on repetition and remarked that repetitiveness seemed to be an important aspect of the training since one needed to practice the same exercises for many years in order to delve deeper and deeper into the process Seyferth described as a search for balance between doing and non-doing. She replied that repetition in the training is beneficial because it enables the body to learn to let go, something which is necessary but takes time because we are all conditioned in some way. She added that repetition is also important because it helps the performer to become increasingly confident in her abilities as the training evolves, moves forward, and takes her further in the work.

Seyferth's conception of performance practice is grounded in the training she has developed, and during her 2009 work session she introduced exercises that help sustain the organicity of the performer's process. Exploring the passage from stillness to movement, for example, becomes a way of accessing one's individual organic drive, and the exercise she led involved falling out of balance, learning to let go, and following the flow and energy of non-expressive movement. In the course of the training, which included the *plastiques*, she encouraged us to look for fluidity and continuity when transitioning from one movement to the next. When guiding us through the *plastiques*, she told us to avoid staying in the same spot in the workspace and keeping the same rhythm—instead, she instructed us to let the impulses of the actions lead us and move us through the entire space. She encouraged us to take our work on the *plastiques* further so as to avoid making things easy for ourselves. She emphasized the interrelation of spontaneity and precision in these exercises, which required following the flow of impulses leading to rhythmic variations, and which also necessitated sustaining a relationship to the space and to others around us. She asked us to keep searching for a connection inside the body to ensure that our actions did not remain at the level of external movement but instead always started from the spine.

104   *Grotowski, Women, and Contemporary Performance*

We explored how slow changes of balance from one leg to the other enables one to feel the axis that connects the head to the feet, and how the gaze changes with alterations of balance. We also worked on releasing the weight of the body into space and letting this falling action become our impetus for movement, letting it run its course without directing it. Falling forward, sideways, and backwards, we followed our body's own momentum until it eventually came to a stop. She pointed out that this process took time and commitment, and added that deep work generated associations, so that something unknown to us could emerge and surprise us, something that was alive and unpredictable. She indicated that the training was about precision, not about expressing ourselves, and that it was about going towards the unknown, without judging or being judged.

Seyferth also stressed that we should not talk about the training outside the workspace with one another, because refraining from speaking about the work helped everyone to feel free to explore possibilities. This is something which I had learned from the leaders of *Présences en Regards*, and which constitutes an ethical stance shared by all the work leaders I have encountered in the Grotowski diaspora. This includes treating the workspace as a special place by leaving quotidian behavior, daily habits, and everyday attire outside the space, cleaning it regularly, and respecting periods of silence that precede the work and mark a transition necessary for everyone to focus their energy. As with Mirecka, it is by embodying these ethical principles in her creative work and in her teaching that Seyferth transmits them to others.

When speaking with Seyferth after my participation in her work session in southwestern France, I asked her whether it had been challenging to keep up her connection to this way of working and continue to develop her creative research over the years. She replied that if the experience of working in that way is fulfilling, then it becomes a challenge: either one keeps on working that way or one doesn't. She observed that it is something with which everyone has to come to terms, and added with a smile that it is certainly more uncomfortable to keep on going. She suggested, however, that when one remains engaged in this work, the process somehow continues by itself because it is a state of being, which she equates with staying open to possibilities. Trying too hard or wanting to force things is counterproductive because it is a subtle process, like a river finding its way—once there is a source for the river, the water will follow its course, and even when remaining still for a while, it will eventually find some opening through which to flow forth.

IBEN NAGEL RASMUSSEN

All the women with whom I met in the course of my embodied research shared with me the conviction that some form of rigorous training is necessary to effectively prepare the performer's body-mind for creative work.

For Iben Nagel Rasmussen, however, training is first and foremost a way for the performer to claim her artistic independence. A core member of the Odin Teatret, Rasmussen has developed her own approach to training and founded the international group The Bridge of Winds in 1989. It was through her early experience of a series of work sessions led by Grotowski and Cieslak at the Odin that Rasmussen became aware of the importance of daily physical and vocal training as a transformative practice which focuses on what Eugenio Barba, the Odin's artistic director, calls pre-expressivity. She also became convinced of the necessity to adapt, change, and transform the training in order to keep growing, become one's own guide, and reach a level of competence and autonomy which turns performance into an act of self-determination by establishing one's sovereignty over one's creative work. In *Den blinde hest: Barbas forestillinger* (*The Blind Horse: Barba's Performances*), Rasmussen writes:

> Training has become the actor's means of being independent, the key that can open doors to constantly new places. It's all about surprising Eugenio. I love to see him standing there gaping, looking confused—and then, all of a sudden, being the one to surprise us all by giving the work a direction that none of us expected. A perspective or a new meaning that would have been impossible to imagine or calculate. [. . .] I don't really like being directed, having someone telling me what to do. I need to create my own material and develop my own language. This means that I prefer to look on working with the director as an encounter. (138, 153)

Not only is Rasmussen's perspective on the performer-director collaboration necessarily more fruitful from a creative standpoint, but it also means that when the performer becomes the owner of the modes of production, so to speak, her labor of embodiment constitutes an investment in her own self, leading to an accumulation of cultural capital, or expertise, that sets her free from the wants, whims, and woes of her colleagues, critics, and public. Interestingly, Rasmussen derived her personal desire for freedom from her exposure to the unprecedentedly exacting physical and vocal training developed by the Theatre Laboratory actors.

In "Letter to Grotowski," Rasmussen recalls a dream about her relationship to Grotowski which may provide an insight into the source of her thirst for independence:

> The other night I had a strange dream: I was walking into a very exclusive restaurant together with Grotowski and someone who I don't remember. I put my hands slightly on their shoulders which made me start to levitate and fly over this very elegant restaurant. I didn't have my own body but that of a soft, fluffy, pink, cloud-like animal. It felt incredibly funny, and we all began to laugh loudly until I said: Eugenio doesn't like me to fly. And I woke up. (8)

In this text, Rasmussen goes on to qualify what could be interpreted as an indictment of Barba's authority by pointing out that it was her work with him which made her capable of flying, both metaphorically and literally. She then refers to her admiration and love for Grotowski as a master who inspired her greatly, and explains that the summer seminars led by the Polish director and Cieslak became a particularly influential reference point for all the members of the Odin. Rasmussen goes on to recount that when she began to teach other actors she felt that she was holding the hand of Grotowski and transmitting to them something she had received from him. She explains that during one of their last meetings, she told the Polish director about her teaching and about the experience she had with some of the women performers who "would start crying when finally finding the low breast or stomach resonator." Grotowski replied that he was sure this could happen while working with her. Rasmussen comments: "Where he got this confidence in my teaching I don't know. But I felt it all the time—the confidence and the support." She then addresses Grotowski directly as she writes: "I miss you—but I don't find you in the words, the anecdotes or the dreams. You are in my so-called pupils, in their breath, their dance, their sometimes awkward steps and voices. They are what I am no longer" ("Letter to Grotowski" 8).

Rasmussen chose to read this text at the beginning of my interview with her in December 2011, which is why I am including these fragments here. During our conversation, Rasmussen stated that the roots of her training were the exercises that she and the other members of the Odin Teatret had learned from the Laboratory Theatre actors. She mentioned the corporeal exercises and the *plastiques*, both demonstrated by Cieslak in the documentary film shot at the Odin. She stressed that, as far as she knew, these exercises had not been invented by Grotowski and his collaborators but had been derived from other forms such as yoga and mime as well as acrobatics, yet she pointed out that what was unique about the training they developed was the sense of continuous flow which was sought in all the exercises, something which she noted could be seen very clearly in Cieslak's demonstration. Rasmussen recounted that in the first few years of training at the Odin she felt that she wasn't finding the flowing energy she witnessed in Cieslak's work as well as in the work of fellow Odin actor Torgeir Wethal, who worked closely with Grotowski at the time. She felt very slow, couldn't find any flow within herself, and got quite tired from doing these exercises. Then, during the daily training, she began to ask herself for the first time: what is a dramatic action? Looking for a physical answer to this question, she began to search for different ways of falling linked to her work on balance. She explored falling completely to the ground and using that momentum to come back up like a wave in the sea, which she said enabled her to rise again like a Phoenix. She found the precariousness of this type of exercise very dramatic since it entailed some physical risk, and felt that falling and rising continuously each time in a new way replenished her energy.

She discovered that such experiments enabled her to continue to explore new possibilities, which she said was fantastic for her at that stage of her development as a performer.

This first phase of her personal training was documented on film by the Odin, and Rasmussen confided that when she watched this film now she noticed that she was always looking at the ground and that many aspects of her work still needed to be developed, but stated that it nevertheless constituted the nucleus from which she created her own training. She had continued to search for different ways of going down on her knees, turning around in a centrifugal movement, and finding each time another way to come back up, which took her into another direction in the space and led her to find a continuous flow of movement—that sense of flow she said had been lacking so much for her in other exercises. Developing her own training had therefore enabled her to experience the inner life which she said was shining through the work of Cieslak and Wethal, and which she referred to as the transparent body.

I asked her if this meant that finding her own flow hinged upon finding her own way, and she replied that, indeed, finding her own way had made her feel completely free to invent, and that this possibility of devising her personal training had been very important for her. She emphasized, however, that what had enabled her to do so was her very long period of preparation at the Odin during which she had gone to the maximum of her capacity, tiredness, and resources. I mentioned the Odin film *Moon and Darkness* in which she gives a training demonstration that includes a number of acrobatic feats,[7] and pointed out that as far as I knew this was the only film featuring a woman demonstrating the kind of intensely physical training which, in this tradition, is usually associated with Cieslak. She replied that her work at the Odin had always been very demanding and insisted that without having gone through this experience she would have never been able to discover how to create her own training and pursue her creative research for so many years.

This, in turn, had informed her approach to teaching, as she chose not to tell others how to do exercises pertaining to her personal training but instead encouraged each person to develop their own exercises. By guiding performers to help them make their own discoveries, she followed a principle that had become central to her conception of training: she had found out that discovering an exercise was much more convincing, much stronger for her, than being told by others how to do the exercises they had developed. She worked with the members of Farfa, her first group, on a different version of her out-of-balance exercise in which they didn't fall all the way to the floor but instead fell only until a certain point, then stopped and threw the energy in another direction. She felt that this was a definite improvement since stopping the fall before coming into contact with the floor gave the performer an even stronger impulse and enabled her to accumulate more energy that could then be redirected in the space.

The founding members of her second group, The Bridge of Winds, to whom Rasmussen affectionately refers as "the Old Winds" to distinguish them from members who joined later, developed a series of exercises which are still part of the training that my project documentation team and I filmed over the course of two weeks in December 2011. The group's signature exercise is the Wind Dance, and in my interview with her, Rasmussen traced this key element of the training to her first meeting with The Bridge of Winds, during which a young Danish woman contributed an exercise that she had learned from Gardzienice, the Polish group directed by Włodzimierz Staniewski, a close collaborator of Grotowski from the paratheatrical period. Rasmussen described this exercise as a kind of dance with a set step accompanied by rhythmical breathing and a very loose way of moving the head. When the entire group tried it, she saw that it had potential and encouraged them to develop it further. She observed that it was like an egg of Columbus, because unlike some other exercises which needed to be perfected for a very long time in order to find a sense of flow, this simple dance already had a life of its own. Variations of this exercise included performing the dance in an introvert or extrovert manner, changing directions in the space while keeping the rhythm precise, relating to others, and so on. This was a particularly significant breakthrough in Rasmussen's teaching, especially since in her formative training she had been struggling with exercises such as the *plastiques* which, in her experience, could quickly become quite tiring, and which had made it impossible for her to achieve the sense of flow she was seeking.

Rasmussen said she had noticed that when the members of the Odin were young they would work all day, perform in the evening, and then go to a club and dance for a very long time without ever being exhausted. Wondering where this energy came from, she encouraged her group to create dances enabling them to experience this continuous flow of energy. She then discovered that the Wind Dance could be learned fairly rapidly and worked for most people. Having a common rhythm helped the group's precision, sustained their energy, and kept them connected to each other as they moved through the workspace. They added the elements of throwing, pulling, stopping, and relating to each other in a variety of spatial configurations which eventually became fixed patterns in the training sequence they developed. Initially, there were moments of individual improvisation which could last up to half an hour, sometimes longer. The other performers would tap stones together to create the rhythmical background for these solo improvisations. Later, improvisation with a partner became an integral part of the training sequence, and the only constraint was keeping the rhythm of the dance steps. The Wind Dance therefore began as a basic exercise that evolved into a defining feature of the international group's homegrown approach to training which they have continued to practice to this day.

Practice: Mapping Out Interconnections 109

Figure 2.7 Iben Nagel Rasmussen teaching the Wind Dance. *Meetings with Remarkable Women*, Grotowski Institute, Wroclaw, Poland, July–August 2009—photo by Francesco Galli.

During the training sessions we filmed, Rasmussen observed her group attentively, wrote down comments as she watched, and gave very specific notes at the end. When I asked her what she was looking for in her group's training and what she considered to be a successful training session, she pointed to particular moments of connection. She remarked that sometimes you repeat what you know, but sometimes something is really happening and you can feel it in the room. She said that she could sense when the members of her group came together in a special way, when something was different, when something was really there, really living, which was impossible to repeat. Whereas the point of the training is to create the necessary conditions for these moments of connection to emerge without knowing when this might happen, she noted that such creative moments, which are the most productive outcomes of the training, do not systematically occur every time.

Rasmussen then acknowledged that she had always wanted to ask her group members why having some kind of training is important for the actor, but she said that it was a difficult question to bring up because she had been working so closely with them. Nevertheless, she felt the need to ask why they still wanted to practice the Wind Dance after so many years, why they continued to do this training or any form of training. She wanted to ask them: what is it good for? In her view, training is inextricably linked to the actor's independence, and she emphasized that the moment the actor gives up and says, okay, I'm not going to do it anymore, then comes the director (she made a threatening sound while gesturing with her arms as if attempting to grab hold of someone), and the actor is reduced to a puppet, unable to resist. She added that although one's training can change and become, for instance, a way of preparing the material for a new performance, it is above all about creating one's own space, an inner and outer room which is and remains one's own. Then, she observed, even if the director completely misunderstands or misuses what the actor has been doing, the latter can still derive a sense of fulfillment from the work process. She stressed that having this space of one's own, which one needs to find in the early years of one's training, had been a way for her to remain in contact with the creative sources of her work. She specified that maintaining this connection through some form of personal training entailed thinking with one's whole body, which she described as meditating in action.

I experienced Rasmussen's teaching during the three-day work session which she led for *Meetings with Remarkable Women* in 2009 at the Grotowski Institute, and in the course of which she introduced the participants to the main elements of the training she has developed with her group, including, of course, the Wind Dance. This work session was documented on film by Francesco Galli and is featured on the Routledge Performance Archive. For the *Meetings with Remarkable Women* Festival, Rasmussen performed *Ester's Book*, a beautifully poignant piece that she wrote and directed, and in which she embodies her own mother towards the end of her life.

Practice: Mapping Out Interconnections 111

Figure 2.8 Iben Nagel Rasmussen rehearsing *Ester's Book* for the *Meetings with Remarkable Women* Festival. Grotowski Institute, Wroclaw, Poland, August 2009—photo by Francesco Galli.

In the summer of 2010, I met Rasmussen again in Milan, where the Odin was on tour, to discuss with her the possibility of organizing a meeting for The Bridge of Winds so that her work with her group could also be documented on film. In December 2011 I organized and funded a meeting which brought together the group members from Poland, Finland, Denmark, Italy, Colombia, Argentina, and Brazil for a two-week closed session hosted by the Odin Teatret in Holstebro, Denmark. Francesco Galli, Celeste Taliani, Chiara Crupi, and I worked closely with Rasmussen and her group on the film documentation process, our goal being to devise effective ways of filming the different elements of the training and to document the group's community involvement through their voice concerts and cultural barters.

In the course of these two weeks, I conducted individual interviews with each member of the group and with the children of the founding members who had grown up in this small transnational community of artists. Rasmussen herself explained that she had always encouraged group members to bring babies and young children with them when working with her, and she said that it had functioned very well since everyone happily took turns taking care of this new generation of "little Winds" to enable the parents to continue to participate as fully as possible. She told me that just before my arrival at the Odin she had attended the wedding celebration of two group members: an Italian woman who belonged to the "Old Winds" and a Danish woman who was part of the "New Winds" and who was about three quarters through her pregnancy, yet still took part in most of the group's activities. While witnessing the dynamics of this itinerant global village struck a chord with me because of my own experience at a United World College, what I found particularly striking about this diverse configuration of unusually dedicated individuals was that even though they clearly consider Rasmussen to be a master-performer/teacher without whom The Bridge of Winds could not have thrived for so many years, its intergenerational artistic longevity hinges upon a non-hierarchical model which is inclusive, participatory, and self-regulating. To her credit, Rasmussen's relationship to the group is neither that of a teacher to her students nor that of a director to her actors, and even less that of an emblematic Odin Teatret actress to her devoted followers, but rather that of an exceptionally experienced and compassionate creative collaborator whose generosity of spirit and commitment to her craft provide an alternative model of artistic leadership.

3 Towards an Ecology of the Body-in-Life

Prior to my meetings with Grotowski's foremost women collaborators, I wondered how working with these artists and learning about their experiences might inform and transform my perspective of and relationship to a type of performance training that had been important to me for a number of reasons. What I felt was most valuable about the experience I had with my Paris-based group led by students of Flaszen and Molik were the ways in which this work stretched in a literal and figurative sense the boundaries of what was defined as theatre in my culture. For the creative process activated by this work was intensely engaging: although the training was quite challenging, it provided me with a deep sense of psychophysical fulfillment, a feeling of being fully alive which I had never experienced in my previous theatre training. It also gave me an insight into the potentialities that could be harnessed through the cultivation of a dynamic and fluid energetic balance between the imagination, the body, and, importantly, the voice, which I will address in this chapter.

SEEKING BALANCE: LIFE AS PRECARIOUS EQUILIBRIUM

While it is difficult to put into words how the body-mind *feels* when fully engaged in this form of creative practice, I would submit, along with Favel who shared with me his experience of working with Mirecka, that the ultimate purpose of this type of training should be to make practitioners feel balanced, in the sense of physical and mental well-being. Within the specific context of his culture and community, Favel envisions performance as a point of convergence between theatre and tradition by relating the function of performance to that of traditional practices and rituals. He refers to what he calls "being clean," which he defines as the absence of obstacles in one's relationship to others, to one's natural environment, to one's ancestors, and, consequently, to one's self. Grotowski himself often mentioned the need for the work to be clean (*propre*) and stated in his seventh Collège de France lecture that everything depended on the quality of what was being accomplished, and that one should not work for the sake of pleasing others in order to be accepted. Within the historical context of Communist Poland, putting one's trust in the wrong person could have dire consequences, so that being clean connoted being trustworthy, in the sense of not having been corrupted by a system which often required people to dissimulate and compromise their ethical, political, and spiritual convictions in order to survive. To some extent, then, it might be possible to draw some parallels between life in occupied Poland and the on-going experience of colonialism by Indigenous people in North America, insofar as survival in such circumstances often entails having to forfeit a part of oneself.

When Favel suggests that Mirecka's teaching fulfills a specific need pertaining to the shortcomings of modern living and its negative impact on people's mental and physical health, he is pointing to a lack of balance which also manifests itself in the ecological crisis that may be interpreted as resulting directly from industrial and technological development in service of capitalist productivity. Indigenous scholars observe that destroying the environment is a form of self-destruction, and foreground the interconnectedness of human beings and all other forms of life, a principle which Manulani Aluli Meyer argues is fundamental to Indigenous epistemologies. This is echoed by Kenneth J. Gergen who contends in *Relational Being: Beyond Self and Community* that a sustainable relationship between human beings and the natural world is critical to the survival of all forms of life on earth: "To understand the world in which we live as constituted by independent species, forms, types, or entities is to threaten the well-being of the planet. [...] Whatever value we place upon ourselves and others, and whatever hope we may have for the future, depends on the welfare of relationship" (396). This compelling notion of welfare as relational, which Gergen associates with the well-being of the planet, supports an ecosystemic view of our relationship to the environment which has become increasingly informed by Indigenous ecological knowledge.

Linda Tuhiwai Smith hence states in *Decolonizing Methodologies* that

> indigenous communities have something to offer to the non-indigenous world [such as] indigenous peoples' ideas and beliefs about the origins of the world, their explanations of the environment, often embedded in complicated metaphors and mythic tales [which] are now sought as the basis for thinking more laterally about current theories about the environment, the earth and the universe. (159)

Smith points to the strategic essentialism that characterizes the way in which Indigenous peoples have managed, in spite of colonial epistemic violence, to preserve an embodied knowledge of their identity which is rooted in the land of their ancestors. She specifies that, although "claiming essential characteristics is as much strategic as anything else, because it has been about claiming human rights and indigenous rights [...] the essence of a person is also discussed in relation to indigenous concepts of spirituality"

(*Decolonizing Methodologies* 74). Indigenous perspectives are thus informed by "arguments of different indigenous peoples based on spiritual relationships to the universe, to the landscape and to stones, rocks, insects and other things, seen and unseen," which, she remarks, "have been difficult arguments for Western systems of knowledge to deal with or accept" (74). She asserts that this place-based conception of identity and the spiritual dimension of its relationship to the natural environment "give a partial indication of the different world views and alternative ways of coming to know, and of being, which still endure within the indigenous world [and which are] critical sites of resistance for indigenous peoples" (72). Honoring Indigenous worldviews that colonial powers attempt to systematically suppress therefore constitutes a fundamental aspect of the healing process fostered by Indigenous research and pedagogy. Performance, which is vital to the embodied transmission of traditional knowledge, sustains cultural and spiritual identity through material practice, thereby significantly contributing to this healing process, as argued by Favel.

By allowing access to their creative practice, the first-generation women whom I consider to be the Elders of a small transnational and intergenerational community of artists have enabled me to gain an embodied understanding of the principles and values binding the members of this community. I am especially struck by how deeply connected they still feel to their lived experience of the theatrical and paratheatrical phases of Grotowski's research. The consistency of their testimonies reveals, on the one hand, the extreme level of commitment required to engage in this type of long-term artistic research and, on the other hand, the deep sense of fulfillment derived from such an engagement. Indeed, the rewards must have been so substantial that they compelled Grotowski's collaborators to abide aspects of the work which, from an outsider's perspective, might appear to make this extremely challenging research unduly demanding.

When I last visited Wroclaw in the summer of 2012, Gardecka and I spoke about this and she remarked that this total commitment to creative research was very unusual even at the time. She stressed that in her experience as Grotowski's main administrator such a commitment was never dependent on the type of financial compensation that would be required nowadays to motivate people to do a fraction of the work. Having acknowledged that the Laboratory Theatre's activities took place in very different social, political, and economic circumstances, she said that she nevertheless missed the cultural vibrancy and artistic passion that had characterized the theatrical and paratheatrical periods and had made her administrative work creative and fulfilling. Even though Gardecka was not involved in the artistic work, she was deeply committed to the company and her testimony is representative of how the artists themselves view their experience at the Laboratory Theatre. Gardecka has maintained strong ties to most of them to this day, and it was thanks to her on-going relationship with members of the Grotowski diaspora that I was able to develop this project.

My bearing witness to the consistency of women's testimonies and to the vitality of their on-going engagement in creative research has led me to consider the members of the first generation in light of their accomplishments rather than as the disenfranchised Others of a performance tradition whose legacy appears to remain anxiously guarded by its male inheritors. Consequently, I have become increasingly interested in the implications of women's contributions to this type of research beyond dominant notions of artistic merit that pertain to the evaluation of more conventional performance models. What I am therefore proposing in this chapter is an examination of the ways in which their practice challenges such conventions and proposes alternative possibilities related to an ecological understanding of performance, in the broader sense of ecology articulated by Indigenous scholars who foreground relationality and interconnectedness.

AN ECOSYSTEMIC CONCEPTION OF ORGANICITY

The performance practice I am investigating supports a performance paradigm positing an interconnection between the organic processes of the body-in-life and the organicity of the natural environment. In some of the experiments of the post-theatrical period, the performer's psychophysical relationship to nature may even be said to have supplanted the relationship to the performance space inhabited by other performers and spectator-witnesses that was central to the theatrical period. Borrowing Grotowski's way of speaking about artistic experimentation, I would contend that, in the post-theatrical period, it was *as if* nature had become both a partner and a witness, a double function also embodied by human beings as partner-witnesses of nature. The notions of actor and spectator thus became irrelevant simply because the exchange that took place between partner-witnesses no longer belonged to the realm of theatre.

Scientific inquiry also employs an "as if" when formulating a research hypothesis, and the "ecosystemic life hypothesis" articulated by environmental biologist Daniel A. Fiscus constitutes a particularly imaginative "as if" that provides a useful lens through which to view the performance processes explored by the women participating in my project. Attempting to define ecological health, Fiscus responds to the question: "What is life?" by suggesting that "a reciprocal relation with environment is arguably as important for understanding life as it is for understanding ecosystems" ("The Ecosystemic Life Hypothesis I" 248, 250). He goes on to assert: "This, combined with the historical scientific trend to explain ecosystems in ever more physical terms, says to me that the concepts of life and ecosystem are necessarily linked and naturally convergent" (250). Fiscus points out that scientists who posit an ecosystemic origin of life propose to adopt a holistic treatment of life and its environment as a single evolving system. He notes that R. Rosen reframes the question "What is

Towards an Ecology of the Body-in-Life 117

life?" by asking instead "Why are organisms different than machines?"—a query related to the argument according to which "the explanatory powers of the mechanistic worldview cannot help understand the realm of living systems" ("The Ecosystemic Life Hypothesis II" 95). For Rosen, "life is not divisible like a machine and the mechanistic/reductionist approach will not work to understand it," an observation which leads him to contend that, unlike machines, life is characterized by "two integrated functions—metabolism and repair" (96).

Fiscus links these fundamental life functions to the composer-decomposer functions in ecosystems and posits that "the ecosystemic organization of life from its origin onward is more fundamental than the cellular or organismic forms of organization. The composer-decomposer system is the common ancestor of both metabolic and genetic processes, both of which are processes of molecular string composition and decomposition" ("The Ecosystemic Life Hypothesis III" 147). Expanding upon this argument about the primacy of the ecosystemic organization of life over cellular and organismic forms of organization, Fiscus develops the hypothesis that "the ecosystem [. . .] is the general, self-perpetuating form of life, and cells and organisms are special case subunits of life which cannot persist in isolation" (147). He goes on to argue that such a hypothesis provides insights into "life's capacity for open-ended evolution" (147), and posits that the ecosystemic organization of energy flow is key to understanding life itself.

Fiscus's ecosystemic life paradigm therefore hinges upon the principle according to which life and natural systems possess a comparable capacity to restore themselves. He concludes: "The ecosystemic life hypothesis inverts the current working assumption that life originated and developed from the cell or organism in the general to the ecosystem in the specific" (148), a repositioning which he states is supported by "reformed systems ecologists [who] tend to view organisms as very tightly integrated ecological systems" (148). Fiscus ends by observing that, if this systems ecological approach to understanding life proves to work better than an organism-centric approach, such a perspective could have significant implications for scientific research on both ecology and biology.

What is interesting about this alternative conception of organic life is that, as with the neuroscientific conception of the embodied dimension of brain functions, it seems to be pointing to possibilities that artists such as Stanislavsky, Grotowski, and their collaborators intuitively apprehended through their practice-based research on the body-in-life. Drawing from both the theatrical and post-theatrical periods, the women in my project hence envision the body-in-life as a microcosm of the ecosystemic organization of the natural environment and convey through their teaching that it is possible to experience the human organism "as if" it were a natural ecosystem regulated by energy flow and animated by a self-perpetuating and self-restoring form of life with a capacity for open-ended evolution. This is reflected in their creative work by the importance of connection to space/

place as well as by the fluidity of the notion of organicity which, for them, encompasses all forms of life, human and non-human.

THE LIFE OF THE BODY: SOURCES AND HORIZONS

This ecosystemic conception of organicity is particularly pivotal to Mirecka's teaching, and while the ritualized aspect of her creative work significantly structures the way in which she transmits her embodied knowledge of performance processes, it is the primacy of organicity in her teaching that has enabled me to make connections between the multiple layers of her wide-ranging artistic perspective. When leading the physical and vocal training, Mirecka thus foregrounds organic processes within the exercises that mirror in both a metaphorical and material way the organic circulation of energy within natural ecosystems. In my interview with her, she explained that after many years of work on herself she understands her inner creative process to be a river: she is aware of the power of that river and familiar with the different stones, plants, and animals within. During her work sessions that take place in areas such as the forest base of Brzezinka and the wilderness of Sardinia, she encourages participants to take the time to be with and listen to nature, which she notes speaks without words. She stresses that everything around us is made of the same energy: forest, ocean, sun, wind, and sky, hence the importance of working within the embrace of nature. Mirecka relates this vast natural ecosystem to the inner garden of our organism and suggests that we are in this world to try to understand how to fulfill all of our potentialities so that our whole being may exist in relationship with all other forms of life. She emphasizes the importance of daily practice that begins with breathing exercises based on the system of the chakras and chants from the Indian and Tibetan traditions precisely because these practices are designed to activate the inner circulation of energies within the human organism and connect it to the circulation of energies in the natural world.

When discussing energy during his sixth Collège de France lecture, Grotowski stated that the system of the chakras represented one possible version of the cartography of the various energetic centers within the human body. He said that he did not use ancient texts on the chakras and experiment with the passage from one chakra to another, but resorted instead to an approach that was much more European in that he used the phrase "as if" when conducting his practical investigation. Having distinguished seven different areas of the body, Grotowski explained that in his practical work he had been able to identify various qualities of energy related to these different areas; for example, energies that were connected to the lower area of the body clearly had a much more vital quality, whereas the upper part of the body was related to more subtle forms of energy. Grotowski

Towards an Ecology of the Body-in-Life 119

Figure 3.1 Rena Mirecka in Brzezinka. *Meetings with Remarkable Women*, Poland, July 2009—photo by Maciej Stawinski.

noted, however, that the focus should be on observing the emergence of this phenomenon without manipulation of any kind, so as to avoid the pitfall of autosuggestion. Linking this conception of energy to the notion of organicity, he specified that although artificiality was absolutely fundamental to structure and composition, he personally favored organicity, as did Stanislavsky who considered the latter to be the life force animating both human beings and nature. In the preceding chapter, I referred to Carnicke's discovery in the Russian director's rehearsal notes that he associated this life force with the Hindu concept of *prana* (*Stanislavsky in Focus* 141). Mirecka also employs the Sanskrit word *prana* in her work on the chakras, and the breathing exercises she leads constitute a form of inner observation focused on the circulation of breath in the body. She links breath to energy, which she equates with a source of inner light that is always alive within the human organism and always changing. She refers to the base of the spine and the area of the lower back as the mouth of the serpent, the place in the body from which all movement begins, as well as the voice, which she considers to be an extension of movement.

Such an embodied understanding of organicity in which the voice is envisioned as an extension of movement, that is to say, of physical actions rooted in the flux of impulses and connected to personal associations, is pivotal to the conception of vocal training the artists involved in my project transmit through their teaching. When working with voice, they often evoke non-human forms of movement by referring to natural elements through the use of imagery, thereby inviting performers to experience sound and movement as the source of organic life. In light of the ecosystemic conception of organic life processes that I have begun to articulate, I propose to consider the body-voice connection in relation to this ecological understanding of performance, and examine the extent to which the principles governing the physical training also apply to the interrelation of body and voice.

I would argue that what most significantly distinguishes Grotowski's work from Stanislavsky's lies precisely in the Polish director's focus on the body-voice connection throughout the various phases of his practical research. Over the course of his nine Collège de France lectures, Grotowski foregrounded his long-standing interest in the relationship between voice and embodiment within the context of the performance processes he had been investigating. The body-voice connection may thus be perceived to constitute one of the most fundamental elements linking the theatrical and post-theatrical experiments carried out by Grotowski and his collaborators. Furthermore, I would contend that examining the implications of the body-voice connection for performance practice can provide an insight into what Grotowski called "the second horizon" of his research which, in his seventh lecture, he linked to achieving another level of perception of life and another kind of presence. While he acknowledged that these words fell short of describing what he meant, he noted that what mattered was to have a motivation that was not directly linked to profit whether moral or material. For Grotowski, then, it was necessary to have some form of professional competence in a particular domain and, in addition, to have a second horizon or what he called an aspiration. Accordingly, it was Grotowski's own aspiration for something beyond theatre that compelled him to abandon theatre productions in order to focus on post-theatrical investigations linked to traditional cultural practices.

While the women involved in my project explore their own second horizon in different ways, they consider that this other dimension of creative research gives meaning to their work beyond what is usually confined solely to the realm of artistic practice. Their focus on the body-voice connection hence reflects a conviction they share with Grotowski about the embodied nature of performance, which for them is not limited to the physical manifestation of human psychology in the performer's body, but encompasses other aspects of human existence. Grotowski stressed in his sixth Collège de France lecture that the Laboratory Theatre actors had struggled to reach a certain mastery of the body only in order to eliminate *blocages* within the organism so that it could become an open channel. In order to provide a concrete example related to performance practice, Grotowski screened film excerpts of Cieslak's training demonstration and encouraged the audience to pay attention to the fluidity, lightness, or "non-physicality" as he put it, in Cieslak's exercises, which he noted were accomplished without so much as a creak on the wooden floor, so that the workspace in which the actor moved remained completely silent in spite of the intensity of his actions. Grotowski observed that the final stage in this training session featured Cieslak's work with personal associations, and he specified that the physical transitions in Cieslak's demonstration were informed by his memories, his relationship to the space around him, to his inner life, to human contacts, and so on, yet the actor did not lose his technical ability linked to physical precision. Grotowski thus pointed out that Cieslak followed the flow of his personal associations while carefully keeping the necessary details in place. When Mirecka and Seyferth lead the *plastique* exercises they also emphasize that it is crucial to respect the precision of physical actions in all their detail and to let transitions be informed by the flow of personal associations, since it is the interdependence of structure and spontaneity that sustains the organicity of the performer's process.

Although Grotowski reiterated in this lecture that his alleged interest in the body was an eternal legend which had plagued him throughout his career, he acknowledged that working with the body was necessary; otherwise, it became inert, heavy, and lost its abilities. He underlined that in this form of training the body became a conduit, and that consequently it was not the body in and of itself, or, as he put it, the meat (*la viande*) that was important, but rather the flux of living impulses within the body. Hence, the point of the training was not to foreground the physicality of the body but to render this flux visible.

Grotowski nevertheless considered embodiment to be pivotal to performance processes, and in his seventh Collège de France lecture he addressed the performer's relationship to the body in the training, suggesting that one could derive joy from watching one's body become alive again, and pointing out that one needed to let the body do what it must do in its own way. He compared this process with riding a horse, and observed that the rider should not try to manipulate or direct the way in which the horse positioned its legs: it was impossible to do so as this would only result in incapacitating the horse. Instead, the rider should help the horse to let itself go, cooperate with its way of letting itself go. Grotowski inferred that the relationship between the body and the process that took place inside (although not solely inside) the body hinged upon an understanding, a cooperation. He noted that this approach could be described as joyful although it did not constitute a form of identification, and he insisted that this important dimension was often forgotten. On the one hand, when one directed the body as if it were a puppet it became incapacitated, as was so often the case with actors who manipulated the actions of their body. On the other hand, identifying with one's body led to developing a narcissistic relationship to it. He concluded that one had to let the body have its own experiences of joy, freedom, possibilities, and suggested this was the foundation for another departure, as if riding towards something higher, both ascending and descending, which was not identification but a much deeper relationship between body and process.

As evident in Cieslak's demonstration as well as in Mirecka's and Seyferth's teaching, the *plastiques* can enable the performer to explore the joy, freedom, and possibilities of an embodied process combining discipline and spontaneity, this conjunction of opposites which, "far from weakening each other, mutually reinforce themselves" (*Towards a Poor Theatre* 121) as quoted by Komorowska in her book. Moreover, although such physical training is executed in silence, I will now examine how it constitutes a preparation for creative work that fosters an organic connection between the body and the voice. The analogy of the rider and the horse may thus also be applied to vocal work in the sense that vocal training relies on a deep relationship between body and process. This delicate form of relationality was linked to a search for balance by Mirecka when she explained in one of her work sessions that experiencing the organic connection between body and voice, movement and sound, physical action and vocal vibration, is like stepping lightly into a canoe—only after developing a friendship with the water can we navigate the river.

TRANSMISSION PROCESSES: BACK TO THE ROOTS

Transmission processes themselves can be said to form a network of interconnections through which embodied knowledge circulates from person to person within this small transnational community of artists. Navigating this river of knowledge with its currents and countercurrents has taught me that it flows within this community "as if" its various modes of transmission modeled the very organic processes being transmitted. Recalling Absolon's central image of the flower, with its roots corresponding to paradigms, worldviews, and principles, while its leaves, stem, and petals convey the different yet interrelated pathways through which knowledge circulates in the course of the research journey, I am compelled to interpret the image of the tree summoned by Mirecka in relation to Grotowski's legacy as an ever-expanding network of organic connections. These connections are rooted in the foundational work of the Laboratory Theatre actors informed by a particular conception of performance, a culturally and historically specific worldview, and the guiding principles that regulate a certain type of artistic practice. The energy generated by the multidirectional flow of transmission between the branches and leaves may be envisioned as the sap running through this organic network "as if" it were the breath, or *prana* in the sense of vital energy, sustaining this complex ecosystem.

Tracing the flow of transmission related to vocal training within this map-like image of the tree leads to an interesting discovery: although the body-voice connection, which may be represented as one of the main roots of the tree, is linked to Molik's development of vocal training as the Laboratory Theatre voice specialist, this particular root is closely intertwined with another major root through its interconnection with the work of Mirecka, the specialist of the *plastique* exercises. For it is through their focus on organicity in the physical training that both Mirecka and Molik create the necessary conditions for the performer to experience the body-voice connection as deeply rooted in the flux of impulses and personal associations.

The vocal training at the Laboratory Theatre was led by Molik, who is acknowledged by Mirecka, Komorowska, and Albahaca for helping them (as well as their male colleagues) to develop their vocal capacities. Molik's teaching is therefore an important link in the transmission processes through which vocal work has been practiced and disseminated not only by the members of the Laboratory Theatre but also trans-generationally within the Grotowski diaspora. In my conversations with Albahaca, for example, she outlined three aspects of the vocal work: the initial work led by Grotowski which focused on resonators, the training subsequently developed by Molik, and later, during the Art as vehicle period, the research on vibratory songs carried out by Richards and Biagini at the Workcenter in Italy. Albahaca, who is familiar with these three aspects of the vocal work even though she only witnessed the third, told me that she perceived a continuity between them. She remarked that whereas Molik's work was not concerned with tradition, it was very much focused on the vibratory quality of the voice, and that whereas ancient traditional songs engage the body—especially the spine—in a way that is specific to these songs, this specificity is very closely linked to their vibratory quality, so that in her view there are significant overlaps between these different phases of the research on voice conducted by Grotowski and his collaborators.

While I initially learned about the body-voice connection through my practical experience of the physical and vocal training, using the image of the tree as a map has helped me to understand that the type of training transmitted to me in Paris when I worked with Molik's students is the result of complex transmission processes in which Mirecka's *plastiques* play a central role, even though they do not seem to be directly linked to vocal training per se. It is because of this connection between Mirecka's *plastiques* and Molik's voice-body work that I feel a particular affinity to the *plastique* exercises although I had never encountered them before working with Mirecka—or so I thought. An important clue about this connection is provided by Molik himself towards the end of *Zygmunt Molik's Voice and Body Work* when asked by Giuliano Campo: "So at that time, around the mid-seventies, you started composing the 'Body Alphabet.' How did the 'Body Alphabet' start? What was the process of creation of the 'Body Alphabet' like? Was it your own research to create your own system, or was it like recalling your experience and trying to select some actions?" Molik replies: "To tell the truth I don't remember, but if I try to reconstruct it in my mind, to come back to that time, it must be that since I knew the actions of the *plastiques*, I took from them those that I knew could be useful, and I simply had to invent the rest. I had to invent everything. There was no precursor that I knew from whom I could take my experience" (141). Later, when Campo mentions Mirecka as the Laboratory Theatre member who created the *plastiques*, Molik confirms that she was the leader of these exercises (147), which induces Campo to remark: "You had to follow her when she was leading." Molik responds: "Yes, she was leading the lessons of the *plastiques*." Campo then boldly suggests: "So practically, she influenced you," which prompts Molik to exclaim: "Why not? We influenced each other, yes" (148).

What this exchange between Campo and Molik reveals is not only that everyone at the Laboratory Theatre influenced everyone else, since each core member led the specific part of the training in which they specialized, but, more to the point, that if Molik drew directly from Mirecka's teaching of the *plastiques* to develop his Body Alphabet, then it is fair to say that his approach to voice and body work is substantially indebted to Mirecka's own contribution to the Laboratory Theatre training. At the very beginning of the book, Campo asks Molik about the *plastique* exercises and Molik states: "I use these exercises a lot. In particular a part of my 'Body Alphabet' is based on the *plastique* exercises" (11). Molik later differentiates action from gesture, a distinction which, as we have seen, was key to Mirecka's development of the *plastiques* since she was asked by Grotowski to use Delsarte's investigation of gestures as a starting point and to take it beyond the superficial level of gestures into the realm of actions that were deeply rooted inside the body. Molik hence states: "Real action is real action.

It's not a gesture. Because when I move my arm faintly, it's a gesture. But when I want to open the space, I do a precise line, with both arms, for example. This is action, and that is gesture" (45). The actions which are part of the Body Alphabet are therefore designed, as with Mirecka's *plastiques*, to engage the spine and, consequently, the whole body, in organic action.

CULTIVATING THE BODY-VOICE CONNECTION

In my understanding of the training, physical exercises *precede* vocal exercises as a way to prepare the ground by making the soil of the body fertile, thereby enabling the voice to grow organically from its connection to the body-in-life, considered to be the source of vocal vibration. It is important to note that Molik's Body Alphabet is *a series of physical actions that do not entail any kind of vocalization*. The precise, organic physical actions comprised within the Body Alphabet are performed silently in the workspace, which vibrates with the energy of movement, not sound. In my experience of the vocal training first with Molik's students and later with Molik himself, only a few specific physical actions were used in the vocal work and these actions were not the same as those used in the Body Alphabet. The physical actions pertaining specifically to the vocal training were performed while vocalizing and were dynamic but stationary, often making use of the floor or of a wall in a very precise manner. I would therefore like to emphasize that in Molik's training the performer does not move vigorously through the workspace while vocalizing.

In his book, Molik distinguishes the preparatory physical training of the Body Alphabet from the subsequent work he does with voice by pointing out: "I can only say that too much action is not good for the voice. But some actions are necessary. [...] [I]n a given moment you must be able to do the action, the right action of the body in order to get the right sound. But if you do too much, the energy is dispersed. And then the voice is empty, it gets empty. So you must be very careful about it" (Campo and Molik 51–52). The difference between the actions of the Body Alphabet and the actions used during the vocal work can be clearly seen in the film documenting the demonstration by Molik's student Jorge Parente featured on the book's companion DVD. Molik thus describes the Body Alphabet as a form of physical training designed to open up the body and prepare it for vocal work:

> There are around thirty actions from which I construct a kind of body language. You must learn these actions by heart and then improvise the Life with these [...] doing these actions with the arms, with the hands, with the pelvis, with the legs [...] Nothing is mechanical. [...] You don't anticipate what will be next. [...] All the exercises are done

to serve the voice. I just conceived them in that way, the whole 'Body Alphabet.' (56–58)

When Molik speaks of improvising "the Life" using the actions of the Body Alphabet, he is referring to a process which is similar to Mirecka's *plastique* exercises: what makes both the actions of the *plastiques* and the actions of the Body Alphabet alive, rather than mechanical, is the flow of impulses linked to personal associations. While the structure of the actions needs to remain precise, what must constantly change is the life of these actions, so that improvising with them may be described as a way of modulating energy, which includes variations in tempo-rhythm, in the quality of energy, and in the scale or size of the actions. This modulation of energy, however, is not the result of mental calculation, but takes place in the present moment of doing as the performer follows the impulses of the body-in-life and the images connected to personal associations that emerge from this process.

Consequently, whereas the ultimate objective of the training developed by Molik is to enhance the performer's vocal creativity, he stresses that the goal of the Body Alphabet is "to wake up the connections in the body, to make the body alive and ready to give and respond to impulses. The body must also be prepared for [vocal work], because otherwise you can only do some vocal exercises, and this is quite a different thing" (142). In both the *plastique* exercises and the Body Alphabet, impulse-based physical actions must be connected to what Stanislavsky called the actor's inner life, which Molik and Mirecka awaken by employing images of nature or natural elements in their teaching, images that they relate to the performer's creative encounter with the unknown. Molik describes such an encounter as follows:

> And then in this very moment something unexpected suddenly happens. You find yourself in a quite different place, like somewhere you are very often in your dreams, when you're lying in bed but you dream that you're in a wonderful orchard, [...] where looking far away you see wonderful landscapes, maybe somewhere that you feel as if you have the wind in your face. [...] [T]hen also your physical behavior is changing completely. [...] You're no longer in this room where you are working but [...] in something that's very personal to you, where you have this very special meeting. [...] After the training is over, you remember [...] that you have had such a meeting with the unknown. And that it was interesting and important for you. (111)

In his work sessions, Molik would closely observe everyone while the group worked on the Body Alphabet in order to catch these fleeting encounters. He would then ask each person whom he sensed had experienced a meeting with the unknown during the training to recall what they were doing in that moment and to use their actions and personal associations as the structure, or physical score, for a text which they had memorized.

In his book, Molik addresses this work with text when he states: "And then you have the monologue, which is built on the personal life, which is found in such circumstances during the training. Because if you don't have such a thing, how can you build a monologue? Only by the imagination which comes out of the text, from the words, from the text itself? This isn't so very interesting" (111). This way of layering a text onto the physical score structured by the training and emerging from non-verbal, physically-based improvisation, corresponds to my experience both with my teachers in Paris and with Molik himself, and confirms that the point of the training is to prepare the body for creative work so that the performer's organic process may instill the written text with the flux of impulses and associations characterizing this process.

As can most clearly be seen in the film *Acting Therapy*, the vocal work in Molik's teaching is comprised of exercises focusing on the body-voice connection, collective vocal improvisations, and individual work on songs and text. Critical to this approach is the passage from singing to speaking: the vibratory quality of the voice, rooted in the body-in-life, enlivens spoken words which become deeply embodied and connected to the emergence of personal associations, thereby creating a tension with, resistance or opposition to, the literal meaning of the text. I also experienced this way of working with Mirecka when, during one of her work sessions, I created a physical score which became the structure for my work on a textual montage of *The Waves* by Virginia Woolf. The power of the body-voice connection, then, lies in the interdependence of the physical and vocal processes, which are experienced as a single unified organic process by the performer. My own embodied understanding of what may be called body-voice integration techniques, which are rooted in a conception of body and voice as inseparable from one another, is thus the result of complex transmission processes combining the influence of Mirecka's *plastiques* on Molik's Body Alphabet, my experience of Molik's and Flaszen's teaching transmitted to me by the French actors with whom I trained, and my participation in Molik and Mirecka's work sessions.

THE VOICE AS VEHICLE

The most significant implication of the body-voice connection is arguably that singing itself can become a vehicle for experiential cognition, as noted by Flaszen when writing about the practice-based research on voice he conducted during the post-theatrical period. He describes this experimental work in his text "Meditations Aloud":

> Everything is improvised. Performing some ready-made pieces, chants or song is, as a rule, out of the question: [what is] at stake [is] the penetration of our own vocal stream. [...] You forget whether you sing

nicely or uglily, and that the sounds you produce ought to be impressive, odd, fascinating, funny, or extraordinary. The voice in you, as a voice, and all its music, is not the thing of value here—more precisely: it has a subsidiary value. It's a vehicle. The Vehicle of Experience. [...] It's a catalyst of Experience. A vehicle which takes us into something that is not voice. It's like a flying carpet, taking us to a rare dimension. (*Grotowski & Company* 140–41, 145)

Molik seems to share Flaszen's view when declaring in his book that he employs the term "vehicle" to "explain the role of the human voice in the human organism" because he established through his experience of teaching vocal training that the voice is "like a vehicle which brings out the whole Life. So, not only the sound, not only the breath, but also the soul" (103). This interconnection between life, breath, sound, and soul or spirit is also evoked by Flaszen when he suggests that singing calls into question the type of agency pertaining to an individualist view of creativity:

The fact that you are singing is completely meaningless. You sing because there is singing. And you just don't know who is singing here. Certainly not you. It sings you, through you, it has chosen you, your body, as an instrument. But it could have chosen someone else. [...] The Voice-Vehicle has no author [...] The Voice-Vehicle becomes possible when [...] you understand with your entire being that everything which is, exists and that you exist in it, and that in this wholeness with which you are so tangibly in contact, you are only a small particle, a spark, a straw, a grain of sand, oh, how small, how meaningless John or Jan is. (145–46)

Flaszen goes on to acknowledge, however, that such experimentation cannot unlock the mysteries of the human voice: "[W]hen we break through the zone of the unknown with vibration, at last you break through to the visual without form, to the light, the light that fills us with a mild warmth, and every breath seems to have unlimited length, as if we didn't need air, because everything is a breath—all this happens in conditions, which—frankly speaking—are not exactly known to me" (147). Incidentally, the enigmatic dimension of vocal processes was memorably brought to my attention by Flaszen's ex-students through what retrospectively appears to have been a fortuitous coincidence.

During one of my Paris group's training sessions, my teachers brought out a small stack of hand-written cue cards and asked each member of the group to randomly draw one of these cards and read it. I have kept the card which I picked on that day, a little over twenty years ago, and which states: "*La voix est énigme pour le corps qui ne sait pas s'il la crée, la reçoit ou s'en délivre*" ("Voice is an enigma for the body which does not know whether it creates it, receives it or frees itself from it"). Although I wasn't aware of it at the time, the author of this sentence is Marie-France Castarède, a French psychologist whose research posits voice as the metaphor for all human relations. In *La Voix et ses sortilèges*, Castarède investigates various forms of collective singing practices, as well as the use of voice by mothers and their babies whom she argues communicate through playful vocalization. She observes that it is through the creative use of voice that a baby and its mother establish a non-verbal, embodied relationship which includes facial expressions, gestures, and movements.

The very fact that newborns can hear sounds before they can see images seems to support Castarède's privileging of voice over other modes of expression at this early stage of infancy. Envisioning vocal music as a way of playing with all the intermediary phases between presence and absence, including expectation, desire, tension, and repose, Castarède submits that this early intimate relationship to voice informs a range of voice-related activities, from children's spontaneous vocal improvisations to the most artistically sophisticated forms of vocal expression, arguing that the latter can reconnect "*parole*" (in the sense of orality) to the sources of the Sacred. She refers to the phrase "*de vive voix*," which signifies "in person" but whose literal meaning is "with/through the live voice," and contrasts it with phrases such as "*lettre morte*" (dead words, written down yet without consequences) and "*langue de bois*" (wooden language, a willfully obfuscating use of discourse), thereby foregrounding embodiment as a particularly significant dimension of voice linked to lived experience (*La Voix et ses sortilèges* 416–20).

In her published doctoral thesis titled *Et dedans Et dehors, la voix*, psychosociologist Bernadette Bailleux builds upon Castarède's perspective to develop a psychophysical approach based on the relationship she establishes between voice and embodiment. Grounding her investigation of this relationship in Ivan Fónagy's bioenergetic theory of voice as "*geste vocal*" (vocal gesture), she begins from the premise that our initial experience of sound during infancy constitutes the foundation for *parole*, in the Saussurian sense of the term, which distinguishes itself from *langue* because it is rooted in the lived experience of individuals situated within an historically and culturally specific context. Although *parole* is usually associated with individual agency, Bailleux explains that Fónagy sees in vocal gestures traces of an ancestral relationship to sound, a form of embodied cultural memory which connects us to the lived experience of those who came before us. Fónagy's notion of "vocal style," which he equates with its linguistic equivalent "verbal style," refers individuals back to their relationship to others as well as to their society, culture, and ancestral past. This is particularly relevant to the larger context of my discussion of the body-voice connection since it implies that the voices of our ancestors might still be resonating within our body memory. However, Bailleux argues that an individual's vocal style is also constituted by all her experiences throughout the course of her life and, most importantly, by the various ways in which she might consciously or unconsciously identify with some of these experiences, including class-based identifications that manifest themselves vocally through accents.

Taking this analysis further, I would submit that gender constitutes a major factor in the reproduction of normative vocal behavior, so that speaking with a high-pitched voice, for example, becomes associated with being a woman, a form of conditioning which may be perceived as the vocal equivalent to the type of physical behavior which Pierre Bourdieu defines as *habitus*. Bailleux includes within the category of vocal style the kind of vocal work that performers undertake to train their voices for the purpose of artistic practice (203–06, 210). She specifies that, as a professional psychotherapist, she works very closely with actors and singers, some of whom she credits on her website where she also provides links to the international Festival "Voix de Femmes" which supports women vocal artists from different cultures and traditions, and to the website of Evelyne Girardon, a traditional music specialist based in Lyon, who was my singing teacher for two years prior to my pursuing Grotowski-based training in Paris (http://www.resonancesvoix.com).

Bailleux's choice to include in her website links to the work of these women artists is pertinent to my discussion since the women in my project investigate the body-voice connection in part through their work on traditional songs. As I mentioned in the first chapter, it is through the influence of their teaching that I have become reconnected with traditional songs in the Occitan language which was my maternal grandmother's mother tongue. The first Occitan song I learned was transmitted to me by Girardon about two years after I graduated from Pearson College, and I remember experiencing a very strong connection to the musical tonality of the song and to its language. Occitan was not transmitted to my mother's generation and it hence lies outside my own linguistic competency, yet when learning to sing this song I experienced what may be described as an embodied understanding of its cultural meaning at the level of *parole* instead of *langue*.

Years later, when I first worked with Molik, participants were required to come prepared to sing a song. I felt strongly about working with a traditional song, and of all the songs I had studied with Girardon, the one I best remembered was the only Occitan song I knew. Somehow this song had stayed with me and I still felt connected to it. To some extent, encountering my teachers' master and singing this song during my first work session with him was a kind of test that constituted the preliminary phase of my meetings with women in the Grotowski diaspora, for I first needed to verify, so to speak, the value of what I had learned from Molik's students by working directly with him.

My Occitan song was very short and composed of only one stanza, so Molik instructed me to sing it three times consecutively as if it were a three-stanza song. He asked me to sing each stanza in a different way: while the first should be sung normally, the second should be filled with some form of love, and the third should be sung in a heroic way. As I followed Molik's instructions to the best of my ability, something occurred that I had never experienced before: by the time I reached the second and third stanzas, I sensed that my breath was flowing, that my jaw was quite dropped and my mouth wide open, and I discerned the loving and the passionate qualities of the song as if it were singing through me and had a life of its own. I was also aware that Molik stood across from me, watching from a distance, and during the heroic stanza I noticed that he was moving his forearms up and down rather vigorously along with the energy of the song. When it was over, Molik briefly commented: "Yes—very simple, but very powerful." Later on, during the break, we stood in the field outside the workspace when Molik walked towards me and said: "You did this song very well, you were very brave." Yet, it seemed that all I did was to get out of the way of this traditional song whose life I thus discovered for the first time.

I am grateful that this moment is not included in the film *Dyrygent*,[1] which was shot during this work session, as I feel that this kind of discovery is best remembered from inside, as a body memory. I had trepidations when first seeing this film, which is quite impressionistic and reveals very little about the work as Molik himself notes in his book. At some point, the whole group is seen vocalizing for an extended period of time while Molik walks around as he listens and watches. Then, in a close-up shot, he stops next to me. Only the back of my head can be seen with his head in profile as he listens intently. He lowers his jaw with his fingers to instruct me to open my mouth wider. Then, after listening some more, he slowly nods his head, and moves on.

Reflecting upon my experience with this particular Occitan song, I am compelled to think of the people who worked the land owned by kings, aristocrats, and religious dignitaries. Once a year, they would march in a large procession and sing this song to announce their arrival to their masters and let them know that it was time to give back a small portion of the fruits of their labor through the symbolic offering of a feast. I am only one generation removed from these people's immediate descendants, whose lives were still very much regulated by the cycles of seasons and conditioned by grueling physical labor and stark poverty. What the song conveyed to me was the energy and spirit of those who had survived these difficult circumstances in part thanks to a rich oral tradition transmitted through story-telling, music-making, singing, and dancing. The significance of this cultural legacy lies in the vibrancy and resilience of traditional practices hinging upon deep ecological knowledge and an extremely concrete and practical savoir-faire rooted in an age-old relationship to spirituality.

SINGING THE BODY ORGANIC

What I find compelling about Bailleux's bioenergetic approach to voice is that it emphasizes embodiment, creativity, and a form of pleasure which she considers to be potentially therapeutic. Acknowledging that vocal work can bring up emotions connected to painful life experiences, she suggests that vocal training can be beneficial when, as an embodied practice, it provides access to an empowering form of creative agency. A parallel can be made between Bailleux's observations and Rasmussen's experience as a performer and teacher for whom voice is an important part of actor training. In her "Letter to Grotowski," a text to which I referred in the second chapter, Rasmussen recounts sharing with Grotowski her experience of teaching voice to women. She explains that when transmitting her knowledge of vocal work to women to help them to explore their vocal potential, some of them start to cry. When I asked Rasmussen to elaborate in my interview with her, she told me that this had happened on several occasions when women reached the low resonator. Bailleux would probably suggest that this vocal breakthrough constituted for these women a new embodied experience of their human potential. Rasmussen stressed that this, of course, did not occur exclusively when working with women, and she provided the example of one of her male friends who had a comparable experience when his singing teacher helped him to find a very high voice. He said that he started crying as he touched this particular quality of his voice because, although he was a trained singer, he had never used it in his entire life. Rasmussen observed that while he obviously had this vocal possibility within him, he had never been aware of it.

In my conversation with Rasmussen I asked whether she thought that, for women, developing the range of their vocal power by learning how to ground their voice in their lower body instead of privileging the head resonators that produced higher pitched sounds, played an important function in the vocal training. Rasmussen replied that the problem was the pervasive assumption not only that women's voices were supposed to be high, but that they should also be gentle, fine, and never too provoking. She emphasized that the goal of the vocal training was not to become vocally forceful or aggressive, but to find the depth of the voice. She explained that at the Odin, actors were encouraged at a very early stage of the training process to focus their work on themes or images in both physical and vocal improvisations. She recalled that Barba would give her a theme and ask her to improvise vocally while lying down on the floor, sitting, or standing. She noted that what she really appreciated was that he would give actors a lot of time for this kind of exploration, so that individual vocal improvisations could last up to half an hour. She said that this was how she had learned to discover what she reluctantly called her inner world, a phrase which she noted sounded awkward. She described such a process as a way of finding her space, which, for her, constituted a very important aspect of the training.

Towards an Ecology of the Body-in-Life 133

Rasmussen recalled that when she saw the first Odin production, titled *Ornitofilene* and performed by Anne-Trine Grimnes, Else Marie Laukvik, Tor Sannum, and Torgeir Wethal, she was extremely impressed with the group's high level of physicality, but she was especially drawn to the unusual quality of the women's voices which she said were incredible and went straight to her stomach. Although the psalms they were singing were well known in Scandinavian culture, she felt that their voices were expressing something inside these songs that she had never heard before. This was partly why she became interested in joining Barba's company. Later on, the women members of the Odin began giving public work demonstrations which included elements of the vocal training that they have continued to transmit through their teaching until now. When I asked Rasmussen about the roots of the vocal training at the Odin, she explained that the work on vocal resonators which was the foundation of her approach had initially been transmitted to the Odin by the Laboratory Theatre actors themselves. She added that, although Grotowski had eventually moved away from working directly on resonators, she had continued to rely on this aspect of the vocal training because she had discovered in her own teaching that it was an extremely effective way of helping actors to develop their vocal capacities.

During his sixth Collège de France lecture, Grotowski discussed the vocal exercises which the Laboratory Theatre had developed from two different perspectives which he said were both very technical: on the one hand, the group worked on unblocking the larynx, which Grotowski noted was crucial since this part of the vocal apparatus closes off completely in stressful situations. Given that the actor is always under some form of stress, he pointed out that it is absolutely essential that the larynx remain open so that the power of exhalation can carry the voice. On the other hand, the group developed vocal training based on the body's resonators. Grotowski said that in classical theatre actors are only familiar with the facial resonator, which he called the mask, and the chest resonator used especially by opera singers. He stressed, however, that there is a wide variety of resonators in the human body. While one can manipulate them very easily in a technical way, he observed that such manipulation leads to the deadening of vocal production. He stated that there is another way to proceed, which entails getting the resonators to function in an organic manner by directing the voice towards different parts of the workspace. For instance, when one directs the voice towards the ceiling, the higher resonators are engaged. He also remarked that one can study resonators by observing different languages, suggesting that Russian speakers, for example, speak from the belly—as he pronounced these words, Grotowski used a lower, deeper voice to illustrate what he meant. He noted that, although resonators are usually associated with a vibrating bone structure and there is no such structure per se inside the belly, it is nonetheless clear in practice that this part of the body can function as a resonator even if this is difficult to explain anatomically.

Grotowski remarked that the members of the Laboratory Theatre had conducted this technical research not with the intent to prepare the actors but simply to address the specific problems they each encountered when performing. These problems may include a blocked larynx, weak breathing, and lack of vocal power, the latter being specifically linked to the function of the resonators. Grotowski added that while the Laboratory Theatre actors were confronted with problems that had initially appeared to be merely technical, they had also learned to rely on associations to help them in their practical research. Hence, whereas the Laboratory Theatre investigated the power of the human voice in a very technical way, and the body-voice connection was, to some extent, the object of a laboratory experiment that appeared to be almost scientifically precise, this practical research eventually led the group into the post-theatrical period when the body and the voice became a vehicle for something which, as Flazsen suggested, was other than the body and the voice.

Grotowski continued his investigation of the body-voice connection across cultures and traditions throughout the Theatre of Sources, Objective Drama, and Art as vehicle periods. In his inaugural Collège de France lecture, he spoke about the vocal training developed by the Theatre Laboratory actors and linked it to the research on ancient vibratory chants he was then leading with Thomas Richards at his Workcenter in Italy. The Polish director stated that he was interested in the fact that the sonorities of certain traditional songs were rooted in the body, so that the body could become a conduit, enabling a passage towards something delicate, translucent. He contended that if singing was connected to impulses and actions, and if the body was not excluded, then singing could serve as a kind of yoga in the larger meaning of this term. This type of approach, he remarked, existed in different cultures, and he provided the example of the de-conditioning work of alchemists dealing with notions of time and space, of the Indian, Islamic, and Christian Orthodox traditions, and especially of certain Afro-Caribbean traditions whose ritual chants involved total participation of the body.

Grotowski specified in his sixth Collège de France lecture that it was thanks to Molik's research that he had come to understand that, when training the voice, it was impossible to do so without engaging the whole body along with personal associations. Indeed, Molik states:

> Voice is a complex thing, a very complex thing. [...] If you are in a real process the whole body [...] must breathe. All, from the feet, the whole body. [...] From the earth. The energy must be taken very often from the earth. [...] By the feet, by the legs, by the lower part of the legs, by the upper parts of the legs, by the hips, and then you give yourself the energy to create the sounds and it starts from somewhere. Very often it's taken directly from the base of the spine and then it goes by different resonators and then you can shape it, you can make it soft, or you can make it very strong. [...] I try never to use the head for

speaking or singing. Of course, [...] you ultimately speak with the mouth. With your tongue, with your mouth, with your teeth. But this is only when you give the sound, the voice, its final shape. (Campo and Molik, *Zygmunt Molik's Voice and Body Work* 9, 50–51, 103–04)

Molik's description of this organic vocal process clearly shows that it requires the mobilization of the entire body, with a focus on the base of the spine, that is to say, the area of the pelvis and the hips. By putting the focus on the lower part of the body, including the legs and feet, Molik takes the focus away from the head and mouth, which are often the site of extraneous tensions when privileging this part of the body generally assumed to be central to the production of sound. Warning that placing too much emphasis on the resonators can become counterproductive, Molik indicates that he favors an indirect approach through a form of creative vocal exploration structured by the principles of the training which mobilizes the resonators organically rather than in a purely technical way.

For Mirecka and Molik, who both prioritize organicity, working with the voice is an embodied process which requires sustaining a fluid circulation of energy within the entire organism experienced as an open channel, so that the principles guiding the physical training also apply to vocal training. The main focus of the vocal work is on the vibratory quality of the sound. Grotowski himself defines vibratory quality by pointing out that when playing the same melody with a piano and a violin, what changes is the vibratory quality of the music, whereas the melody remains the same ("Tu es le fils de quelqu'un" 299). Molik, who was a man of few words in his teaching, frequently stated during the work sessions in which I participated: "Less voice, more vibration"—for although performers may derive self-satisfaction from the power of volume alone, the latter should not be confused with vibration. While he invites performers "to give the maximum of [themselves] on the level of the vibration of the sound," Molik states that one should "never force the voice" (Campo and Molik, *Zygmunt Molik's Voice and Body Work* 107). He suggests that "it is possible to touch the impossible with a sound which is pure vibration, without a high voice, without a strong voice" and asserts that it is very important to "find the balance between the power of vibration and the sound," cautioning that "the voice should never be dominating in the sound, but rather the vibration should be, if something is to be dominating. And usually, there should be a balance between the sound, the voice and the vibration. [In the] work on voice, the most common mistake is to abuse [the voice]" (107). The need to search for this kind of balance is also fundamental to Mirecka's teaching, and, like Molik, she stresses that the voice should never be forced, pushed, or manipulated in a result-oriented manner.

Expanding on Grotowski's example of the difference in vibratory quality between the piano and violin, it is possible to explain vibration in a very concrete way: with a string instrument, it is the tension exerted on the strings by the musician that produces the vibration. The action of drawing on the string creates an opposition, a resistance, and an accumulation of tension, and the action of releasing the string results in a form of vibration, so that the combination of these two consecutive actions produces sound. One may therefore suggest that there is a *jo-ha-kyu* in this sequence of actions, for, as Barba explains in *The Paper Canoe*, "*jo*" means to retain, "*ha*" means to break, and "*kyu*" means speed or culmination (33). In the case of the human voice, however, the instrument is the body, or the entire organism, and vibration is produced by the breath circulating in the body-in-life, through the ever-changing modulations of inner organic oppositions, resistances, and tensions. The body may be compared to a string instrument which reacts in very subtle ways to its own actions, for the performer is simultaneously the instrument and the musician, and must therefore fine-tune the body-in-life whose organic actions affect the vibratory quality of the voice. What is at stake for the performer working on text is the passage from the singing to the speaking voice, a delicate process wherein lies the secret of the body-voice connection—a secret which, within the realm of performance practice, the actors of the Laboratory Theatre have perhaps most thoroughly investigated.

Mirecka's vocal virtuosity is a living example of the value of this secret, for the vibratory qualities of both her singing and speaking voice render her words expressive beyond their literal meaning. This is a tangible phenomenon cultivated over more than fifty years of work, and Mirecka's voice can truly be said to resonate with her lived experience, like the strings of a finely tuned instrument whose acute sensitivity responds to the slightest psychophysical variations. In her teaching, she takes vocal work into the realm of paratheatre, in which the Voice-Vehicle is linked to what both Stanislavsky and Grotowski identify as the work on oneself. This is why, when speaking of the body-voice connection, Mirecka compares the organic connection between movement and sound to the action of delicately stepping into a canoe to navigate the river of one's creative process. Such a continuous search for balance does not take place only within the ecosystem of one's organism, which Mirecka describes as our inner garden, but also in one's relationship to the workspace, to others in that space, and to the world outside. The voice can thus help to establish an interconnection between the inner and the outer, between our energies and the energy of natural elements, as if the human body were a microcosm of the universe.

At the end of her July 2010 work session in Sardinia, Mirecka spoke to us about what she had learned. She said that the more she lived, the more she became "nothing," stressing that the point of the work on oneself was to be empty like a bamboo so that the energy could flow through us—and she asked: the energy of what? She suggested that it was a mystery, the unknown, something that we could sense, become conscious of, but not know with the mind. However, as noted by Seyferth, this does not mean that one should do nothing, since it is about finding a balance between doing and not doing. In my interview with Mirecka, she explained that through her many years of creative work she had come to understand that it is not the small "I" of the ego that has the power to do. She acknowledged that, initially, she was convinced that she had to push herself, push people, in order to be stronger, faster, but she eventually realized that all this was only physical presence. She added that it was her mind that was pushing, not the source of inner energy that can surprise us by opening our imagination, our fantasy, and enable us to do something we have never done before. She observed that the problem with pushing is that it is not healthy, neither for the body nor for the mind, whereas singing and making music can become a way to call for energy through the vibration of our body, through a connection between sound and energy. Like Grotowski, she referred to *wu wei* in the Chinese Taoist philosophy, a phrase which she said meant "to do without doing" and which, in the case of the voice, is related to an inner process that is both passive and active, enabling us to be open and to create a relation, a meeting with others, through a continuous flow of the voice, of the breath, which she said also had to do with involving the heart, with not being cold. For she believes that while every single detail must be attended to as precisely as possible, there must be joy and sorrow in the work because that's part of life, and doing things mechanically or technically is not alive.

In May 2011, Mirecka led a work session hosted by Double Edge Theatre in Ashfield, Massachusetts, during which she observed that when we are singing or dancing, everything flows, the body and mind are connected, the mind is not leading, judging—Rasmussen had made a similar observation in my interview with her when speaking about the Wind Dance. Mirecka reminded us in Ashfield that this process should not be understood as "something I am doing," but as something that one allows to happen. As with the physical training, much of the vocal work consists in letting things happen by learning to be open, to receive, and to give. Music is an important part of Mirecka's teaching: she asks work session participants to bring an instrument and invites them to create the rhythmic soundscape that often supports movement-based improvisations.

While this kind of work with musical instruments usually takes place in the evening, the mornings are devoted to more meditative exercises during which Mirecka, sitting with the group in a circle, leads breathing exercises linked to the chakras and teaches the chanting of Indian and Tibetan mantras. During her summer 2012 work session in Brzezinka, she asked us to write down the words of several mantras in our notebooks and encouraged us to learn them precisely so we could use them in our lives. As we practiced these mantras with her, Mirecka reminded us: Don't do it for me. Do it for yourself. Smiling, she declared that she too was doing this for herself. Employing the phrase "to be, not to have," as in Zbigniew Cynkutis's published manifesto,[2] Mirecka indicated that the work on oneself entailed searching for simplicity, for that which is essential in life, something that was once familiar to our grandmothers and grandfathers.

French Buddhist monk Mathieu Ricard, who holds a doctorate in molecular genetics, addressed the benefits of spiritual practice in his 2004 TED talk titled "The Habits of Happiness." He suggested that the repetition of certain activities, which include meditation in nature, can lead to a modification of brain structure, as demonstrated by recent discoveries about the plasticity of the brain. He screened photos of Buddhist monks practicing these activities in awe-inspiring natural landscapes, and stressed that such practice can transform our way of perceiving and being in relation with ourselves, others, and the world in which we live, thus creating new embodiments of who we are. Ricard described our being as a stream and consciousness as continuous transformation, and pointed to an alternative conception of agency which can be cultivated through body-mind training, that is to say, a form of work on oneself. Such a perspective challenges the deterministic dimension of Bourdieu's notion of *habitus*, and I would suggest that a parallel can be made with performance training since the process of productive disorientation I discussed in the first chapter operates through an alteration of balance in the performer's body and produces a de-conditioning which eliminates daily behavior, and a reconditioning which turns "extra-daily" behavior into a new *habitus*. In the Japanese Noh, Chinese Opera, and Indian Kathakali traditions, for example, performers learn highly stylized and codified forms at a very young age while their body-mind is still open and flexible.

Perhaps this is why Mirecka, in her teaching, often assigns particular tasks to individuals: although these tasks may appear to be simple, they somehow feel like a kind of challenge or test for they require one's full attention to details yet they should somehow be accomplished effortlessly. During her 2012 summer work session, for example, she asked me to lead the group's chanting of the mantra "*Shante prashante*" during a procession-like walk which took us from the workspace into the open field outside the building. I didn't know this mantra very well as we had learned it quite recently, but based on what Mirecka had told us I understood its meaning to be the joyful assertion: "No, no, I will not be afraid." It was ironic that I was afraid to sing this mantra improperly because I felt responsible for remembering the words and maintaining the rhythm to keep the chanting precise. As I struggled to do this consistently, I noticed that other participants seemed to remember it better than me, and it felt as though they were leading me. Walking and singing with the group, it occurred to me that I was in the process of embodying the meaning of this mantra, and I was reminded by way of association of the many times during my project when I had to overcome a variety of obstacles, including doubts about my personal abilities to carry it through. Learning to sing this mantra challenged me to consider the work on oneself as a form of training that could help me to complete the journey of my research process.

ANG GEY PIN

While Mirecka is the eldest among the women involved in my project, Ang Gey Pin is the youngest, and represents a new generation of artists whose connection to Grotowski corresponds to the last two periods of his research: the Objective Drama Project at the University of California, Irvine, and Art as vehicle at the Grotowski Workcenter in Italy. It is therefore particularly significant that Ang, who is from Singapore, has chosen to look to the past and study the traditional songs of her own culture. Through her dedication to this research she has become the voice specialist of the new generation and developed her own approach to the body-voice connection.

Ang began her theatre training in Singapore in 1986 and went on to study world performance traditions at the University of Hawaii-Manoa. She then participated in the final session of the Objective Drama Project at the University of California, Irvine in 1992. She is the co-founder of Theatre OX, which she directed in Singapore from 1995 to 2006, leading the company's research on Chinese performance traditions. Ang was a member of the Workcenter of Jerzy Grotowski and Thomas Richards in 1994 and from 1998 to 2006. She performed the lead role in *One Breath Left* (1998–2002), the first performance piece created by the Workcenter and presented publicly. I was fortunate to see this piece two evenings in a row when I visited the Workcenter in 2001, and the movements, singing, and images of the dying elderly woman embodied by Ang in *One Breath Left* have stayed with me to this day. Ang's inspiring work was like an unexpected gift, and it was very emboldening to witness a non-European woman perform this leading role. When I asked Ang whether *One Breath Left*, which received the UBU Special Award in Italy, had been documented on film, she said that only photos had been taken. It was the realization that women's work remained for the most part undocumented, hence very little known, that led me to conceive of a project that would focus exclusively on women and provide access to their work through film documentation as well as through writing.

Ang continued her collaboration with the Workcenter when the group toured Europe and Asia with *Project The Bridge: Developing Theatre Arts*, performing in the piece titled *Dies Irae: My Preposterous Theatrum Interioris Show*. In 2006, she began to work as an independent artist and has since been performing, directing, and teaching in Europe, Asia, and North America. I participated in three work sessions led by Ang in 2007, 2008, and 2009 all held at the Grotowski Institute in Wroclaw. For the 2009 *Meetings with Remarkable Women* Festival, Ang performed in *Feast of You Shen*, a piece which she conceived and directed, and which was documented on film for my project by Maciej Zakrzewski, who photographed her work session. In 2009, Ang was also a guest speaker, along with Mirecka and Gardecka, on the panel titled "Women in the Grotowski Diaspora: Training, Transmission, Creativity" which I chaired for the conference "Tracing Grotowski's Path: The Year of Grotowski in New York" organized by Richard Schechner. Ang explained during this panel that although she later realized that Grotowski was the same age as her father, the Polish director had appeared to her as a grandfather figure, an ancestor whose influence on her had shaped the trajectory of her work. During her first year at his Workcenter, she was inspired and challenged by Grotowski's extensive knowledge of Eastern philosophies and traditions, which compelled her to further explore her connection to her cultural heritage and conduct research on Hokkien traditional songs.

140 *Grotowski, Women, and Contemporary Performance*

Figure 3.2 Ang Gey Pin rehearsing *Feast of You Shen* for the *Meetings with Remarkable Women* Festival. Grotowski Institute, Brzezinka, Poland, August 2009—photo by Maciej Zakrzewski.

As with first-generation women, Ang speaks rarely when teaching, yet her energy on the floor is contagious. The training she leads retains elements from the theatrical period, such as the exercise known as "the Cat," immortalized in a photo of Cieslak featured in *Towards a Poor Theatre* as well as in the film of Cieslak's demonstration, and which is also part of the physical training in Mirecka's and Seyferth's teaching. However, Ang transmits the Workcenter version of this exercise, which features slight variations that may be attributed to the transformations that occur within trans-generational modes of transmission. Although the *plastiques* are not part of this training, it is nevertheless intensely physical, and Ang invites participants to treat the exercises as a game and to develop a kind of playfulness, especially during the most strenuous parts of the training. A lightning-quick presence, she darts around the space and expects participants to move with her at the same time she does, without any lag between her and the group. The challenge is to follow the impulses of the whole body, to be light yet grounded, to walk, run, leap soundlessly across the floor, and to remain in relationship with the movement of others. Ang also introduces participants to the discipline of Chen-style *Taijiquan*, which she has been studying with Master Foo Shang Wee in Singapore and Master Chen Xiaowang in Europe. Practicing this Chinese martial art requires anchoring the body in the ground while following the energetic flow of continuous movement, whose source springs from the fluid inner tension between rootedness and lightness. In Chinese traditional medicine, *Taijiquan* is considered a beneficial practice which improves internal circulation linked to breath, increases balance and flexibility, and promotes mental and physical well-being.

When leading the vocal work, Ang shares *Hokkien* traditional songs with the participants and encourages them to receive and follow these songs with the whole body, neither ahead of nor behind her voice, trusting that the song is a map. As in the physical training, she hence expects everyone to sing with her "as if" in complete synchrony, even though participants are familiar neither with the songs nor their language. Singing, in this case, is about having the courage to dive in, and while the structure of each song provides the map, finding the life of a song is like finding a path to freedom. This is similar to working with a text through building a precise line of organic physical actions, or physical score, which is both the source and the channel of a river of images, sensations, and memories born from the interplay of actions and words. Just as acting, in this kind of work, is not about reciting a text but about letting the text speak through the physical score, singing is not about reproducing a melody but about embodying the song's structure and letting the song sing you. Ang explains that it's about singing with the heart and asking for something, as if searching for the secret life of the song.

At the end of her 2008 work session at the Grotowski Institute in Wroclaw, prompted by a participant's question about the body-voice connection, Ang

142 *Grotowski, Women, and Contemporary Performance*

Figure 3.3 Ang Gey Pin leading her work session. *Meetings with Remarkable Women*, Grotowski Institute, Wroclaw, Poland, July 2009—photo by Maciej Zakrzewski.

shared her perspective on the embodied nature of the voice. Having suggested that the voice lives everywhere in the body, she conveyed its ever-changing flow through the image of an ocean wave or a waterfall, which she linked to the flux of personal associations rooted in one's lived experience and memory, including what one thinks one has forgotten—for example, when one first learned to use one's voice, or when one first learned to walk, not by being taught but simply by discovering how to speak, how to walk. Ang inferred that vocal work entails a confrontation with oneself because the voice is composed of our imagination, desires, and personal experiences. This includes what we don't want to remember, which can create tensions in the body in the form of muscular contractions that can block the flow of the voice. She emphasized that it takes many years of daily work to develop an embodied awareness of this very delicate and ever-changing process, and observed that it is important not to try to analyze it but to cultivate instead a deeply visceral sensitivity to this process. She specified that such embodied knowledge cannot be gained by reading theory but must be acquired through practical work. Yet, paradoxically, the vocal process is something that happens by itself, as if many different doors or gates opened up, one after another, letting the voice flow through the body, passing through gate after gate, full of our past—what we remember and what we don't remember.

Ang compared this process to a journey leading to a memory, an association, and insisted that although these may be linked to the past, they affect us in the present moment. What matters in this journey, she observed, is to become aware of each subtle change, including contractions in parts of the body that might never have been allowed to speak, so as to accept these areas of the body and let them live. She noted that it takes a lot of work for space to open within the body so that the voice can flow, and it takes a lot of time to discover in the voice what she described as another little universe with a whole big world inside. Gesturing to her body as she spoke about this space, Ang evoked the image of flowing water passing underneath a rock, then becoming a little stream, going with the current, and then against the current, perhaps due to some tension in the body which might be related to something never before expressed, generating a struggle with oneself, and then, in time, leading to a great sense of release. Ang cautioned, however, that blocks in the body change from day to day, so that it is never possible to repeat the same thing, hence the necessity to search anew every time. She added that while in her teaching she guides participants in this search, each person has to engage in it on their own by sharpening their senses to be able to see, to hear, the changes happening beneath the skin.

EMBODIMENT, SPIRITUALITY, AND THE PEDAGOGY OF PLACE

Traditional songs can thus provide an opportunity to explore the body-voice connection since the life of these songs, encompassed in repetitions and subtle variations, is what enables them to reach us across hundreds of years. According to Grotowski, what keeps a song alive is the particular vibratory quality linked to the precision of the song's structure, so that it is necessary to search for the vocal and physical score inscribed within each particular song. When a competent performer actively and attentively embodies a traditional song, it can become a vehicle that reconnects her/him to those who first sang the song. If ancestral embodied knowledge is encoded in traditional songs, and if the power of these songs hinges upon the embodied experience of singing them, then trusting that the body can remember how to sing, as if traces of this ancient knowledge had been preserved in the body memory, can become a way of recovering that knowledge and reclaiming cultural continuity.

Qwo-Li Driskill might be referring to a similar process when writing about learning to sing a Cherokee lullaby:

> As someone who did not grow up speaking my language or any traditional songs and who is currently in the process of reclaiming those traditions—as are many Native people in North America—the process of relearning this lullaby was and is integral to my own decolonial process. The performance context provided me an opportunity to relearn and perform a traditional song, a major act in intergenerational healing and cultural continuance. As I sang this lullaby during rehearsals and performance, I imagined my ancestors witnessing from the corners of the theatre, helping me in the healing and often painful work of suture. ("Theatre as Suture" 164)

The relationship between performance, embodiment, and cultural continuance expressed here by Driskill points to a creative agency which is intimately linked to lived experience and yet which is not limited to or defined by a single individual perspective.

Rasmussen's experience of teaching voice to women also shows that working deeply on oneself can be extremely challenging and even painful at times. As I continue to pursue vocal and physical training, my sense is that, in time, the desire to acquire the skills and techniques usually associated with artistic know-how gradually dissolves until one becomes confronted with one's perceived shortcomings and limitations. At that point, working on oneself becomes a way of learning to trust embodied creativity as a source of knowledge that can be activated, cultivated, and transmitted to others, and this embodied way of knowing oneself may provide an alternative form of agency that can be particularly empowering for women.

Indigenous scholars consider embodiment to be key to self-knowledge, and Meyer affirms that "the body is the *central* space from which knowing is embedded" and stresses that "our body holds truth, our body invigorates knowing, our body helps us become who we are. [...] Our thinking body is not separated from our feeling mind. *Our mind is our body. Our body is our mind.* And both connect to the spiritual act of knowledge acquisition"

("Indigenous and Authentic" 223). She specifies that she derives this understanding of embodiment from engaging in the culturally specific knowledge which is her legacy, and points out that Indigenous scholars "are defining places science can follow but not lead or illuminate. Other ways of knowing something *must* be introduced if we are to evolve into a more enlightened society. It will not occur with scientific or objective knowledge only" (224–25).

For the Hawaiian people, cultural continuity vitally depends on performance-based practices such as ritual chanting and dancing, experiential ways of cognition that rely on trans-generational oral transmission. Meyer explains: "Mentors' belief that they are links in a Hawaiian chain reaching back to antiquity helps to prioritize how knowledge is acquired, exchanged, and valued [. . .]. Knowledge as a 'sequence of immortality' summarizes this sense of spiritual continuity, as does the notion that we, by ourselves, cannot bring about the kinds of knowing that endure" ("Our Own Liberation" 128). The *Kumulipo*, a Hawaiian genealogical prayer chant, is a case in point. Martha Warren Beckwith remarks that "since writing was unknown in Polynesia before contact with foreign culture," it was the responsibility of the *Haku-mele*, or master of song, to memorize and perform this sacred chant made up of over two thousand lines. The oral transmission of this chant entailed the acquisition of specific vocal techniques combining vibration (*kuolo*), a guttural sound (*kaohi*), and a form of gurgling (*alala*), produced by different parts of the vocal apparatus. Beckwith notes that "such a feat of memory [. . .] was hence common to the gifted expert in Polynesia" (*The Kumulipo, A Hawaiian Creation Chant* 35–36). Hawaiian Elder Halemakua's evocation of a "rhythmic understanding of time and potent experiences of harmony in space" (Meyer, "Indigenous and Authentic" 231), to which I referred in the first chapter, can thus be perceived as a reminder of the extent to which the body and the voice constitute a vehicle for the type of spiritual continuity that sustains Hawaiian identity and cultural sovereignty.

While highlighting the specificity of traditional ways of knowing, Meyer contends that Hawaiian epistemology is relevant and valuable beyond the confines of its geographical and cultural boundaries. She posits an Indigenous conception of universality based on the notion that it is specificity that leads to universality. She defines the latter as hinging upon "respect and honoring of distinctness" and ties it to Halemakua's provocative statement "*We are all indigenous*" ("Indigenous and Authentic" 230, italics in original). Fending off potential controversies, Meyer cautions that "to take this universal idea into race politics strips it of its truth" (231). The notion of Indigeneity evoked by Halemakua and supported by Meyer is grounded in a place-specific understanding of universality predicated on the interrelation of land and self, experience and spirituality, embodiment and knowledge. Meyer therefore proposes to redefine epistemology as necessarily linked to direct experience and to a "culturally formed sensuality."

In "Our Own Liberation," she observes that "the genesis of Hawaiian knowledge is based on experience, and experience is grounded in our sensory rapport" (133), inferring that knowledge itself is shaped by the senses, so that awareness, intuition, and insight depend on sensual maturity, or what she describes as the art of paying attention, a "culturally specific 'deep internalized knowledge' [...] achieved only through practice" (134). Cultivating a sensory and empathetic connection to all non-human entities in the natural world is part of this embodied practice, which relies upon a form of sensory perception and embodied awareness related to both intelligence and spirituality, and associated with the body's center.

As with the performance experts participating in my project, the Hawaiian mentors who shared their embodied knowledge with Meyer speak of a center point in the human organism, which they call *na'auao*, or "enlightened stomach," experienced as "the place of wisdom" (143). Meyer thus reports performance master-teacher *kumu hula* Pua Kanahele stating: "It's a cosmic center point. It has to do with your ancestors coming together with you. It has to do with your spiritual being coming together, it has to do with our physical being (Pua Kanahele, 15 January 1997)" (144). Interestingly, the notion of an energetic center situated in this particular area of the human body recurs in a number of performance traditions, as noted by Barba and Savarese in their *Dictionary of Theatre Anthropology*. Pua Kanahele goes on to explain:

> *Na'au* [stomach] is the center of who you are [...] the center of your body [...] between your very spiritual and your very earthy, or your very airy and your very earthy. I think that when your whole body or when your whole self reacts to something it all comes to that center. [...] To me, *na'auao* [enlightened stomach] is when everything, not when *you*, but when everything kind of centers for you [...] that's *na'auao*. [...] It's being centered, it's when everything comes together (Pua Kanahele, 15 January 1997). (145)

Hence, according to this perspective, the physical, intellectual, and spiritual dimensions converge through a central point of the human organism, as if "being centered"—a phrase shared by a large number of performance practitioners—offered a more material or organic way of referring to relationality, which may be conceived as a balancing process sustaining endless interconnections occurring at all levels of life, human and non-human, from the cellular to the cosmic.

I would suggest that it is possible to draw a parallel between this relational conception of balance and the ecosystemic performance paradigm I have articulated. The relational dimension of this paradigm is epitomized by the body-voice connection since the vibratory qualities of the voice depend on the resonance of both body and space, or body and place. In "Tu es le fils de quelqu'un," Grotowski hence suggests that traditional songs are connected not only to those who first sang them but also to the natural environment in which these songs were created: people living in the mountains had different ways of singing than people living in the valleys, and traces of these places therefore subsist in the modes of transmission of traditional songs (304).

Significantly, Wilson observes that, from an Indigenous perspective, "knowledge itself is held in the relationships and connections formed with the environment that surrounds us" (*Research is Ceremony* 87). He notes that relationships made with people and relationships made with the environment are equally sacred, and defines knowledge of the environment as the pedagogy of place (87). He remarks that experiencing place as relational and sacred is key "within many Indigenous peoples' spirituality," and concludes that "bringing things together so that they share the same space is what ceremony is all about" (87). For the women in my project, bringing people and things together within a shared space is, to some extent, what defines their creative work, whether that shared space be an enclosed workspace or the open space of our natural environment. This raises the question of how space/place sustains the type of relationships that contribute to shaping who we are as individuals, community members, citizens, and co-habitants of the same planet. Is it possible to conceive of performance as a relational practice whose healing properties derive from experiencing the space between us as shared, hence sacred?

In my experience, relationship to space is what makes space sacred in a secular sense of the term. This means acknowledging that the workspace is not an ordinary space and that it can therefore only be used for particular purposes and in specific circumstances. Treating the workspace with respect is a way of respecting oneself and one's work partners, and of honoring the work accomplished by the group. This, in turn, encourages the group members to be generous with their energy, to focus completely on what is taking place in the here and now, and to learn from their mutual engagement in the creative process.

Treating the space as shared hence sacred is an extremely effective strategy that extends to the shared living space of residential work sessions, during which participants are responsible for daily cleaning and cooking tasks, in addition to washing the floor of the workspace and preparing it carefully. There is a long history for this communal way of caring for a shared space that can be traced to the early days of the Laboratory Theatre in Opole, as Komorowska recalls in her book:

> The Theatre of Thirteen Rows was in constant danger, they would close it down, then they would extend the permit. Each time they were about to close us down Jerzy Grotowski would call us all in and say our place was uncertain, there was no money, etc. etc. In Wroclaw we started guarding the working space. Literally, because we didn't know whether they would take it away from us and because of that we were on duty day and night. We kept watch and we looked after that space;

we scrubbed it, we washed it and we were very strict about it...all those floor exercises...a lot of our sweat soaked into that floor. We cleaned it, polished, and prepared the space ourselves—that was hard work. We prepared our own costumes, sometimes somebody would help with laundry or ironing but generally we did everything ourselves. That was an important experience. To this day when I leave the theatre I clean after myself. That stayed with me. (Komorowska and Osterloff, *Pejzaż* 20, 27)

This way of guarding the workspace has clearly shaped aspects of the training itself, and the principle of "taking care of the space" was central to the physical exercises led by Dora Arreola during her 2009 work session.

DORA ARREOLA

I first met Arreola in 2003 when we both participated in a Butoh workshop led by Katsura Kan at California State University, San Marcos. Arreola's focus, discipline, and quality of energy stood out in the group, and when I asked her about her training she told me she had encountered Grotowski's work during the final period of his research, namely, Art as vehicle. Arreola recounted that after working in the mid-80s with Jaime Soriano, who collaborated with Grotowski from 1980 to 1992, she visited the University of California, Irvine in the spring of 1987 during Grotowski's Objective Drama Project, and was selected to participate in the research activities being carried out at Grotowski's Workcenter in Italy, where she was a member of the Upstairs Group from February 1988 to September 1989. This group was composed at the time of nine women and one man of different nationalities, and directed by Haitian master-performer/teacher Maud Robart.[3] Arreola went on to pursue Suzuki training, contemporary dance, and Butoh. She received a Masters of Fine Arts in Directing from the University of Massachusetts-Amherst in 2009 and is currently an assistant professor at the University of South Florida. As the artistic director of the all-woman dance theatre company *Mujeres en Ritual* which she founded in 1999, Arreola works with dancers and actresses from Mexico and the United States committed to exploring women's issues and experiences in the border region. Arreola performed *I, Rumores Silencio* at the 2009 *Meetings with Remarkable Women* Festival, a solo piece based on the creative research she has been conducting on her cultural legacy and the traditional ritual practices of Indigenous communities in northern Mexico.

In her work session, Arreola emphasized the need to take care of the space by making sure that it was occupied evenly at all times, which she called "balancing the space." This required participants to work together and constantly focus on the group dynamics in order to maintain an ever-changing

Towards an Ecology of the Body-in-Life 149

Figure 3.4 Dora Arreola rehearsing *I, Rumores Silencio* for the *Meetings with Remarkable Women* Festival. Grotowski Institute, Wroclaw, Poland, August 2009—photo by Francesco Galli.

sense of balance between people in the space. Such a search for balance is not meant as a metaphor by those who practice this form of training developed in the post-theatrical period, and Arreola stressed that it is a concrete way of being in direct relation with others, a way of working together to defend and save the space, as if in a constant state of emergency. I was introduced to this approach by Jairo Cuesta and Jim Slowiak when I participated in a work session they led in October 1999 at the University of California, Irvine for the Symposium "Grotowski at Irvine—and Beyond." Slowiak was Grotowski's assistant at Irvine and in the early years of his Italian Workcenter, and Cuesta was a core member of The Vigils, along with Seyferth, as well as of the Theatre of Sources and Objective Drama projects. Slowiak and Cuesta co-founded the New World Performance Laboratory based in Cleveland and are the co-authors of *Jerzy Grotowski*, a book in which they describe the exercise "Watching" developed at Irvine in 1985. They write: "At first sight, Watching looks like a game of follow the leader. In reality, however, the structure functions to give participants the freedom to follow their own stream or flow while executing the technical aspects with precision" (130). This exercise, whose aim is to train performers to watch actively through movement, is composed of ten different sections that take place in silence.

In the first section, named "Control of the Space," Slowiak and Cuesta indicate that the leader's movements in the space are followed by everyone so that the group functions as one. They state: "The task is to place yourself in the space and in relation to the other participants in such a way that the entire room is balanced: no big empty space; not everyone in the center or on the periphery; not forming a big circle" (131). They provide the following instructions:

> Immobility: To see. To listen. To be ready. [...] Control the space with only your eyes. Movement without displacement: You see; you listen. You open your attention to the environment, to the others. [...] Displacement in the space: [You] begin to explore the space around you. You change location and react to the displacement of others. Remember to control the space. Always serve the space. Always serve your partners. (131)

This way of balancing the space recurs in the tenth and final section, called "Control of the Space II," where the initial order is reversed: the participants control the space with displacement, then control the space with movement but no displacement, until the group achieves immobility (136). Slowiak and Cuesta go on to identify horizontal attention: "When control of the space arrives to this certain quality (there are no collisions and the group is moving as one organism), [...] we often introduce [...] horizontal attention [which] involves a merging of action and awareness, a basic element of the experience of the space" (127). Referring to Spanish philosopher José Ortega y Gasset's depiction of the hunter as exceptionally alert,

Towards an Ecology of the Body-in-Life 151

they equate the actor to the hunter and assert: "The actor in Grotowski's theatre is the 'alert man'" (128).

Although in her work session the training led by Arreola was informed by the same sensitivity to space, she associated the alert performer not with a hunter but with a bee when she emphasized the need to work together "like bees looking for honey or gold." She also replaced the notion of controlling the space with that of taking care of the space in an effort to achieve a kind of balance. She first introduced a sequence of physical actions, which she specified must be performed in the correct order and which she asked participants to list precisely in their notebooks. She later invited the group to work on a different sequence which she said had been developed at the Workcenter and whose principles overlapped to some extent with the principles of the training led by Ang Gey Pin.

These two movement-based sequences, or collective physical scores, were made up of individual actions which participants memorized by practicing them with Arreola. Such actions ranged from watching and listening with the whole body, Arreola's version of the hunter's horizontal attention, to yoga-based exercises that challenged the body's balance in various ways. These exercises were used by the participants to engage in a structured exploration of space which Arreola linked to a network of images: specific patterns on the floor changed from a string of pearls to a chain of puddles scattered along a trail that wove around a mountain like a spider's web until

Figure 3.5 Dora Arreola leading her work session. *Meetings with Remarkable Women*, Grotowski Institute, Wroclaw, Poland, July 2009—photo by Francesco Galli.

it reached the summit where one experienced the "dance of the beginner." Once this network of actions and associations became inscribed in the body memory, there was no more need for explanations or for writing things down. The group of bees led by Arreola set out to search for gold, taking care of the space together, looking for balance, following the momentum of collective movement, charged with energy, yet always in silence.

THE ENERGY OF SILENCE

The importance of silence when engaging in creative work recurs within transmission processes and across generations in the Grotowski diaspora. Not only do these artists clearly privilege embodied understanding achieved through doing, but in spite of the centrality of the body-voice connection in much of their work, they all embrace, cultivate, even mandate silence. There are a number of reasons for such a stance. Firstly, by choosing not to rely on verbal communication and explanations in their teaching, they make it possible for participants to experience working conditions free from the daily reflexes of small talk, the interference of the controlling mind, and the tendency to judge oneself and others. Secondly, silence is considered to be a fundamental aspect of the training because it is linked to time and duration as well as precision and rigor. For being silent and taking time requires delving deeply into the organicity and flow of the body-in-life. Working in silence thus helps the performer to bypass the discursive circuits of verbalization and to become acutely receptive to the personal associations that emerge from her total commitment to what might be called 'deep work', an immersion in the here and now, which is the first step in her journey into the unknown.

In his book, Molik recalls his time at the Laboratory Theatre: "Yes, silence. That was the best for us; we did it all the time. At first it was obligatory. And later it became usual. We got so used to it that we felt we should be silent. But it was no longer obligatory" (Campo and Molik 55). Flaszen further extends this propensity for silence to the Laboratory Theatre audiences when arguing in his text "Grotowski and Silence" that Grotowski was a "silencemaker," as in "rainmaker" (17), since silence was paramount in his work with actors and critical to the impact that such work had on audiences. Flaszen recounts that Laboratory Theatre spectators "delayed leaving and remained in silence for long minutes on end, not talking even after the action had ended. It was running its course in them. Stanislavsky would have called it inner action, referring to the intangible process taking place in the actor" (20). He goes on to observe that, cast in the role of witnesses, spectators "refrained from the atavistic reflex of clapping one's hands at the end of a production. Shock? Astonishment? Agitation? Anxiety? Pondering about oneself and life? State akin to meditation? Contemplative feeling that one has brushed against the unknown, the inexpressible, the unnamed? Or was it simply emotion?" (20). Leaving these questions open-ended, Flaszen specifies that, for the Laboratory Theatre, the need for silence "proved to be one of the basics of creative work hygiene" (18), thereby becoming an integral part of the actor's organic process:

> Just like voice was for Grotowski an extension of the reaction and impulses of the entire body [...], so listening was not with the ears but with the whole body, the whole of oneself. It was active silence, action-silence. [...] Listening—silence—voice was a single, living, pulsating process between partners. A real exchange of impulses and reactions; exchange of action energy; energy of sound; energy of silence. [...] Work of this kind changed the spirit, the presence of space where it took place. (19)

Fueled by the energy of silence, the performer's process thus unfolds in time and space as physical impulses become embodied intuitions that can be trusted. This kind of experience crucially depends not only on the conditions in which it takes place, or what Flaszen calls creative work hygiene, but on the ability to trust that there is value in the embodied nature of this process. It is precisely this other way of knowing that Grotowski and his collaborators would go on to explore in the paratheatrical period as well as during the Theatre of Sources and Objective Drama projects, and the final period known as Art as vehicle.

Flaszen equates these post-theatrical phases of Grotowski's investigation of performance processes with the "forested silence" of Brzezinka, "a real place of solitude, with trees, a pond, a real sky above [our] head[s]." He goes on to quote Grotowski's evocation of a productive silence, which "is at the root of everything: the silence of words, the silence of sounds, the silence of movement. It is silence that gives important words and songs a chance, silence which does not disturb the speech of birds. The body is induced into motion which is seeing, listening, perceiving" (22). This experience of silence which becomes an impulse to listen and see with the whole body is then linked by Flaszen to Grotowski's vivid conception of awakening: "You feel that all your senses are active. You feel as if everything was flowing from inside you, from the centre [...]. From the centre and from things. Awakening of this kind is awakening in the full sense of the word" (22). Flaszen concludes by pointing out that Grotowski started from "a concrete fact" to approach in his own way "the traditions that are concerned with awakening" (22). Indeed, as with Stanislavsky's own insights into performance, the embodied sense of interconnectedness described by Grotowski appears to be an intuition grounded in years of practice and experiments, which eventually led him and his collaborators away from theatre and closer to the relational dimension of traditional ways of knowing.

THE VOICE OF NATURE

During Seyferth's 2009 work session, participants experienced the "forested silence" of Brzezinka when she guided the group on nocturnal expeditions that entailed walking, running, rolling, or lying down without verbal instructions, explanations, or commentaries. The only sounds were those of the forest surrounding us. Although thirty years had elapsed since Seyferth had worked in Brzezinka, her knowledge of this forest was obviously still alive in her body memory.

The feeling of complete trust which takes over when following someone into the depth of the forest at night is both daunting and exhilarating, especially once it becomes clear that if the guide were to disappear in that darkness, one would be very unlikely to find one's way back to the comfort of light and shelter. I had a second opportunity to experience this kind of night-time peregrination the following summer in southwestern France. Some of the young people who had participated in the month-long

Figure 3.6 Forest of Brzezinka. "Brzezinka Landscapes Project" funded by the Grotowski Institute and the University of Kent, Canterbury, 2008–09—photo by Francesco Galli.

Towards an Ecology of the Body-in-Life 155

Laboratory of Creative Research I organized in Poland in 2009 decided to meet again at Seyferth's center near Bordeaux for a three-week work session led by her in July, and I participated in the second week of this session. One evening, Seyferth took us on what turned out to be a four-hour-long exploration of the beautiful natural area in which the center is located. We started by doing the Motions outdoors at sunset, then formed a long line, and walked off into the countryside as night fell and the moon rose above the open fields.

Seyferth led us through a wide variety of natural spaces, passages, and paths: between the rows of a vast cornfield, through thick thorny bushes and narrow gullies, down a muddy slope, across a stream, then past a rushing watermill, and up a hill into the woods from which we distinguished, as we peered through branches, the reflection of a wide expanse of water. At some point, we arrived in a very large field with a single tree showered in moonlight. The tree was speaking-singing as the breeze gently stroked its leaves. Sitting near the tree in the open field, we listened to the rustling sound, with the moon and stars above us in the summer night sky. We then lay down on the earth and gently rolled across the field like waves, as we often did on the hardwood floor of the workspace during the training, but now the soft blades of grass felt like feathers against our bones and skin. Later on, we followed one another again in a long line, this time with a silent pageant of shadow silhouettes accompanying each of our steps on the paved road, as if projected by a magic lantern. We then entered a thick wood with the moon shooting rays of light through the trees and painting bands of white on the ground in dream-like effects.

About half-way through the walk, it felt as if we were making our way back, and I expected to come across some landmark indicating we were retracing our steps, but each time I thought I recognized the way some new obstacle challenged my impression that we were making progress: more bushes, more thickets, more meandering paths in the woods, the sounds of wild animals, possibly boars or stags, an owl calling out, a string of ducks following each other along the wall of a farmhouse as if mimicking us, fenced-in cows staring at us through the darkness, free-ranging cows running away as we approached. I began to suspect that Seyferth had somehow lost her way, perhaps because she was forced to make circuitous detours when we encountered natural barriers, such as this ocean of prickly shrubs suddenly rising up in a giant wave blocking the way forward. After a bold attempt at making our way through it, Seyferth turned back as if searching for a better route. Convinced that we must really be lost, I was resigned to the idea of spending the whole night outside—and then we crossed the stream again, finally a sign that we were on our way back. When we reached the familiar area where we had performed the Motions it was close to two o'clock in the morning. Everyone sat at a small outdoor table with lit candles in glasses, and as we quietly drank cups of hot tea I noticed that Seyferth was sitting with her head slightly tilted and her eyes seemed filled with images of all the previous nocturnal journeys that had led to this one.

In my interview with Seyferth, which took place shortly after this experience, she compared her creative work with going out at night on expeditions. She observed that everything kept changing: sometimes there would be unpleasant things around, then you would find yourself in an open space, then in some place where you could hardly move, then suddenly it would be very dark, and then it would get bright again, and so on. The point, she observed, was to keep moving through all these changes. I smiled and told her that what she had just described had certainly been my experience of this particular night-time odyssey. I explained that when writing about it afterwards in my notebook, I had begun to think of this journey, with many unpredictable events occurring on the way, as a kind of metaphor for this creative work as well as a metaphor for life—not only life as a journey, but also life as an organic phenomenon. This was perhaps what Grotowski had in mind when he said that the tree moving in the wind is not trying to express anything—it is simply alive. Thinking of the night expedition in this way has helped me to understand what Seyferth means when she asserts that the value of paratheatre is that it is very simple. It is simple because it is about what is alive, and there is something very valuable in experiencing what is alive as that which is always changing. This applies to human and non-human life, to natural ecosystems, as well as to the body-in-life experienced *as if* it were an ecosystem, sustained by the flow of energy animating the leaves of the tree which continues to sing in the moonlight even when there is no one there to listen.

4 At the Crossroads of Theatre, Active Culture, and Ritual Arts

Ritual studies scholar Ronald Grimes employs the term "pilgrimage" to describe his experience of Active Culture, the participatory paratheatrical activities initiated by members of the Laboratory Theatre in the 1970s. Grimes writes:

> A pilgrim is a person in motion [...] an ordinary person [...] proceeding through extraordinary space—in-between space, liminal, threshold space, boundary crossings, [...] paraordinary space. Grotowski calls this space 'paratheatrical.' It is parareligious as well [...] Yet 'paraordinary' does not mean 'supernatural.' It means very-natural, very-ordinary, authentically simple and direct. [...] The form of a pilgrimage is makeshift, improvised, spontaneous. ("Route to the Mountain: A Prose Meditation on Grotowski as Pilgrim" 248–49)

Like Grimes, the women who walked the roads of Active Culture, either as guides or participants, understand authenticity—one of the most contested terms in theatre and performance studies—in relation to simplicity, and directness in relation to embodied experience. The liminality of the pilgrimage process evoked by Grimes guarantees the instability of these terms which belong to the paraordinary and resist categorization precisely because they lie "outside the bounds of such carving-ups of reality" (248). Moreover, the makeshift dimension of pilgrimage precludes the kind of normative *communitas* which, according to Victor Turner, characterizes institutionalized spiritual practices. Grimes thus states: "The strength of pilgrimages as ritual processes is that the theatre of the sacral deed does not perform by virtue of a priestly office. All are lay persons in the pilgrimage process" (250). Active Culture, which may be considered to constitute the most open-ended and inclusive phase of Grotowski's research, thus offered a secular experience of spirituality to a large and very diverse group of lay persons.

This final chapter follows the journeys of women at the crossroads of theatre, Active Culture, and ritual arts, a parareligious pilgrimage in the course of which notions of belief, trust, and spirit will be addressed. I am therefore grateful to feminist performance theorist Jill Dolan for her bold endorsement of the words faith, belief, hope, and even love, as well as "the capacious holding place called 'humanity'" (*Utopia in Performance*, 163)—terms which, from a critical theory standpoint, are often considered to be as suspect as the notion of authenticity. Stressing that her "longing to articulate a spiritual effect in performance" should not be reduced to religiosity or fundamentalism, Dolan specifies that what she defines as the utopian performative is "grounded in the humble, messy attempt to seek out human connectedness" (136). She goes on to assert that utopian performatives are "transformative doings of what *if*" (141) and contends:

> This kind of hope represents an opening up, rather than a closing down, of consciousness of the past and the future in the present; this kind of hope relies on the active doings of faith. [. . .] Hope, like faith, demands continual reaffirmation [. . .] Despair could break us; theater might renew us, by inviting us to imagine [. . .] ways to be fully human together. [. . .] [T]he privilege of relief from banality and the pleasure of working at creating the ever shifting, always partial understandings that [performance] allows, models a way of being together, as human beings, in a culture and historical moment that's working much harder to tear us apart. (141, 163, 165)

The necessity to actively practice acts of consciousness hinging upon faith in what makes us fully human, or fully alive, was central to the experiences of women who, in the turmoil of 1968 Poland and its aftermath, believed in the possibilities of post-theatrical utopian performatives. These embodied practices, which often entailed crossing the boundaries between art and life, gave them hope in their capacity to create different ways of connecting with others, as well as different ways of being themselves.

GENDERED BEHAVIOR AS CODIFIED PERFORMANCE

In *Volatile Bodies: Towards a Corporeal Feminism*, Elizabeth Grosz calls for an alternative approach to the body, arguing that "it must avoid the impasse posed by the dichotomous accounts of the person which divide the subject into the mutually exclusive categories of mind and body. Although within our intellectual heritage there is no language in which to describe such concepts, no terminology that does not succumb to versions of this polarization, some kind of understanding of *embodied subjectivity*, of *psychical corporeality*, needs to be developed" (21–22). Developing such an understanding is especially important when investigating women's lived experiences within the context of a performance practice in which psychophysical processes and embodied consciousness are paramount, as is the case with the artists in my project. Dance scholar Karen Barbour, to whom I referred in the first chapter, provides the example of Maxine Sheets-Johnstone's phenomenological inquiry into "the wholeness of dance in the immediate encounter," which Sheets-Johnstone proposes as "a way of reflecting backwards and illuminating the structures of consciousness." Barbour notes that such a perspective has contributed to redefining lived dance experiences as "a source of self-knowledge, a way of knowing about the world, and a way of generating knowledge" ("Beyond 'Somatophobia'" 36). In dance improvisation, for instance, the performer "perceives the possibilities of her environment, the possibilities of her own body, and responds by instantaneously integrating her perception, exploration and responses in dancing" (36). Barbour further remarks that in order to be able to immediately respond to "the specific information present in the moment," performers cannot afford to separate body and mind, or doing from thinking, but must instead be able to "think in movement" (36). I previously discussed Barba's understanding of this process as "thinking in motion," which he contrasts with "thinking in concepts." Pointing to ethnomusicologist John Blacking's notion of "a thought which does not become a concept," Barba reports that Blacking "speaks of the body which 'thinks' when dancing," and builds upon Blacking's perspective in order to ask "whether *thinking in motion* might not be the best way to define the teaching of 'physical actions' which Stanislavsky tried to pass on to the actor, the teaching of which Grotowski is now the true master" (*The Paper Canoe* 88). This consideration is relevant to my discussion of the Stanislavsky-Grotowski lineage inasmuch as it is through their teaching that the women involved in my project remain in dialogue with this lineage as they transmit their own ways of thinking in motion to the younger generation.

Barbour, whose focus is on women performers, points out that Sheets-Johnstone's argument may be undermined by what Iris Young has identified as the gendered socialization of women, a process beginning in early childhood through the acquisition of "a specific positive style of feminine body comportment and movement" ("Throwing like a Girl" 153). Young contends that girls learn to embody a gendered identity through the development of what I propose to call their feminine *habitus*, that is to say, a form of socially codified behavior which, for Young, includes running, climbing, swinging, throwing, hitting, walking, standing, sitting, and gesturing "like a girl" (153). Since Young herself employs the term "style," I would further submit that this gendered codification of behavior may be compared with the kind of stylization pertaining to performance training. Codified acting, which is highly stylized, is defined by Schechner as "performing according to a semiotically constructed score of movements, gestures, songs, costumes, and makeup. This score is rooted in tradition and passed down from teachers to students by means of rigorous training" (*Performance Studies: An Introduction* 177, 185). While Schechner associates codified acting with the high degree of stylization characteristic of Western ballet and of Asian and African performance traditions, I propose to envision the gendered codification of movement described by Young as a form of stylization of the female role which women are taught to embody very early on in their everyday lives. Although this codified style of behavior, once it becomes 'second nature', may appear much more 'natural' than the highly stylized femininity embodied by male performers specializing in female roles in the Kathakali and Kabuki traditions, it also involves specific training through which young girls acquire a semiotically constructed way of moving, gesturing, and speaking, and which includes learning to wear the appropriate type of costume and makeup. This codified physicality is rooted in the culturally specific conventions of what acting as a woman looks like, conventions that are transmitted by means of the rigorous training of gendered socialization, a process that relies on repetition, as demonstrated by Judith Butler, and which, in the field of performance studies, is identified by Schechner as the restoration of behavior.

It is precisely this gendered stylization of behavior that Young indicts in her influential text since such learned behavior restricts the range of movement available to women and undermines their self-confidence by focusing their attention on how to avoid getting hurt, getting dirty, and tearing their clothes, which amounts to teaching girls to assume they would fail at activities in which their male counterparts are expected to excel. Young describes this enculturated female embodied experience by stating that "the woman lives her body as *object* as well as subject" (143, 153, 155), a positionality which is produced by a form of psychophysical conditioning that drastically limits women's embodied experiences.

TRUSTING EMBODIED WAYS OF KNOWING

From the perspective of performance practice predicated on the body-mind connection, conditioning the body also means conditioning the mind, so that restricting the range of movement available to women also imposes limitations on how they think in motion. Consequently, the lack of confidence identified by Young can be said to be produced by the pervasiveness of the feminine *habitus*. This, in turn, leads to a lack of trust in embodiment which devalues the kind of awareness, intuition, and insight linked by Meyer to sensual maturity achieved through practice ("Our Own Liberation" 134). Accordingly, Young points out that the gendered socialization process she describes induces women to experience their body as objectified, an unhealthy relationship to the body which is further exacerbated in the age of globalization by what McRobbie identifies as the insidious effects of the beauty-fashion industry complex.

Advocating a feminist phenomenological perspective that might enable women to restore their trust in embodied knowledge, Barbour remarks that although phenomenological inquiry as conceived by Heidegger and Merleau-Ponty challenges the Cartesian body-mind division by positing the living body as the center of human experience, its implicit reference point is a generic male body, so that it fails to account for the individualized lived experience of both male and female bodies. She contends that the perspective articulated by Young in "Throwing like a Girl" is informed by Merleau-Ponty's instrumentalist view of the person, a view which betrays an "account of body comportment, motility and spatiality [...] based on male experiences of movement" ("Beyond 'Somatophobia'" 38). Barbour remarks that Young herself acknowledges that such an instrumentalist perspective privileges "plan, intention, and control," and that these are "attributes of action most typical of masculine-coded comportment and activities" (38). Barbour infers that instead of looking for plan, intention, and control in women's ways of moving, dance researchers must take into account "first-person descriptive phenomenological investigation of a dancer's lived movement experience" (38). She notes that this is especially important if the researcher is to avoid positioning herself as an external observer assuming that she is able to decipher and interpret the lived experience of others from the outside.

Interestingly, Young concludes her essay by suggesting that researchers need to further investigate women's embodied experience, including "less task-oriented activities, such as dancing" (155). She goes on to write: "I have an intuition that the general lack of confidence that we frequently have about our cognitive or leadership abilities, is traceable in part to an original doubt in our body's capacity" (155). Young's usage of the pronoun "we," along with her reliance on the intuitive mode to confide in her reader about her intimate understanding of the challenges faced by women, seem to indicate that she might be on the verge of producing a personal testimony in which she might ask other women to compare their lived experience with her own. This could be interpreted as a call for the type of embodied research that Barbour advocates and which entails embracing first-person narratives that privilege reflexivity, dialogism, and intersubjectivity.

It is significant that both Grosz and Young explicitly identify with their reader. Grosz links "the dichotomous accounts of the person which divide the subject into the mutually exclusive categories of mind and body" to the use of a language which is part of what she calls "our intellectual heritage" (21–22). As for Young's notion of "original doubt," it is arguably as culturally specific as the concept of "original sin" upon which gendered socialization itself can be said to rely in Judeo-Christian cultures.[1] Just as Grosz's use of language is restricted by what she considers to be the limitations of her intellectual heritage, the range of analytical movement available to Young in her examination of socially normative modes of female identity production is necessarily constricted by an enculturated conception of embodiment tied to the gendered constraints experienced by women within a particular culture and society.

In light of such enduring limitations, perhaps the time has come for Western women to stretch their body-minds in new directions, beyond the confines of an intellectual heritage which many of us experience as particularly disempowering, and set out to investigate alternatives without being afraid of getting hurt or getting dirty. Thinking in motion can help us to engage in the kind of creative thought which "proceeds by leaps, by means of a sudden disorientation which obliges it to reorganize itself in new ways," defined by Barba as "*thought-in-life*, not rectilinear, not univocal" (*The Paper Canoe* 88), and from which I have derived the notion of productive disorientation. For if "[t]he growth of unexpected meanings is made possible by a disposition of all of our energies, both physical and mental"—a disposition which Barba equates with "perching on the edge of a cliff just before taking off in flight" and which he notes can be "distilled through training"—and if it is possible, by means of training, to "develop a new behavior, a different way of moving, of acting and reacting" (88), then we might have to spread our wings and fly into the unknown, that is to say, "the always dialogic space of performance" envisioned by Dolan as a space of endless potentiality in which "thinking and creating propels movement through *something*" (170, italics mine).

In *The Invention of Women*, Yoruba sociologist Oyèronké Oyewùmi links the privileging of sight over other senses in Western cultures and societies to the conflation of sex and gender, and contends that Western modes of social organization rely on what she defines as "bio-logic": the physical body, she states, provides visual data about sex (biology), which determines social gender roles. She then contends that in traditional Yoruba culture social roles and identity are not conflated with biology. Having demonstrated by means of cross-cultural comparison that the man/woman dichotomy and the mind/body/soul division, as well as the association of man with mind and woman with body are fundamentally Western, Oyewùmi argues that "woman" is essentialized by Western feminism and patriarchy alike into a universal category, so that "woman" becomes universally equated with the subaltern/victim. She contrasts the Eurocentric worldview whose "bio-logic" justifies a body-politic in which the Gaze establishes physical differences between individuals, with the Yoruba (and non-Western) "world-sense" which does not privilege sight over other senses. She infers that non-Western identity formation processes offer an alternative that is nullified by hegemonic Western categories, and provides the example of oral traditions in which the spiritual and the material are not dissociated and where words carry the world-sense of a people.

I would suggest that a parallel can be drawn between Oyewùmi's notion of "world-sense," in which the spiritual and the material are indivisible, and Meyer's conception of embodied knowledge transmitted trans-generationally through the channels of traditional cultural practices, a knowledge which is inclusive of the senses and the intuition. Meyer thus argues that feeling something is not strictly emotional but reflects an "instinctual sense" ("Our Own Liberation" 142). She specifies:

> This distinction fine-tunes how feelings shape epistemology and brings us back into our *senses*, 'our basic perceptions,' and how they shape how and what we know. Knowledge is not carved from anger or joy. Knowing something is *feeling* something, and it is at the core of our embodied knowledge system. Knowing something, however, is metaphorically housed in our stomach region because that is also the site of our emotions, our wisdom, as if knowledge also shapes how we emote. Perhaps then, feelings precede emotions, then wisdom develops. (142)

Meyer derives this perspective from her relationship to mentors who explain that, in Hawaiian epistemology, while the brain is considered to be the seat of power, intelligence is located in the area of the stomach, liver, and guts, so that the head, associated with logic, and the stomach, associated with the heart, must be connected for people to make sensible decisions. She refers to "the merging together of 'head and heart'" as a "dual system of knowing" in which "information, experience, *and* feelings" are interdependent (142–43). Teaching, for Indigenous peoples, therefore entails reaffirming the value of an experiential way of knowing which challenges dominant views of what constitutes intelligence.

Embodied wisdom rooted in an instinctual sense is also pivotal to the teaching of the artists whose work I am investigating, for the training they transmit brings about a deconditioning of the body-mind's enculturated *habitus*—which is gendered in different ways for women and men—and a reconditioning process through the cultivation of an embodied way of knowing which makes it possible to trust one's senses, instincts, and intuitions. In their testimonies, several of the women recalled behaving like "tomboys" in their childhood and being resistant to social gender norms when growing up, consequently developing a very strong sense of independence experienced by some as a form of rebellion. One of them spoke of being androgynous and unsuited for normative gender roles, while another proudly self-identified as a gay woman. Although during their formative years, first-generation women did not necessarily articulate their experience in terms of gendered oppression, several of them retrospectively acknowledged that they had struggled as young women yearning to develop their creative abilities, and my sense is that this may be partly why they so passionately embraced Grotowski's alternative conception of performance practice.

Not only are the unconventional life choices made by these artists informed by the very principles that underlie their teaching and creative research, but the uncompromising integrity and fierce sense of self-determination that characterize the ways in which they conduct their work and lives clearly defy the dominant gender norms that Young indicts. Accordingly, the confidence which these women demonstrate in their cognitive and leadership abilities is rooted in the trust they have developed in their body's capacity. Acquiring confidence in one's abilities to direct one's own life is politically significant for women, especially in the case of artists who are placed in a particularly precarious position by a profession in which both women and experimental performance practice tend to be marginalized and receive little support.

Furthermore, these women belong to a transnational community of artists which is becoming increasingly culturally diverse. Whereas all first-generation women are European except for Albahaca, what distinguishes Ang and Arreola is not only their age difference—they are both in their mid-forties, hence more than thirty years younger than some of the eldest members of the first generation—but also their cultural background, since they are respectively from Singapore and Mexico. Cultural diversity is also found among the performers who participated in the five work sessions I organized in Poland in 2009: they came from eleven different countries with an average age of about twenty-five years old: the youngest participant, a Peruvian woman, was nineteen, and the eldest was Arreola, who chose to take part in the work sessions led by Ang, Seyferth, Mirecka, and Rasmussen. When advertising for the month-long Laboratory of Creative Research comprised of these five work sessions, I sent out calls for participants internationally, inviting both male and female performers to apply. I used my research funds to keep the work session fees quite low compared to the usual rate for this kind of training opportunity, and I also offered participants free accommodation and food during the two weeks spent in the forest base of Brzezinka; finally, I provided scholarships to those who could not afford the work session fees. I received a much greater amount of applications from women than from men, and although I had initially hoped to have almost equal gender representation and even greater cultural diversity, we ended up with a group composed of fourteen women (including myself) and three men, from Spain, Italy, Greece, Germany, England, France, Brazil, Peru, Mexico, the United States, and Canada. I had a fairly substantial waiting list of people who expressed interest in participating, but whom I unfortunately was not able to invite because having too large a group would have affected the quality of the work sessions. While my main concern when selecting applicants was diversity, I was also looking for signs of previous experience in physically-based performance training combined with an interest in the type of creative research developed by the work session leaders.

The group's demographics clearly demonstrate that young women from a variety of cultural backgrounds are seeking this kind of training today, and Ang and Arreola, who have both chosen to research their own cultural heritage, provide non-European role models for this younger generation of women. These recent developments would thus seem to indicate that in the post-Grotowski era—which we have entered relatively recently given that the Polish director died in 1999—creative research influenced by his legacy will most likely expand in unforeseen directions well beyond its European lineage. What I am suggesting is that the modalities of such an expansion are already operational in women's current creative research precisely

At the Crossroads of Theatre, Active Culture, and Ritual Arts   165

because the latter focuses on performance processes open to change and transformation. As discussed in the preceding chapter, such processes mirror those of natural ecosystems, and I would submit that through their on-going engagement in this kind of research, these artists support an alternative performance paradigm in which cultural, traditional, and ritual practices significantly contribute to sustaining health or well-being experienced as ecosystemic balance between all forms of life. In light of the increasing cultural diversity that characterizes the Grotowski diaspora in the twenty-first century, this alternative paradigm points towards a vision of performance in which bio-diversity and cultural diversity mutually reinforce one another.

CROSSING THE BOUNDARIES OF AESTHETIC AND RITUAL PERFORMANCE

As I previously argued, embodiment, nature, and spirituality are defining features of the paradigm emerging from the current artistic work of women, yet the vision of performance fostered thereby should not be conflated with a perspective on artistic practice shared exclusively by women. This is an especially important distinction to make, for Oyewùmi cautions against associations of "woman" with the body and nature, and of "man" with the mind, that is to say, associations supporting culturally specific processes of identity formation that essentialize femininity and masculinity by constructing them as radically opposed. It is therefore significant that visual artist Bill Viola, whose discipline seems bound to privilege sight over the other senses, also argues that it is necessary to overcome the body-mind dichotomy and its visualist bias indicted by Oyewùmi in her critique of dominant Western knowledge systems. Viola thus states in "Putting the Whole Back Together":

> There has been much discussion about the result of the famous dualism of Descartes, and it is obvious that today we view body and mind as separate from each other, and we consider the intellect, senses, emotions, and so on, as separate parts of the mind. If we take a broader view of culture, past and present, [...] it becomes apparent that the present division that we in the industrialized West have developed is a kind of distortion. Going back to ancient times, the body was always a necessary part of the process of learning and in many cultures it was even considered to be a key instrument of knowledge. [...] You learn something so much more deeply when you move, when you move through it—in fact, thinking *is* a form of movement. (*Reasons for Knocking at an Empty House* 266)

By relating learning and thinking to moving, Viola extends Barbour's and Barba's respective understandings of the relationship between thought and movement by positing the body as the source of the thinking self. Viola further contends that in order to counterbalance the "scientific materialist point of view that holds that the way to understand is to divide, to separate, to isolate, to categorize, to specialize," what we need to do is "put the whole back together," an alternative perspective which he notes is already evidenced "in developments as diverse as chaos theory in mathematics, the management of natural resources, nutrition and psychology entering into clinical medicine, as well as the emergence of areas such as conceptual, performance, and installation art of the late twentieth century" (270). Importantly, for Viola, putting the whole back together begins with acknowledging that our basic models "come from nature, because we are a part of nature" and understanding that the natural world is "about *change and process*" (270). Viola compares human life processes with natural life processes when he asserts that "the layers of human experience become like sedimentary layers of the earth. As these layers build up they move from the levels of the 'conscious' and reason at the visible surface, to the deeper layers of the unconscious and the intuition below" (271). He points out that artistic practice itself begins with training, a period during which one cultivates the necessary technical skills followed by a sedimentation process through which creative work deepens, and that he posits as the necessary condition for being inspired: "[W]e learn something in order to forget it, to get the conscious mind out of the way, [. . .] to reach the unconscious, the deepest submerged layers of the self, [. . .] and this process creates a deeper structure, [which] is in itself the architecture of inspiration" (271).

Viola links the function of creative practice to "the original sense of art, in the sense of *ritual*," stating: "You can use it to learn something in your life, to go deeper" (282). Incidentally, Viola's references to Meister Eckhart and St. John of the Cross, whom he relates to "the other side of the Western tradition, a tradition that was carried on in the East," tracing it to early Christianity's "desert fathers in the Nile valley and Syria, staying out in the wilderness like Zen monks on retreat," are also key references for Grotowski. Viola testifies that finding these roots in the history of his own religion was a revelation to him, since "this is religion in the negative way, the *via negativa* as it is called, as opposed to the accepted *via positiva*" (283). This is, of course, also fundamental to Grotowski's approach to performance, which he memorably describes as a form of *via negativa* in *Towards a Poor Theatre* (17).

Furthermore, Grotowski refers to what Viola envisions as the other side of the Western tradition in his talk "Holiday [Swieto]":

> a singular phenomenon which occurred two thousand years ago in the peripheries of the huge empire encompassing the entire Western world, as it was then: some men walked in the wilderness and searched for truth. They searched in accord with the character of those times, which, unlike ours, was religious. But if there is a similarity between

At the Crossroads of Theatre, Active Culture, and Ritual Arts 167

> that time and ours, it consists in the need to find meaning. If one does not possess that meaning, one lives in constant fear. [...] This is why there is a direct connection between courage and meaning. The men who walked in the vicinity of Nazareth two thousand years ago [...] talked about strange things and sometimes behaved imprudently, but in the air there was a need to abandon force, to abandon the prevailing values and search for other values on which one could build life without a lie. (in *The Grotowski Sourcebook* 216)

Suggesting that there are similarities between such a quest and the creative research he and his collaborators accomplished in response to a lack of meaning in the twentieth century, Grotowski observes: "In the fear which is connected with the lack of meaning, we give up living and begin diligently to die. Routine takes the place of life, and the senses—resigned—get accustomed to nullity. [...] With great agility, through hiding our gloom, we busy ourselves about our own funeral. [...] And what is this death? The dressing, covering, possessing, escaping, canonizing of one's burden" (in *The Grotowski Sourcebook* 217). As with Viola, who proposes nature as a model, Grotowski points to the natural world: "And what remains? What lives? The forest"—and, citing the Polish saying "*We were not there—the forest was there; we shan't be there—the forest will be there*," he goes on to ask: "And so, how to be, how to live, how to give birth as the forest does?" (217, italics in original). In response, he suggests that if we say to ourselves: "I am water, pure, which flows, living water," then the source becomes "*he, she*, not *I*: [...] only if *he* is the source can *I* be the living water." Grotowski thus seems to be evoking an intersubjectivity in which human and non-human life merge together: "To be 'looked at' (yes, 'looked at,' and not 'seen'); to be looked at, like a tree, a flower, a river, the fish in that river. [These] are not metaphors. This is tangible and practical. It is not a philosophy but something one does. [...] This has to be taken literally, this is experience" (217–18). Hence, although the embodied experience of being guided by Seyferth in the forest at night may be perceived as a metaphor for the journey into the unknown for which the training prepares the performer, it is first and foremost a tangible and practical way of abandoning force and letting someone else be the source of one's doing. Physically sinking into the darkness of the forest to descend deeper and deeper into the layers of embodied experience, the sediments of body memory, towards an instinctual sense of what it means to be alive, may also become a way of reclaiming one's roots within the primordial forest whose existence not only precedes ours but extends indefinitely into the future.

In "Performer," Grotowski suggests that "one access to the creative way consists of discovering in yourself an ancient corporeality to which you are bound by a strong ancestral relation" (39). One can start from one's body memory of certain details, for example "the distant echo of a color of the voice" through which one discovers within oneself somebody other: first, it is the corporeality of someone known, a close relative, perhaps one's grandmother, and then "more and more distant, the corporeality of the unknown one, the ancestor" (39). Grotowski specifies that one does not discover this corporeality literally as it was, but as it might have been: "[E]ach time I discover something, I have the feeling it is what I recall. Discoveries are behind us and we must journey back to reach them" (39). For Grotowski, journeying further and further into the past can lead to a breakthrough "as in the return from an exile—[...] as if very strong potentialities are activated," and he derives the notion of a breakthrough back to one's origin from the following statement by Meister Eckhart:

> When I was in my first cause, I did not have God, I was my own cause. [...] What I wanted, I was it and what I was, I wanted; I was free from God and from all things. [...] This is why I am unborn, and by my mode unborn, I cannot die. [...] When I return, [...] in the breakthrough [...] I am what I was, what I should remain now and for ever. [...] There, I am what I was, I do not increase nor diminish, because I am—there, an immobile cause, which makes move all things. (40)

John Eckhart was a kind of Medieval trickster condemned as a heretic by the Inquisition for inciting his followers to cultivate a form of creative power linked to disinterestedness, a notion close to the Buddhist concept of detachment. He posited the presence of God in all living things, including human beings, who could therefore have direct access to the divine. In one of his sermons, he declared: "[W]hen [God] finds you ready he must act, and pour into you, just as when the air is clear and pure the sun must pour into it and not hold back [...] You need not look either here nor there. He is no farther away than the door of the heart" ("Another Sermon on the Eternal Birth" in *Late Medieval Mysticism*, 189). Viola describes this "union with the Divine" as a process by which the individual connects her spirit directly to the divine without the intermediary of a priest, and warns: "Of course, this is politically dangerous to the established powers." Accordingly, Eckhart believed that such creative agency inspired by spirituality was accessible to all rather than the privilege of a few, a radical perspective Viola relates to William Blake's conviction that "*all* people are capable of having visions and being in contact with the Divine Imagination" (*Reasons for Knocking* 283). Eckhart's supporters included the Beguines, a movement of women who adopted a free style of religious life in the twelfth and thirteenth centuries. In the introduction to *Meister Eckhart and the Beguine Mystics*, Bernard McGinn specifies that the Beguines "were the only new form of 'apostolic life' (*vita apostolica*) in which women took the leadership role" (3) and suggests that the teachings of Marguerite Porete, a French Beguine who was burned at the stake in 1310 for disseminating her views through her book *The Mirror of Simple Souls*, most likely influenced Eckhart himself. Incidentally, during a work session, a participant showed me a copy of Porete's book, a connection which leads me to wonder whether the Beguines may be perceived as the spiritual ancestors of Grotowski's women collaborators, with the image of Porete signaling through the flames across centuries as a total act of resistance and sacrifice.

My sense is that the type of politically dangerous creative agency evoked by Viola and to which Grotowski appears to be referring via Eckhart subtly underscored the Laboratory Theatre's post-theatrical activities. Paratheatre itself seems to have emerged organically from the creative process leading to the company's final theatre production, *Apocalypsis cum figuris*, which arguably constitutes the most collaborative, experimental, and influential of all Laboratory Theatre creations. This was especially the case among members of a younger generation who were deeply marked by this piece and who participated in the experiments that took place during the transitional period in the course of which the theatrical and the paratheatrical substantially informed one another. Although Grotowski's controversial decision to "abandon" theatre was perceived as a betrayal by a number of theatre scholars and practitioners, it was experienced as a particularly fruitful time by the women who spoke to me about this mostly undocumented period.

According to the information provided on Grotowski.net, a website created and maintained by the Grotowski Institute, Active Culture, a designation that was more commonly employed than paratheatre at the time, is considered to have lasted from 1969 to 1976, although the website entry on paratheatre indicates that these dates are the subject of on-going debate. The problem is two-fold: on the one hand, the paratheatrical period can be said to have overlapped with the beginning of the Theatre of Sources, during which some of Grotowski's collaborators remained engaged in paratheatrical experiments, and, on the other hand, the phrase Active Culture itself is employed in different ways when discussing Grotowski's post-theatrical research. In "The Theatre of Sources," Grimes suggests the following periodization: "(1) the 'poor theatre' phase (1959–1970), (2) the 'paratheatrical' phase (1970–1975) and (3) the Theatre of Sources or 'active culture' phase (1976–1982)", thereby distinguishing paratheatre from the Theatre of Sources, the latter being equated with Active Culture (271). However, in the unpublished document titled "On the Road to Active Culture: The Activities of Grotowski's Theatre Laboratory Institute in the Years 1970–1977," a collection of testimonies that appeared in the Polish and foreign press and was edited by Leszek Kolankiewicz and translated by Boleslaw Taborski for a symposium that took place in June 1978, Flaszen states in the preface that these testimonies were compiled by Kolankiewicz in order to provide information about the paratheatrical activities of the Laboratory Theatre, hence suggesting that Active Culture encompasses all the post-theatrical activities that took place during these seven years. Finally, Slowiak and Cuesta propose the following periodization in the list of contents of their book: the Theatre of Productions (1959–69), the Theatre of Participation/Paratheatre (1969–78), the Theatre of Sources (1976–82), Objective Drama (1983–86), and Ritual Arts or Art as Vehicle (1986–99)—which indicates that paratheatre and the Theatre of Sources overlapped from 1976 to 1978 (*Jerzy Grotowski* ix).

When reflecting on the transition from theatre to paratheatre, Grotowski states: "I suspended my work as constructor of performances and continued, concentrating on discovering the prolongation of the chain: the links *after* those of performances and rehearsing; thus emerged paratheatre, that is to say, participatory theatre (meaning, with the *active* participation of people from the outside). Herein was the *Holiday: the day that is holy*: human, but almost sacred, consisting in a 'disarming of oneself,'—reciprocal and total" ("From the Theatre Company to Art as Vehicle" 120). Grotowski observes that in the first years, when this work was carried out by a small group over a long period of time and a few new participants eventually joined in, "things happened on the border of a miracle" (120). Albahaca's testimony corroborates this assessment of the early phase of paratheatrical research, which she stated was structured by the principles developed at the Laboratory Theatre yet explored new possibilities beyond the limitations of theatre. She felt that it was a very rich and very important period which she found extremely stimulating, from Holiday, the first paratheatrical project, to the Tree of People, the final project that synthesized the various elements of Active Culture and was led by some of the Laboratory Theatre core members, including herself.

Grotowski concludes from these various experiments that, when attempting to include more participants or when the core group "had not passed first through a long period of intrepid work[,] certain fragments functioned well, but the whole descended to some extent into an emotive soup between the people, or rather into a kind of animation" ("From the Theatre Company to Art as Vehicle" 120). However, he acknowledges this phase to be a necessary passage when stating that "from paratheatre was born (as the link *after*) Theatre of Sources, which dealt with the source of different traditional techniques [. . .]. Often working outdoors, we were looking mainly for what the human being can do with his own solitude, how it can be transformed into force and a deep relationship with what is called the natural environment" (120). Grotowski specifies that this research focused on "the living body in the living world" (121). By emphasizing the chain linking each of these periods, he points to the continuity of his research in spite of its periodization. He also provides a sense of this continuity when observing that "paratheatre made it possible to put to the test the very essence of determination: to not hide oneself in anything. Theatre of Sources revealed real possibilities. [. . .] I never broke with the thirst that motivated Theatre of Sources" (121). This research hence led Grotowski to focus on ritual arts and to engage in the final period of his work which he named Art as vehicle. He describes the focus of his investigation during this period as a primordial elevator, "some kind of basket pulled by a cord, with which the doer lifts himself toward a more subtle energy, to descend *with this* to the instinctual body. [. . .] The point is not to renounce part of our nature—all should retain its natural place: the body, the heart, the head, something that is 'under our feet' and something that is 'over our head'," a vertical line which he states should be held taut between organicity and awareness (124–25).

The testimonies of the women who experienced the transition from the theatre of productions to Active Culture provide evidence that the post-theatrical experiments that overlapped with *Apocalypsis cum figuris* and preceded Objective Drama and Art as vehicle opened up what Grotowski himself acknowledged to be "real possibilities," whose creative potential some of these artists have continued to explore and have taken in various directions by developing their own research. Moreover, the hybrid nature of their work often blurs boundaries not only between the theatrical and the "para"- or "post"-theatrical, but also between performance and the traditional techniques related to what Grotowski called ritual arts, as well as between the notion of Art as presentation and Art as vehicle.

I asked Grotowski during his seventh Collège de France lecture whether he thought that the theatrical work accomplished by someone involved in Art as presentation could encompass aspects of Art as vehicle. I was curious about the possibilities that might emerge from developing a hybrid approach connecting the two extremities of the chain, and wondered whether performance could be experienced as a vehicle by both doers and witnesses. Grotowski wryly protested that I had made him suffer by forcing him to listen to his own terminology. He pointed out that he usually preferred that people refrain from using the terms he had coined since they were informed by the specific experience of a particular individual, and consequently could not be used to convey possibilities or experiences pertaining to someone else. That being said, Grotowski replied that it was probably possible for Art as vehicle to exist within Art as presentation, although it would have to come from someone who had—and he paused briefly as he searched for the right phrase—a personal passion or interest. He suggested that it was possible to discover other terms, and added that while a particular approach may provide an example which could become fruitful (*fécond*), it could only show us that it was possible to take the work in that direction, but it could not be imitated.

Grotowski further observed that when carrying out long-term investigations into ancient songs and the actions linked to these songs, it was possible, for example, to focus on different traditions than the ones with which he had worked, such as the songs of the Greek and Russian Orthodox Christian traditions which were not part of his research. He noted that there was yet another possibility that had been developed in Bengal by the Bauls, who were constantly recreating very old songs as if they had been new ones. Furthermore, when watching the work of Decroux towards the end of his life, Grotowski had sensed that this kind of orientation also existed in his approach. He stressed that it was linked to Decroux's aspiration, his attitude, and his immense competence. While Decroux did not use his voice at all in his work, Grotowski felt that he had achieved something very similar to what could be accomplished when working on traditional songs. He remarked that although pantomime usually precluded such possibilities because of the dominance of artificiality, Decroux clearly had an aspiration towards something that lay well beyond the level of performance.

Grotowski then suggested that certain connections between the two extremities of the chain could certainly exist in the case of an individual who was from a culture or tradition that was ancient. He specified that he was thinking about a particular person with whom he had worked and who had selected a sacred text from their own tradition and carried out a type of research akin to monodrama on the basis of that text. Grotowski also referred to the work of the famous Polish actor Jacek Woszczerowicz, about whom he had spoken during his second Collège de France lecture, explaining that Woszczerowicz had been a great friend of the Laboratory Theatre even though his way of working belonged to the artificial pole of acting. Towards the end of this actor's career, Grotowski had noticed that something in his work had changed, and when he asked Woszczerowicz about it, he found out that the actor was suffering from a serious heart condition and that performing had become very dangerous for his health. He had nevertheless decided to keep on working, yet Grotowski observed that something fundamental in his attitude had changed: he was no longer interested in controlling the spectators' reactions, as he so masterfully did before, but instead focused his energy on doing something that had a meaning of its own, something that had to be accomplished as well as possible, and, consequently, he no longer addressed his performance to the audience as he had in the past. Woszczerowicz had found another way to approach his work by becoming very deeply connected to what Grotowski called a "second horizon." While the Polish actor continued to work with the text and physical score of the roles he performed on stage, Grotowski remarked that it was as if he had redirected the technical aspects of acting towards another perspective induced by the awareness he had of his situation. It was this different mobilization of energy which gave another dimension to his work and showed that it was, indeed, possible to do both.

Grotowski derived from these examples that for this connection to exist between the two extremities of the chain, it was necessary to have some form of professional competence in a particular domain and, at the same time, a second horizon. He concluded that anything was possible if one had competence along with this kind of motivation, curiosity, or aspiration. However, he acknowledged that the circumstances of one's life and work could, of course, interfere with such an aspiration, and stated that, in that case, there was no solution, except perhaps if one searched for an *efficacious* way of changing this context.

I would submit that the women who have shared their work with me all seem to have changed their circumstances in an efficacious way in order to

At the Crossroads of Theatre, Active Culture, and Ritual Arts 173

pursue what constitutes their second horizon. Some of them have chosen to search for their own way in theatre and/or paratheatre, in spite of the wide-spread conviction in the Grotowski diaspora that the achievements of the Laboratory Theatre cannot be matched, as emphasized by Albahaca during my conversations with her. Others have pursued their second horizon through professional accomplishments that are not directly linked to theatre or paratheatre and yet are significantly informed by what they found to be valuable in Grotowski's research. Prepared by the training and challenges characteristic of this unusually demanding way of working, these women have explored new possibilities, engaged in independent research, and taken the risk to trust their impulses, commit to their passions, and follow their aspirations. They have continued to draw energy, courage, and determination from their past experiences without letting the latter weigh them down or deter them from moving forward. Perhaps most significantly, they have succeeded in maintaining a sense of integrity in their work that is also reflected in their lives, which follow the principles of their creative research through the rejection of social conformism and normative gender roles.

This was clearly conveyed by the testimonies of a group of women who, having participated in the 2009 Meetings, initiated a follow-up meeting that Gardecka and I organized in the summer of 2010 and that I will discuss in this chapter. Benesz generously offered to host this meeting at her house in Sardinia, and although I initially thought that the isolation of Casa Blanca and the lack of basic amenities might perhaps dissuade the seven women who wished to participate in this new meeting, Gardecka was enthusiastic about such a gathering taking place in Sardinia and she convinced me that the women would enjoy this kind of adventure. Prior to our meeting, I participated in a six-day work session led by Benesz, and I will now address the interrelation of performance, tradition, and ritual practice within her creative research, which is situated at the intersection of the theatrical and the post-theatrical.

THE QUESTION OF BELIEF

The hybrid nature of Benesz's perspective was reflected in the diverse backgrounds of her work session participants. Conversely to my previous experiences, where most participants had been young performers searching for alternative approaches to theatre, this group was composed of people of different ages working in a variety of professions, with only a few self-identified theatre practitioners. Three middle-aged men from Sardinia, Germany, and Belgium, who have been continuously involved in Benesz's creative research over close to three decades, were introduced by Benesz as her collaborators, yet only one of them, Vincenzo Atzeni is a performer. Almost everyone else in the group had previously participated in work sessions led by Benesz, including Daniela Marcello, a Sardinian woman who has been working with her for six years, and Karina Janik, a Polish doctoral student who is conducting research on paratheatre with a focus on Benesz's approach. The non-actors, who comprised the majority in the group, seemed extremely trusting of the process through which they were guided by Benesz and her collaborators, even though it required everyone to sing, move, and perform ritualized actions whose efficacy depended upon the ability to focus one's energy and fully commit to the work.

Benesz foregrounds seasonal cycles in her teaching so that the activities which she invites participants to experience change according to the season. This particular session took place at the end of August, which in Sardinia is the grape harvest season, and this significantly structured the work we did. The impact of this work became clear to me when the group began to engage in ritualized actions linked to traditional practices connected to the harvest. One morning, Benesz announced that we were to prepare for a gathering that would take place under the shade of the *carrubo* tree. At some point during this preparation, Benesz showed me a postcard which was a reproduction of a Chagall painting featuring a large blue crucified Christ on a red background. As we delineated the outdoor space designated by Benesz, she assigned various tasks to us and attended to every detail while we worked together to transform this particular area into a ritual space.

Creating a special gathering place is also something which Mirecka invites participants to do, and in the month of July of that same summer I took part in a work session led by her at Casa Blanca during which we built a large bamboo hut with white fabric walls covered with colorful paintings created by the participants. We also bedecked the branches of the *carrubo* with large pieces of light fabric that the *sirocco* turned into the billowing sails of a ship. A month later, there were no traces of these makeshift artifacts, which led me to reflect on the ephemeral quality of this kind of work.

Once everything was ready, Daniela covered her hair with a dark red scarf and balanced a basket on her head as she walked up to the *carrubo*. The basket was filled with dark grapes still attached to green stems, and Benesz distributed large handfuls of the ripe fruit as Daniela sang a traditional Sardinian song. We all worked together to separate the grapes from the stems and collected them in large bowls. Benesz then wove together the vine stems into something which strikingly looked like a crown of thorns. Holding the crown, she walked towards Stéphane Lucca, a French man in his thirties. He did not resist while Vincenzo and Daniela dressed him in a white shirt with long wide sleeves, placed the crown on his head, and covered his shoulders with a deep blue cloth.

Through these simple actions, Stéphane was immediately transformed into a Christ figure. The montage effect was surprisingly efficacious: the image was so striking that no one could have denied what it represented,

At the Crossroads of Theatre, Active Culture, and Ritual Arts 175

Figure 4.1 Ewa Benesz under *carrubo* tree. Sardinia, Italy, August 2010—photo by Celeste Taliani.

yet, at the same time, Stéphane somehow remained unchanged. The only perceptible difference was in his eyes, tinged with a shade of wonder mixed with weariness. Nevertheless, there was no sign in his behavior indicating that he was trying to play a character. When someone placed grapes in his hands, he accepted them resignedly and simply looked at us silently. What became clear to me at that point was that Stéphane did not have to do anything, he had become Christ in spite of himself, and we were witnesses to this transformation. Participating in this ritualized action felt as if we had designated him as Christ, as if we had assigned this role to him, perhaps by default, and possibly also against our own will.

I was standing next to Vincenzo when Stéphane took a step forward to offer him a grape. Vincenzo accepted it and, holding it between two fingers, slowly stroked Stéphane's face, and then swiftly touched his forehead as if marking it or perhaps taking off a sign. After Stéphane had offered grapes to everyone in the group, as in the Christian rite of the holy communion, Benesz briefly spoke to him, asking him something which I couldn't grasp. He replied very simply, as himself, and I thought I heard him explain that he would like to believe but that it was difficult for him. Benesz then removed the crown from his head while someone else, a woman, began to wash his feet. I think that it was at this point that Karina made a gesture towards Stéphane as if wanting to touch the body of Christ and suddenly let out a long drawn-out wail. Benesz turned to us as if this were our cue and began to sing a song in which the word "Shalom" recurred as she clapped her hands rhythmically. We all joined in the song, which became our way of bringing this action to an end.

During a conversation I had with Benesz after the work session, we spoke about the progression of the work over the span of six days, which I felt had powerfully culminated in the action with the grapes. As I experienced it, the archetypal figure we summoned through this action brought up images of *The Constant Prince*, featuring a Christ-like ruler whose faith is cruelly tested by his torturers, and strongly resonated with echoes of *Apocalypsis cum figuris*, in which a group of drunken revellers humiliate the Simpleton/Dark One (*Ciemny*), an outcast whom they derisively appoint as the Christ of the Second Coming. Following these associations, I asked Benesz about the Polish tradition of yearly processions, a ritual practice which also exists in southern Europe. In Portugal, for example, I had witnessed members of the community embodying biblical characters, including the Christ figure. In her response, Benesz contrasted this type of practice with the mode by which the figure of Christ had emerged in our work. She suggested that it had sprung from the action with the grapes, from which the possibility of the crown had naturally unfolded. She remarked that although grapes are a great gift from nature, they are separated from the stems which then get discarded, yet, in our action, that which is usually rejected and cast away suddenly became sacred through the process of making the crown, which raised the question of what to do with it.

Benesz asserted that the crown did not necessarily need to be placed on a man's head, and that, in fact, it was the first time that this action with grapes had developed in such a way during a work session. She described the work process as a kind of journey, and noted that while the actions were structured they were also open-ended, so that no one knew how things would unfold and develop. She added that, of course, there was a relationship between actions and associations, and indicated that, prior to the gathering, she had shown the postcard of the Chagall painting to Stéfane and spoken with him about it. I told Benesz that, during the action, I couldn't discern her words to Stéfane but felt that the gist of her question was something like: So, how is it, what can you say to us now? She concurred that it was indeed what she had asked him, and specified that in his response he had acknowledged that he felt the need to believe and that he would like to be able to do so.

This desire to believe deepened by a lack of faith, which I felt was epitomized by the action with the grapes, is something I have personally often experienced when participating in what may be broadly defined as post-theatrical performance practice. Harrowing moments of doubt alternate with peaceful passages and moments of epiphany. Each work session experience feels like a journey that stirs up both the darkness and the light, magnifying what would otherwise go unnoticed, and intensifying life beyond quotidian familiarity. The deep self-questioning which such work elicits is not something to which one can simply become accustomed or immune. When re-reading the notes taken in the course of the work sessions that comprise a large part of my fieldwork, I am still surprised by the extent to which going through this type of embodied experience seems to invariably bring up the unanswerable questions which Chaikin relates to the potential power of performance:

> We are joined to each other by forces. These forces are of two kinds. The first are observable political-social forces which move irrevocably through all of us who are alive at the same time in history. We are further joined by other forces: unanswerable questions to do with being alive at all. These questions cannot be examined. We ask questions in words, and in response we experience a dynamic silence. In effect, we are joined to each other (to all living creatures) by what we don't understand. (*The Presence of the Actor* 12)

THE PATH TO PARATHEATRE

Perhaps relationship to the natural world, then, can instill in us a sense of faith in life rather than belief in a God-like father figure presiding over mankind's destiny. This might be why the forest of Brzezinka became the creative territory of the Laboratory Theatre during the period of Active Culture. I was struck, for example, by Molik's acknowledgment of the importance of paratheatre when, standing with him outside the Brzezinka workspace in 2006, he reminisced that he and his colleagues had worked even harder there than previously in Wroclaw. At the time, the old farm building in which the actors lived was barely habitable, and Molik recalled showering in an icy waterfall. Looking off into the distance as if seeing images of the past, he still seemed astonished by it all, and added pensively that working with Grotowski had changed his life. In his book, Molik explains that although he had initially hesitated to become involved in paratheatre, this period of Grotowski's research had had a profound influence upon him both professionally and personally:

> When we had the first experiences of this kind we knew absolutely nothing, like the other participants. We were leaders but only by name, by rule. Actually we were there with complete non-knowledge, like all the others. [. . .] [In the project called Tree of People], it was just, how to say, getting to know someone without knowing him, being really together without being together, without touching the others, however it functioned. [. . .] I remember that once the night was completely dark, without any moon, and I led everybody through the forest, where there is a very narrow path. Nobody could see anything [. . .]. We just followed the path instinctively, but nobody knows how it was possible. [. . .] Yes, this work with nature was very fruitful. I wasn't the same man, not the same actor, before working with nature as I was afterwards. I was much changed. After this contact with nature I was very much renovated, we can say. So it was a very good experience. (Campo and Molik, *Zygmunt Molik's Voice and Body Work* 31, 117)

The relevance of such a relationship to nature was also emphasized by Seyferth in her talk to the participants of her 2009 work session in Brzezinka, when she recounted that, in her early twenties, she had felt drawn to the paratheatrical work which she experienced when she first came to Poland to participate in the Mountain Project. She explained that participants were taken about two hours away from Brzezinka, walked for two days, spent one night in the forest, and finally arrived at a fortress-like castle. They were then taken to a very large room with a hardwood floor and a fireplace, the space in which the work took place. They ate and slept in an adjacent room, there was no talking between them, only what was necessary, and the guides did not give them any explanation. Seyferth described what happened in the large room as "moving together without speaking," which occurred in the presence of Grotowski, whom she said participated in the work at that time. The session lasted for three days, but Seyferth explained that she liked this experience so much that by the third day she felt a strong desire to stay.

When the guides led participants out of the castle one by one, Seyferth said that, surprisingly, no one came to get her, even though a new group of participants was being brought in for another three-day session. She ended up staying for the entire duration of the project, and at some point was asked to guide participants through the forest. A very big storm broke out, which made this experience particularly intense, and she later found out that the people she had been leading through the forest were Flaszen himself and Antoni Jahołkowski, one of the founding actors of Grotowski's company. The project ended earlier than planned because of torrential rains that led

At the Crossroads of Theatre, Active Culture, and Ritual Arts 179

to problems of inundation. When the groups of leaders returned with Seyferth to Wroclaw, she was asked by Zmysłowski, the leader of the Mountain Project, whether she would like to join his group. Seyferth decided to accept and began working with the group composed of nine members from Poland, France, Germany, the United States, Colombia, and Japan, Seyferth being the only woman.

Under Zmysłowski's leadership, they developed an action named *Czuwania* (The Vigils). Seyferth specified that this work took place towards the end of the paratheatrical period and preceded the Theatre of Sources project to which she also actively contributed. The Vigils was something which could be experienced by anybody since no particular prior knowledge or ability was needed to participate. It consisted in open-ended, movement-based, non-verbal actions which involved a large group of people and took place in an empty room or workspace. It always began with silence and stillness, and the guides initiated simple physical actions to which the participants responded in their own way. Zmysłowski's group took this project to various cities in Poland, and one session held in Milan in 1979 was documented on film by Mercedes Gregory. Although the participatory aspect of this kind of experiment was also explored in other paratheatrical projects, The Vigils became a way for a diverse group of people who did not know each other to meet in a non-daily manner and explore possibilities together without communicating verbally. The events I organized in Poland in 2009 for *Meetings with Remarkable Women* included an open session of The Vigils led by Seyferth.

Figure 4.2 Katharina Seyferth leading The Vigils. *Meetings with Remarkable Women.* Grotowski Institute, Brzezinka, Poland, August 2009—photo by Francesco Galli.

FROM PARATHEATRE TO THE THEATRE OF SOURCES

Seyferth then worked on the Theatre of Sources project along with some members of the group that created The Vigils. The preparatory period began in the summer of 1978 in Brzezinka, a time during which Grotowski asked the guides to develop actions in the forest which would change the perception of the participants. Seyferth compared this process to meditation and specified that Grotowski wanted them to create actions that would touch some more profound level of being and temporarily change one's way of experiencing things. She stressed that these were simple but effective actions developed over a few months and tested by the group—when an action worked, it became part of what was offered to participants during the Theatre of Sources project.

Part of the preparation included trips with Grotowski to Haiti, India, and Mexico, where the group would meet with a variety of people, including holders of traditional knowledge, some of whom were invited to Poland to join the Theatre of Sources project. Seyferth, who took part in the trip to India, recalled meeting with the Bauls, whom she explained are members of nomadic groups who perform songs requiring a highly specialized technique linked to a connection with the chakras and inner energy. She said that these songs belong to secret knowledge transmitted across generations for two thousand years and sharing common roots with Sufism. She remarked that, in Bengal, the Bauls travel from village to village and are honored by the villagers who welcome them and feed them. They sing about ancient stories that are part of Indian mythology, make very irreverent jokes between songs, and tell news from the last village they visited, so that their role is also to transmit information between the villages. Grotowski invited an elder Baul's apprentice to come to Poland, and asked Seyferth, who said she had a good rapport with the Bauls, to take care of this young man during the Theatre of Sources project.

Seyferth explained that this project, which took place in the forest bases of Brzezinka and Ostrowina, was comprised of five-day sessions involving small groups of invited participants who would follow the actions led by the guides. She pointed out that the Theatre of Sources hence differed from paratheatrical activities, which were more open-ended and did not require precisely imitating a specific action. Seyferth added that participants had two days to go through all the actions led by the guides, each of which lasted between an hour and a half and two hours. After the first two days, Grotowski would meet with the participants and ask them which actions they liked and wanted to repeat, and during the next three days they would take part in the actions they had chosen. She stressed that there were very few instructions and all the actions took place in silence since absence of verbal communication was a principle which was observed by everyone at all times in Brzezinka.

It was the era of *Solidarność* in Poland, and Seyferth recalled that there was a recurring joke about the Russians arriving in their tanks to chase everyone away. The political situation was so tense that Grotowski decided to ask the European participants to return home, and the only members of the group who stayed in Poland were those who had come from afar, along with people who had been invited to join during the trips to Mexico, India, and Haiti. Seyferth said that this small group carried on with the Theatre of Sources in a quasi-clandestine way at the Laboratory Theatre's headquarters in Wroclaw and also through visits to people's homes.

Although Seyferth went back to Germany at that time, she remained in contact with Grotowski and accompanied him to Rome in 1982 where he gave a series of lectures about the Theatre of Sources. Grotowski then left for the United States where he developed the Objective Drama Project. Seyferth came in contact with this project during Grotowski's trip to Italy in 1985 for a two-month work session. She observed that during this new phase of Grotowski's research the style of work had changed: it was quite strictly controlled, even militant in some way. She felt that this approach was in stark contrast with her experience in Poland because the atmosphere at the Laboratory Theatre was exceptionally welcoming and everyone was treated in a particularly attentive and sensitive way—she emphasized that as soon as one entered one could sense that it was a special place. This dimension of the Laboratory Theatre was also highlighted by Gardecka when she spoke to me about what distinguished the company from a conventional theatre.

I asked Seyferth how her experience in Poland had shaped her work and her life, and she acknowledged that during the paratheatrical period she had problems with her family, who resented her inability to explain what she was doing at the Laboratory Theatre. She remembered being very quiet because her experience of the work lay outside the context of words, and she suggested that this is one of the reasons why there is so little documentation about this period. She stressed that it was about lived experience, about doing things which, if described, might give the wrong image and create misunderstandings. She said that it was like being on a boat on the ocean with everything one needed on board. She added that during this period of her life she felt so far away from quotidian reality that reintegrating "normal life" after this experience had required quite a bit of readjustment. She then remarked that she had never been on good terms with normal life anyway, especially in her youth prior to engaging in these experiments, so that, to some extent, she had always been searching for another way, a quest which continues to this day.

MEETING IN SARDINIA

The conversations I had with the seven women who gathered again in Sardinia a year after our meetings in Poland helped me to further understand

182　*Grotowski, Women, and Contemporary Performance*

Figure 4.3 Meeting in Sardinia, Italy, August 2010 (seated, left to right: Stefania Gardecka, Virginie Magnat, Ewa Benesz, Danuta Ciechowicz-Chwastniewska, Jana Pilatova; standing, left to right: Elżbieta Manthey, Karina Janik, Marianne Ahrne, Dominika Laster, Daniela Marcello, Inka Dowlasz; rear: Stéphane Lucca, Robert Ornellas)—photo by Celeste Taliani.

the significance of the post-theatrical experiments for the young people who had come into contact with Grotowski's work during the period known as Active Culture. This group of seven was composed of Gardecka, Benesz, Jana Pilatova, a Czech artist-scholar who is a full professor at the Prague Academy of Performing Arts, Marianne Ahrne, a writer and film-maker based in Sweden, Inka Dowlasz, a theatre director and teacher who works in Krakow, Elżbieta Manthey, who directs the *Agencja Dramatu i Teatru* in Warsaw, and Danuta Ciechowicz-Chwastniewska, a therapist and special needs educator who works in northern Poland. Dominika Laster, who was born in Wroclaw and holds a Ph.D. in Performance Studies from New York University, was an important collaborator during this meeting given her expertise as a Grotowski scholar. She kindly accepted to serve as our interpreter, while Robert Ornellas, my long-time research associate, made daily rounds to nearby villages in search of fresh food items that Daniela Marcello prepared with Sardinian culinary savoir-faire. Everyone was determined to make the most of our five days together and we had a busy schedule consisting of semi-structured group discussions as well as informal individual interviews with each woman, which were all documented on video by Celeste Taliani. Recurring themes in our discussions included the final Laboratory Theatre production, the paratheatrical period, and the Theatre of Sources.

MARIANNE AHRNE

Marianne Ahrne, who was a close friend of Grotowski, shared her experience of her first encounter with him during a work session he led with Cieslak at the Odin Teatret in Denmark in 1967. After suffering from a concussion when attempting to perform a difficult physical exercise on the final day, Ahrne was told that Grotowski wanted to speak with her. She was surprised when instead of being critical the Polish director said that he had noticed she was working as if she wanted to get a good grade from a master or be accepted by an implacable judge. He added that it was something he had often observed in women's approach to the work, and stressed that one needed to work for the thing in itself. Ahrne specified that in this particularly challenging work session, participants would drop out every day until only a few remained at the end, and she said that she would have rather died than given up, so that her attitude resembled that of a kamikaze. She acknowledged that, to some extent, she did work hard in order to be accepted, a need which she felt was linked to her personal history, and explained that her mother, who became pregnant but did not want to have a child, left her infant daughter in the care of her grandparents, and Ahrne grew up without parental love. She said that Grotowski had sensed that in her, and when she had told him that her dream was to become a writer, he had rejected her request to be considered to work at the Laboratory Theatre and had encouraged her instead to follow her desire to write. Ahrne explained that it was the first time that someone had believed in her abilities, which had helped her to pursue what she most deeply desired. She observed that writing had also been a way of overcoming the need to be accepted.

Ahrne stated that Grotowski had become a life-long friend and that she often helped him when he was working on texts and translations. She shared several stories about her friendship with him, portraying Grotowski as someone who, in spite of the seriousness with which he treated his work, had a distinctive sense of humor and could be quite playful. She recounted that she particularly enjoyed the strange and wonderful demands he made of people, which constantly required them to do the impossible. He would, for example, send her an unsigned telegram indicating a place and a date without any other details, which was a way of challenging her to find him—and she always did. They shared an on-going joke about her being a witch, and she said that although she felt she had absolutely no talent for magic she was convinced that Grotowski himself was a great sorcerer, and that in his presence her attempts at achieving the impossible most often succeeded.

JANA PILATOVA

Jana Pilatova also shared her experience of working with Grotowski when she was young. In 1968, she was an international *stagiaire* at the Laboratory Theatre and had the opportunity to witness the early rehearsals that led to the creation of *Apocalypsis cum figuris*. In her book titled *Hnízdo Grotowského—Na Prahu Divadelní Antropologie (Grotowski's Nest—On the Threshold of Theatre Anthropology)*, Pilatova recalls that there was discipline and precision in everything at the Laboratory Theatre, from the call time for work to centimeters in set design, from the precision of physical movement to the cleanliness of floors and the clarity of speech. During my interview with Pilatova, she explained that since there was only one workspace, one changing room, and one small office at the Laboratory Theatre, training sessions, rehearsals, and performances took place in the same space shared by the actors and the *stagiaires*, a space that was used fourteen to eighteen hours a day. She noted that the very conditions in which the work took place made life at the Laboratory Theatre particularly intense and stimulating.

In her book, Pilatova describes aspects of the training which help performers to trust their body and foster a heightening of perception. She provides the example of the exercise called "The Tiger," in which the goal is to jump over a partner into a roll. The partner, however, changes their position at the very moment of take-off, to try to surprise the person who is jumping over them. Although there is no time to think about how best to jump so as to avoid hurting oneself or one's partner, she remarks that during her six months of apprenticeship no one was ever injured. She specifies that, in a split second, one has to cross the limits of caution and jump with the same decidedness one uses in the run-up. She infers from this experience that an impulsive reaction, if it is wholehearted, is more reliable and thus safer than a calculated reaction. However, she points out that having the courage to jump must not be confused with sheer risk-taking, or what Ahrne described as a kamikaze-like attitude. Pilatova observes that the purpose of this exercise lies in not stopping the correct reaction, and in experiencing the flight through the air with open eyes, so as to see one's partner and the world spinning during the somersault. She adds that one must then immediately run for the next jump. She concludes that this exercise helps one to learn that in moments of greatest intensity requiring total focus, one must remain open.

While she was a *stagiaire*, Pilatova saw *The Constant Prince* about thirty times, and she told me that this piece was incredibly important to her because it conveyed the sense that it is impossible to enslave someone if that person does not allow it, something which she said had stayed with her and enabled her to survive the twenty-one years of occupation in Czechoslovakia that began shortly after she returned home from her internship. When I asked Pilatova whether she could tell me about the larger context of her experience of 1968 Poland in relation to the political situation of the time, she recounted a particularly powerful performance of *The Constant Prince*. She specified that this piece was structured in such a way that tension kept building until it reached its peak during Cieslak's last monologue, and that, afterwards, his entire body would shake until the closing image, when he finally lay still, covered by a large piece of red cloth. She recalled that in this particular performance, however, the opening scenes were already of a very high level of intensity, and this intensity kept rising higher and higher, so that after Cieslak's last monologue, a seemingly uncontrollable tremor took over his body. She said that the audience members watched in absolute silence and that almost everyone wept. The tremor would not stop, and Grotowski finally had to gesture for everyone to leave.

Pilatova stated that it was only later, for the anniversary of the March 1968 events in Poland, that detailed information about what took place day by day in various cities across Poland became available, and when she checked her notes she noticed that the day on which this memorable performance of *The Constant Prince* took place, Grotowski had told the *stagiaires* not to leave the theatre and to go straight home in the evening after the performance because there was something terrible happening. When reviewing the dates of her notes, she realized that this particular performance, which she felt was the most powerful she had seen, took place on the day police forces and army tanks entered Wroclaw to suppress protests against the regime.

These protests had begun in Warsaw when the authorities closed a production of Mickiewicz's *Dziady* (*Forefathers' Eve*) directed by Kazimierz Dejmek at the National Theatre. Interestingly, Grotowski based one of the early productions of the Theatre of Thirteen Rows on this text, and his version of *Dziady* was described by theatre critic Tadeusz Kudliński as a "dialectic of derision and apotheosis"[2] which can be said to prefigure the later works of the Laboratory Theatre. Grotowski's irreverent staging was deemed especially provocative because Mickiewicz's text, which addresses the Russian partitioning of Poland and the issue of independence, is generally considered by Poles to be a quasi-sacred work of art which defines their nation. The Romantic period in Polish literature, which began in the early nineteenth century, is characterized by a deep yearning for cultural freedom and by the development of national and folk themes. Mickiewicz, who lived in exile, is considered to be one of the main proponents of Polish Romantic Messianism, which informed the Polish people's quest for independence (Lerski, *Historical Dictionary of Poland* 103, 117). Pilatova remarked that the history of the various productions of *Dziady* shows that each staging of this text provides an insight into the political life of the country and reveals how Polish society envisions its cultural identity at a particular moment in time.

Pilatova told me that she had the opportunity to see Dejmek's production of *Dziady* in Warsaw prior to its being banned, and she said that it was attended by about one thousand spectators who were intensely focused and absolutely silent. She recalled that when the well-known actor Gustaw Holoubek, who played the part of Gustaw-Konrad, delivered the famous line: "*Zemsta, zemsta, zemsta na wroga Z Bogiem lub choćby mimo Boga!*" ("Revenge, revenge, revenge on the enemy, with God and even in spite of God!"), the entire audience was suddenly uplifted by national fervor. The production had such an impact that the authorities deemed it anti-Soviet and shut it down after only fourteen performances. Fights over the banning of this production began, which led to a wave of student protest that spread to other cities, including Wroclaw, and Pilatova said that workers joined the protests because the closing of *Dziady* in Warsaw became a pretext to protest against the authorities.

Not only did the government send the police and the army to break the protests, but it also redirected the energy of these events, turning Polish nationalism against the Jewish community, who was said to have incited these riots. Pilatova stated that the regime's political maneuver unfortunately succeeded and this resurgence of anti-Semitism resulted in a large exodus of the Polish Jews who had survived the second world war. She inferred that whereas Polish Messianism had fostered a vision of the Polish people as the Liberator, the disastrous outcome of these events turned the Liberator into the Occupier. Pilatova concluded that placing Cieslak's particularly powerful performance within this historical context had helped her to grasp the political significance of the Laboratory Theatre's work in Poland.

The interrelation of Polish culture, history, and politics within Grotowski's work along with his critical stance on organized religion and his interest in spiritual traditions and ritual practices are arguably the most complex yet most pivotal aspects of his contribution to contemporary performance practice and research. Even in the relatively well-documented period of theatre productions, the culturally specific nature of the creation and reception of Laboratory Theatre performances makes the impact of his work particularly difficult to assess. Grotowski himself emphasized in his third Collège de France lecture that it was very important to understand the extent to which this type of approach challenged the Polish reality of the times. He specified that the work of the Laboratory Theatre broke all the rules of the game upheld by conventional theatre, and that the group's accomplishments were initially disowned by the majority of Polish theatre artists, although there was a small minority of established actors and directors who were extremely interested in the Laboratory's undertakings and became very close allies. Grotowski added that this alternative approach was not only abhorred by the authorities because it went against State doctrine, but was also considered heretical by the Polish Catholic Church, which condemned it as shockingly offensive. He stressed that the Laboratory Theatre was therefore attacked on three fronts: the theatre community, the State, and the Church, a situation which he viewed as a catalyst for the company since it induced its members to develop a very strong sense of solidarity in the face of these constant attacks, and to keep inner conflicts invisible to outside observers. Grotowski described the members of the Laboratory Theatre as an explosive group made up of rebellious outcasts, akin to a gang of anarchists with uncompromising discipline, and remarked that while the company appeared unassailable from the outside, there were often confrontations between individuals within the group, and that, in addition to this inner tension, the company was constantly threatened by outside political pressures.

Grotowski's guidance of the group's creative process was not limited to the daily training and extensive rehearsal periods, but also entailed attending every public performance by the Laboratory Theatre as a spectator and a witness to the Polish audiences' reactions. Grotowski explained that he sensed, along with other Polish spectators, that there was indeed something shocking about these performances, and he wondered whether that might open a door that had been closed before and possibly free what he called "the Polish tribe" from some of the lies in which the members of this cultural community had believed, thereby offering another perspective. He felt that he had to be present to sense what was happening within the audience, including himself, and each one of his colleagues. He experienced this process as a journey that led to the break-down of their own conditioning with its in-built limitations, the uncovering of the hypocrisy linked to the acting out of a history experienced as a "tribal" story that enabled Polish people to save face, and the discovery of a genuine human situation that needed to be explored. Grotowski remarked that the actors had to mobilize associative motivations deeply rooted in their personal lives and memories, and stated that it was this aspect of the work which constituted a common ground, or shared space, between him and his colleagues. He concluded that it was within this vast territory that they engaged in a confrontation with their metaphysical, religious, and "tribal" traditions, in a situation of utmost political tension, so that what emerged from the work was extremely powerful.

To provide a tangible example, the Polish director pointed to the passage in *The Constant Prince* during which Cieslak's body becomes the body of Christ that the others literally consume while chanting the sacred incantation of the communion. Grotowski observed that because this was accomplished in a very serious manner, without ridiculing this ritual practice, it summoned positive associations connected to Polish people's relationship to religion, yet, at the same time, devouring the holy body was experienced as a very blasphemous action. He recalled that the tension thus created between the recognition of the sacred and a sense of blasphemy produced a kind of inner trembling within the actors, the spectators, and within the Polish director himself.

Whereas watching the film footage of *The Constant Prince* can provide an insight into what such an experience must have been like, the film documenting *Apocalypsis cum figuris* was shot in circumstances which everyone at the Laboratory Theatre considered to be detrimental to the representation of this performance. However, witnessing *Apocalypsis* has left traces in the body memory of the women with whom I spoke in Sardinia, and the influence exerted by this final piece is tangible in their testimonies. In my interview with Pilatova, she stressed that, as with *The Constant Prince*, she had been deeply marked by *Apocalypsis*. Her apprenticeship gave her an insight into the early creative process underlying the creation of the Laboratory Theatre's final production, because the *stagiaires* were allowed in the workspace during preliminary rehearsals. Grotowski would at times invite them to share their impressions, and when he asked Pilatova what she felt was at the heart of the piece, she spoke about a particular scene that she still remembers very clearly to this day. She specified that in this scene, which immediately followed what she referred to as the Calvary scene, the actors and the *stagiaires* embodied a crowd which begged, cried, and beseeched in an increasingly aggressive way. She said that it was a very shocking scene, and that, in the midst of chaos, Maja Komorowska as Veronica crossed to the Beloved, raised the edges of her dress revealing her legs, and softly caressed his face with the garment. Pilatova told me that she still shivers when remembering this image because there was something particularly powerful about Komorowska's action which created a moment of complete calm within the madness of the scene, as if in the eye of a tornado. She sensed that Grotowski agreed that this scene was the heart of the piece, and although there was something cruel and merciless about it, Pilatova felt that the point was to show that such a moment of love and compassion, set against this violent background, could actually appear in the world, and she said that it had meant a lot to her.

Pilatova recalled that when she finally saw the Laboratory Theatre perform this piece in public she was shaken by the resonances it had for her. She acknowledged that she cried for a long time afterwards, and linked this strong reaction to her personal circumstances in occupied Czechoslovakia, observing that *Apocalypsis* had led her to confront something which was quite painful and which had to do with people's inability to bear the weight of their own freedom. In her book, Pilatova suggests that Grotowski was able to catch in the air and from the depths of the life around him the symptoms of the upcoming crisis which struck the world in 1968. She notes that, from her perspective, the subject of that crisis was the fight for freedom she experienced in her country, which she considers to be a matter of liberty and impotence, and relates to the tasks she encountered every day while working with Grotowski.

Reflecting upon her experience at the Laboratory Theatre, Pilatova asserts that it immunized her organism and remarks that while some might think that Grotowski was too demanding, he did not expect from anybody more than he expected from himself. She further contends that Grotowski could sense fear, conformism, and idleness from a great distance, and explains that during her apprenticeship she became convinced that searching for possibilities when all options seemed foreclosed was what enabled her to become open and creative, and infers that this kind of confrontation with what appeared to be impossible led her to discover resources and abilities within herself of which she had previously been unaware.

When speaking to me about her interpretation of *Apocalypsis*, Pilatova traced some of the associations generated by the tension between the textual montage and the actions of the actors to the sources with which they had been working. These sources included the chapter entitled "The Grand Inquisitor" in Dostoyevsky's *The Brothers Karamazov*, as well as *Doctor Faustus* by Thomas Mann, which placed the Faust legend within the context of wartime Berlin. In Mann's novel, the composer Adrian Leverkühn makes a pact with the devil and exchanges his soul against creative genius, which enables him to compose his greatest work titled "Apocalypsis cum figuris." Pilatova emphasized that when writing this novel Mann had benefited from the guidance of philosopher and music critic Theodor Adorno, whose question "Is art possible after Auschwitz?" she felt informed the Laboratory Theatre's final creation, because she sensed that the making of this piece had been a way for Grotowski and his actors to fight for their soul.

This struggle was discussed by Grotowski when he spoke about the creation of *Apocalypsis cum figuris* in great detail during his eighth Collège de France lecture. He explained that after their artistic competence had reached its peak with the production of *The Constant Prince*, the members of the Laboratory Theatre had been confronted with their own technical perfection, the temptation to merely repeat the symptoms of organicity, and the impossibility of making new discoveries. Grotowski stressed the fact that as long as one is struggling to surmount technical obstacles, the work is continually enlivened by the need to find practical solutions and thus becomes richer in new possibilities. He stated that it is necessary to keep searching, because if one believes one has found the answer, then the process is interrupted and the research turns into doctrine. *Apocalypsis cum figuris* hence developed out of the company's vital need to question its own process.

Grotowski suggested that what was conveyed through this piece was the ultimate risk one may be compelled to take in order to remain true to one's most intimate, innate sense of freedom. He remarked that both the process which led to the creation of *Apocalypsis* and the content of this piece were connected to the renunciation of all that might prevent one from being fully alive. This included the disavowal of organized religion which, in Grotowski's experience, provided individuals with spiritual comfort and certainty in exchange for their unconditional obedience. He specified that "The Grand Inquisitor" in *The Brothers Karamazov* constituted one of the founding elements of *Apocalypsis*. Grotowski's interpretation of this text was that it highlighted the opposition between what Jesus proposed—in Grotowski's understanding of the Gospels which he traced back to his childhood, Jesus was a human hero who acted as a free man and dared others to do the same—and what the Church imposed upon its followers, namely, the abdication of the freedom to which men are originally condemned. He stressed that, in Dostoyevsky's view, the ulterior motive of the leaders of the Church was to claim responsibility for guiding all mankind, thus superseding Jesus and assuming omnipotence.

Indeed, when addressing Jesus upon his Second Coming, the Grand Inquisitor declares:

> I tell you, man has no preoccupation more nagging than to find the person to whom that unhappy creature may surrender the gift of freedom with which he is born. But only he can take mastery of people's freedom who is able to set their consciences at rest. [...] Instead of taking mastery of people's freedom, you have increased that freedom even further! Or did you forget that peace of mind and even death are dearer to man than free choice and the cognition of good and evil? [...] You did not come down from the cross when they shouted to you, mocking and teasing you: 'Come down from the cross and we will believe that it is You.' You did not come down because again you did not want to enslave man with a miracle and because you thirsted for a faith that was free, not miraculous. [...] We corrected your deed and founded it upon *miracle, mystery,* and *authority.* [...] Yes, we shall make them work, but in their hours of freedom from work we shall arrange their lives like a childish game, with childish songs, in chorus, with innocent dances. [...] Quietly they will die, quietly they will fade away in your name and beyond the tomb will find only death. But we shall preserve the secret and for the sake of their happiness will lure them with a heavenly and eternal reward. (292, 295, 298)

Grotowski made clear that there was great risk in accepting the freedom to which Dostoyevsky was alluding, yet the Polish director posited that risk-taking was intrinsic to artistic work.

Pilatova herself recalled that she had experienced *Apocalypsis* as a moment of complete honesty, and she observed that audience members remained seated after the performance was over, as if no longer able to move. She wondered how Grotowski himself could go on from there and what the Laboratory Theatre could possibly propose to these people: after all, no matter how deeply they were affected by the performance, spectators could not sit there eternally, even though they seemed to want to do so. She explained that, at times, after having washed and dressed in the changing room, the actors would come back into the performance space to speak to the members of the audience who had stayed behind, and it eventually became clear that these were people that they wanted to meet in a different way, which was precisely the reason why a new path had opened up—the path leading to paratheatre.

Pilatova suggests in her book that perhaps Grotowski was dangerous because he was teaching freedom. Linking freedom to risk-taking, she highlights two fundamental features of Poor Theatre: its orientation towards effort and its focus on crisis. She argues that comfort and absence of conflict are sterile both in life and in theatre, pointing out that a child who does not risk falling will not learn to walk, and that theatre without risk is boring. She further contends that when disarray and chaos prevail in the world, it becomes absolutely necessary to value precision and to do simple things that are clean and organic. She then acknowledges that it is difficult for her students to understand why, when she speaks about Grotowski, she speaks about cleaning floors, or why, when she speaks about freedom, she speaks about the need for precision. She nevertheless tells them that, in her experience, it is what this work is all about, and that sustaining the relationship between discipline and spontaneity, structure and freedom, is paramount, since without this conjunction of opposites, everything falls apart.

When I asked Pilatova whether she thought that the different periods of Grotowski's research were connected with each other in spite of the break from theatre, she replied that although she might be mistaken, she thought that Grotowski always did the same thing. She noted, however, that times changed and people changed, so that in order to be able to keep doing the same thing he paradoxically had to take a different path. She suggested that, on the one hand, the different names corresponding to different periods were needed to generate financial support, and that, on the other hand, perhaps such labels were necessary to renew the team of people with whom Grotowski worked, as it otherwise might have been difficult for those who had already given a lot to understand why they could no longer participate. Perhaps most importantly, she felt that, irrespective of this periodization, Grotowski always worked in the moment with a particular person and created a situation which enabled that person to break through a wall.

Addressing the transition from theatre to paratheatre, Pilatova stated that reading Grotowski's text "Holiday" in occupied Czechoslovakia had an especially strong impact on her because she knew to what heights Grotowski could take theatre, and was well aware of the price that needed to be paid to take it to such heights and of the unprecedented level of professionalism and dedication required from actors—and now, in spite of their great achievements, Grotowski said: this is not enough. Pilatova had sensed intuitively when seeing *Apocalypsis* that a change was taking place and that other possibilities needed to be explored, and when reflecting on why this transition to paratheatre had occurred, she suggested that perhaps there is something that, ultimately, is even more important than competence.

Pilatova explained to me that as she was conducting research for her book, she was struck by the fact that Grotowski had announced his decision to abandon theatre in New York in December 1970,[3] which coincided with the protests that were taking place in Northern Poland. These anti-regime demonstrations were violently suppressed by the Polish People's Army and the Citizen's Militia, killing more than forty people and wounding over one thousand. She specified that although the Laboratory Theatre was outside Poland at the time, they knew about the situation back home, and she had become convinced that it must have been what had induced Grotowski to put his cards on the table. In addition to the necessity of moving beyond theatre after *Apocalypsis* since there was nothing higher to be achieved in the realm of theatre, it had become clear to him that theatre was no longer necessary. What these times needed was another form of engagement, commitment, and relationship to the creative research which Pilatova felt had always motivated Grotowski's work.

DANUTA CIECHOWICZ-CHWASTNIEWSKA

Danuta Ciechowicz-Chwastniewska, who actively participated in paratheatrical activities as well as in the Theatre of Sources project, told me during my interview with her that she was eighteen when she first came into contact with the work of the Laboratory Theatre through her experience of *Apocalypsis cum figuris*. She recalled that the first time she saw this piece, she felt that although she did not understand it intellectually, it was like a volcano for her on the emotional level. She was especially haunted by the final words "Go and come back no more" uttered by Simon-Peter to banish the Christ-like figure of the Simpleton. She said that she somehow felt compelled to see the performance again and again even though at the time she worked as a teacher in a remote village in the mountains. She explained that Gardecka would send her telegrams to let her know the next date on which *Apocalypsis* would be performed, and recalled that the journey took four hours by train after which she then had to take a bus to reach the city of Wroclaw. She acknowledged that she had seen *Apocalypsis* so many times that she knew the text by heart, yet she stressed that she experienced the performance differently every time she saw it.

Ciechowicz-Chwastniewska observed that when *Apocalypsis* closed in 1980, her involvement in the Theatre of Sources was a very natural transition for her since she found in that experience what she had been looking for in *Apocalypsis* in another form. Having previously participated in the paratheatrical projects known as the Mountain of Fire, The Vigils, and the Tree of People, she took part in the 1980 summer session of the Theatre of Sources as well as in the 1982 session. She foregrounded the differences between paratheatre and the Theatre of Sources by emphasizing that, in her experience of paratheatre, there was no separation between the animators, as they were called during this period, and the participants. She specified that the role of the former was to create a situation in which every person could be at the same level, that is to say, be participant and animator simultaneously. She then stated that one of the main differences between paratheatre and the Theatre of Sources was that in the latter a clear delineation between the participants and the guides who led the activities was reinstated, and that participants were simply instructed to do as the leaders did. She provided the example of the Motions: initially, participants did their best to imitate the leaders, who would eventually point out specific details such as the placement of the feet, the use of the hands, and the position of the head. She indicated that since these instructions were very minimal, participants had to rely on their personal resourcefulness to learn how to fully engage in such precisely structured exercises. In my experience of the Motions under Seyferth's leadership, complete concentration was required to perform the patterns of movement precisely, and while participants who had acquired a good grasp of the different cycles which constitute the structure of the Motions offered to draw sketches to help others to visualize each pattern, I found that what worked best for me was trusting that my body could understand the Motions intuitively.

Ciechowicz-Chwastniewska told me that although she had never enjoyed making physical efforts, the activity she chose involved running through the forest for three to four hours. She insisted that she had no affinity for running, and recalled that while she managed to get through the entire run the first time she tried it, she was so exhausted and in such pain that she became convinced she had failed. When she told Grotowski that she felt she was not strong enough and would not be able to keep up with this activity, he simply gave her the following advice: "Don't think about the fact that you're running, just run." She decided to give it another try and follow his suggestion, and although she said that she wasn't sure how long it took her to overcome her tiredness because watches were not allowed during the Theatre of Sources session, at a certain point she experienced being pulled up by the sky and propelled forward by the earth, and felt that she could run forever. To her surprise, she discovered that she was able to experience this anew every time she participated in this activity.

Ciechowicz-Chwastniewska pointed out during our conversation that whereas paratheatrical activities were directed toward a meeting with another person, so that contact and relationship with others were central to that phase of the work, in the Theatre of Sources participants were by themselves, focused on their own experience, and activities were not about making direct contact with others. She used the analogy of trees growing next to one another, and noted that, likewise, participants had to find an understanding without resorting to language, a form of symbiosis that can only occur when there is no necessity to say or express anything. She specified that there was one required activity which consisted in a meeting with the Haitian group Saint Soleil, and the only task given to participants was to be attentive and observe very carefully what was taking place around them. She explained that this group, led by Haitian artists Tiga Garoute and Maud Robart, was deeply engaged in Haitian traditional songs linked to specific ways of moving, and that participants had to find a way of entering this situation. She recalled experiencing a communal dance connected to a song, and engaging in drawing and painting as part of an activity rooted in Saint Soleil's visual arts practice.

As with Seyferth's experience of the Mountain project, Ciechowicz-Chwastniewska stayed for the entire three-month duration of the first Theatre of Sources summer session. She was then invited by Grotowski to participate in the Theatre of Sources session that took place in 1982 and involved a small group of participants who were all Polish. In contrast with the previous session, every day was structured in the same way for the entire eight-week period. Grotowski would engage in communal conversations with participants, and every two or three days he would meet individually with each person. She recounted that sometimes these individual conversations took up to three or four hours, and that there was such attentiveness, such internal focus and concentration during the Theatre of Sources that after a four-hour conversation with Grotowski she would be able to write down word for word what had been said. She remarked that never before or since had she experienced such clarity, and stressed that it was fostered not only by Grotowski but also by the conditions in which all this took place. She emphasized that, apart from these communal and individual conversations, silence was part of these particular conditions because not speaking fostered a quiet sense of focus that enabled people to be with their own self and discover the untapped capabilities that lie within everyone. After eight weeks without verbal communication or socializing she felt that she knew the participants much more deeply than if they had spoken with her for many hours. She suggested that this was a way of being clean from external things, and added that what was most distinctive and significant about the Theatre of Sources was that each person had the opportunity to be immersed in *doing* and to remain completely undisturbed while engaged in precise yet non-daily actions, so that it became possible to fully commit to these actions without any sense of shame or embarrassment.

I asked Ciechowicz-Chwastniewska whether she thought that these experiences had had a tangible influence on the way in which she had lived her life. She replied by explaining that she came from a very traditional family and that her path had been clearly laid out for her by her parents. When she came into contact with Grotowski's work, she was struggling with personal problems linked to her circumstances, and discovering new possibilities during her engagement in post-theatrical activities had helped her to choose the right path for herself. She specified that Grotowski was interested in her decision to teach in a remote mountain village where the local highlanders employed a derogatory name to designate people who were not part of their community, so that it took a very long time for her to become accepted. She had told Grotowski about the challenges she encountered in her everyday life with the villagers, and recounted that one morning he had appeared on her doorstep accompanied by one of his collaborators and had announced that he had come to check how she was doing. Grotowski stayed in the village for about ten days, and each day after she returned from her work they would have long conversations during which she expressed doubts about her teaching. Grotowski listened and encouraged her to keep looking for the path which was hers.

She reflected during the interview that although she could have pursued a comfortable academic career, she had decided to follow her passion. She explained that in her work as a special needs educator and therapist, she helps children who struggle with dyslexia to discover that life is interesting, and encourages them to ask questions because she strongly believes every question posed by children should be given attention and considered important, even when adults do not have answers. In her experience, this helps children to acquire a sense of their own self-worth and develop self-confidence, which induces them to open onto the world and become curious about life. She suggested that every person regardless of their age has within them the ability to be surprised and experience a sense of wonder or amazement, and that it is this child within ourselves that enables us, when we are adults, to feel a connection to children.

INKA DOWLASZ

Inka Dowlasz also testified to the impact that *Apocalypsis cum figuris* had on her as a young woman, and told me that after seeing the piece, she had written a letter to Grotowski, and he had replied to her. She quoted a sentence from his letter: "What you experienced in the *Apocalypsis* space is as much yours as what we experienced is ours." She explained that when she first saw the performance of *Apocalypsis* she didn't understand it, and that although it only lasted an hour, after it was over she had the feeling that she didn't remember anything, and that she didn't know where she was anymore. She was affected so deeply that this experience influenced her for many years. She passionately inferred that if a theatre event can have such a powerful effect on at least one person—and she remarked that it had a strong impact on other people as well—then this kind of theatre is important.

Dowlasz also felt the need to re-experience the power of *Apocalypsis* and subsequently became involved in paratheatre while struggling with the plans her parents had made for her. After the second world war, they had created a home for people who were without family and support, and they wanted her to continue their work. This was the reason why she had pursued studies in psychology, yet she said that witnessing *Apocalypsis* had shattered the facade she had been putting up to fulfill her parents' expectations. As she became involved in paratheatre, she felt that the Laboratory Theatre had become the home she was lacking in her own family. Paratheatrical experiences such as The Vigils and the Mountain Project had helped her to quiet her overly analytical mind and had been very nourishing for her. She also realized when working as a psychologist in a psychiatric hospital in Krakow that through her engagement in the Laboratory Theatre activities she had learned that one can approach a person without knowing how. She worked with people who had attempted suicide, and helped them to overcome their difficulties by tutoring them so they could attend university and graduate, and, thankfully, all her patients were survivors.

Dowlasz is now a theatre director, acting teacher, and playwright in Krakow, and in 2010 I witnessed a presentation by her acting students. Their work was very focused, simple, and direct, and I told her during the interview that I remembered that silence had seemed to be an important element in the scenes they had performed. She concurred that it is a subtle thing to which she always pays attention. In addition to teaching acting students in a theatre school, she also directs experienced professional actors, some of whom she said run away from themselves onto the stage because they feel it is a place in which they can safely pretend to be someone else. She stressed that even though such actors might be able to cry on stage, the public remains untouched by their work. She then stated that she had experienced high levels of concentration in paratheatre and that she was interested in ways of creating this kind of deep focus within the actors' relationship to the audience in the theatre. She observed that in the type of theatre work she directed there was nothing to look at, and, indeed, the scenes presented by her students were extremely spare. She concluded that, for her, theatre was about relation, or what she envisioned as a capacity for becoming.

ELŻBIETA MANTHEY

Elżbieta Manthey, who is the director of a literary agency specializing in drama and theatre, shared with me an experience which she said had marked her life. After having been told when taking the Krakow theatre school exam in 1974 that she had a problem with her voice because the structure of her mouth was not well formed for vocal production, she was left wondering how this could possibly be since she had practiced recitation for many years and had even received awards. Having been involved in amateur theatre, she was searching for the right place to study acting when she saw a poster about the Tree of People project and decided to participate. She recounted that this three-week session took place in the main space of the Laboratory Theatre where she had previously seen *Apocalypsis cum figuris* and she felt that it was a special place in which to work. She recalled that the physical training included the *plastique* exercises led by Mirecka, and that participants also took part in improvisations. The last day of the session was particularly intense and ended with individual work on a theme which was not disclosed to the participants in advance. When her turn came, the instruction she received was "You are Mary Magdalene," and as she stood in the workspace she felt as if it were empty and lost contact with the people watching. She then saw a group of men approaching her in a way which she perceived was provocative and she felt that she had to defend herself. She explained that defending herself culminated in a song which did not have words but which she experienced as a song of liberation because it gave her great strength to face the challenge of the situation. She felt as if she was shielded and when it was over it occurred to her that it was her voice that had been the shield. She said that this voice, which she remembers to this day, is what she has been searching for ever since.

Manthey went on to participate in a work session led by Molik and took part in The Vigils in 1975, which she described as a meeting with silence which taught her how to listen. During that summer, she engaged in paratheatrical events named Beehives led by Zmysłowski for the University of Research of the Theatre of Nations directed by Grotowski, and which featured a festival of experimental theatre, meetings with artists such as Brook, Barba, Chaikin, Jean-Louis Barrault, Luca Ronconi, and André Gregory, as well as a series of open paratheatrical work sessions, including Molik's Acting Therapy, Flaszen's Meditations Aloud (*Medytacje na głos*), Mirecka and Cynkutis's Events (*Zdarzenia*), and Special Project led by Cieslak. People came to Wroclaw from all over the world to attend these events, and Manthey described the Beehives as a kind of meeting in which individuals who did not know each other communicated on a different level than that of daily life.

Although her involvement in paratheatre was interrupted by her pregnancy and the birth of her daughter, she was eventually able to participate in the Mountain Project. She recalled that people were moving to the rhythm of drums and songs, there was no script, no theme, and one would throw oneself into the action through an impulse, which she said was like entering a river or the ocean. She felt that time ceased during the project and there was no division between day and night. At some point, she was given the task to go into the forest when it was already dark and wait for someone to come and tell her she could return. She said that it was like a kind of meditation and a meeting with nature. Reflecting on these experiences, she observed that they had shaped her entire life, and still gave her strength today. She added that she felt that it was important to be able to share these memories with others and that our meeting in Sardinia was an opportunity to spend time and interact with women who had different experiences and perspectives. She said this was enlightening because it helped her to better understand her own loneliness. This led me to ask her about freedom, courage, and determination, words that had recurred during our meeting. When I mentioned that women involved in this kind of work had very singular ways of living their lives, strongly believed in what they wanted to do, and followed that path with determination without judging themselves, the sirocco began to gust and howl through the branches of the tree under which we were sitting. Manthey did not respond directly but, in keeping with the spirit of paratheatre, suggested with a smile that the *carrubo* might be trying to tell us something.

POST-THEATRICAL PERFORMANCE AND POLITICS

According to the women with whom I spoke and worked in the course of my embodied fieldwork, exploring performance beyond theatre making became urgent for Grotowski at a very difficult historical juncture, and I would argue that his choice to focus on embodied creativity, relationship to nature, and non-religious forms of spirituality had significant political implications within the context of Communist Poland. While theatre had traditionally played the role of a powerful social forum for Eastern Europeans, as evident in Pilatova's testimony, the violence perpetrated by the regime called for a response that put the techniques of theatre in the service of the community in order to empower its members in a more direct and effective way. Since Soviet totalitarianism and Catholic absolutism sought to systematically preclude what Viola describes as creative agency accessed by individuals through their own embodied experience of spirituality, fostering such agency became key to the Laboratory Theatre's post-theatrical activities. As stated by Viola and expressed in *Apocalypsis cum figuris* through Dostoyevsky's monologue of the Grand Inquisitor, such agency is politically dangerous to the established powers because it is more difficult to control and repress than overt resistance dependent on more conventional means, such as the anti-regime protests that were eradicated by tanks and rifles in 1968. My suggestion that Grotowski's post-theatrical activities constituted a form of political resistance might very well seem paradoxical and counterintuitive to theatre scholars who view Brecht and Brecht-inspired performance models as the only viable way of using theatre to impact the community in a politically efficacious fashion. My contention is that the canonization of Brecht's approach, as with Stanislavsky's, has led to an institutionalization of his legacy supported by a particular construction of the figure of Brecht in which his perspective is defined in opposition to that of Stanislavsky on the one hand, and to that of Grotowski on the other. However, just as I argued that there are important connections between Stanislavsky and Grotowski, I would contend that Brecht and Grotowski are not as radically opposed as has been posited by historians eager to categorize theatre practices according to clear-cut criteria.

It is important to note, for instance, that Grotowski admired Brecht's artistic accomplishments, and in his second Collège de France lecture he recounted seeing Brecht's production of *Mother Courage* when he was a student, a piece which he felt was a great work of art. During this lecture, the Polish director screened the moment during which Mother Courage, performed by Helene Weigel, reacts to the shooting of her son with a highly stylized physical action—the famous scene known as the silent scream. Using this example to speak about form, Grotowski differentiated Chinese Opera from Brecht's approach by observing that in the German director's production of *Mother Courage*, the form was very precisely structured and everything was accomplished by the actors in a way that was overtly dispassionate (he employed the term *froid*, or cold). He then remarked that in Chinese Opera, while the form was also extremely structured, the performers did not need to show that they were dispassionate. Grotowski stated that, unlike Chinese Opera, Brecht's theatre foregrounded this aspect through the work of his actors, whose technique enabled them to hurl images of ideas at the spectators. Grotowski added that although Brecht seemed to be disturbed by what the Polish director described as the actor's inner process, when he saw *Mother Courage* in Poland his sense was that Weigel's work, while never tending towards identification, was not merely empty (*vide*). Similarly, Albahaca told me during our conversations that she had seen the Berliner Ensemble perform in 1965 and found the actors excellent and very alive, although in a different way than Grotowski's actors. This observation led her to point to the counterproductive debates that had famously opposed European academics who favored Brecht to those who defended Grotowski.

To provide an example of the absurdity of such a polemic, Albahaca referred to Ionesco's 1955 play *L'Impromptu de l'Alma*, a mordant satire featuring grotesque renditions of the theorists Roland Barthes and Bernard Dort, two fervent proponents of Brechtian theatre, cast by Ionesco as "*Docteurs en Théâtrologie*" who put on trial the artistic competence of the play's author, whom they publicly accuse of not being Brechtian enough. Originally from Romania, Ionesco was an outspoken critic of fascism and totalitarianism, the ideologies of the Nazi and Communist regimes he indicts in *Notes et contre-notes* and *Journal en miettes*. These texts include Ionesco's provocative critique of Brechtian theatre, which scrutinizes Brecht's rejection of the magic of theatre that operates through affective participation, and which calls into question Brecht's assertion that he does not want spectators to identify with the characters of his plays (*Journal en miettes* 23). In the *Routledge Companion to Performance*, Paul Allain states that "Brecht wanted the spectators to rationalize their emotional responses and to evaluate the stage action objectively in order to ascertain the social foundation of the characters' motivations and their own reactions to these" (30). Ionesco argues, however, that Brecht wants spectators to participate in his plays by identifying not with the characters he created but with his thinking or ideology, so that the latter becomes endowed with the very magic Brecht claims to repudiate. Ionesco extends this analysis to politically engaged theatre makers by asserting that what they desire is to convince and recruit their audiences, which he equates with violating spectators (*Journal en miettes* 23).

Ionesco's recriminations notwithstanding, Brecht clearly remains the undefeated champion of a materialist paradigm which has successfully endured the sea-changes of structuralism, post-structuralism, and postmodernism in the academy. Like Stanislavsky, who has been canonized as the father of realist theatre, Brecht is upheld as the father of political theatre, a perspective whose influence reaches well beyond the field of theatre studies since the Brechtian theatrical paradigm also prevails across the humanities and social sciences in the form of Augusto Boal's Theatre of the Oppressed. Denzin and Lincoln, for example, envision in the *Handbook of Critical and Indigenous Methodologies* a performative critical pedagogy grounded in Indigenous perspectives and in Boal's model of political theatre (7).

BOAL AND FREIRE REVISITED: INDIGENOUS AND ENVIRONMENTALIST PERSPECTIVES

The privileging of Boal by proponents of critical pedagogy can, of course, be attributed to their explicit allegiance to Paulo Freire, since Boal's Theatre of the Oppressed is grounded in Freire's pedagogy of the oppressed as well as in Brecht's Marxist approach to theatre. Boal, inspired by Freire, advocates a post-Brechtian theatre in which the separation between audience members and actors dissolves, and where the "spect-actor" can intervene and change the course of events presented by the Theatre of the Oppressed, the latter being defined by Boal as "a rehearsal of revolution" ("The Theatre as Discourse" 97). In her examination of competing scholarly assessments of Boal's approach, Helen Nicholson remarks that "depending on how you look at his work, Augusto Boal is either an inspirational and revolutionary practitioner or a Romantic idealist" (*Applied Drama* 15). She provides the examples of Schechner's and Michael Taussig's diverging perspectives, with the former identifying Boal as a post-modernist who refuses to offer solutions to social problems, and the latter indicting Boal for being a traditional humanist who believes that human nature has the power to transcend cultural differences (116). Nicholson goes on to suggest that it is Boal's relationship to the work of Freire which is most relevant to "those with an interest in applying Boal's theatrical strategies to pedagogical encounters" (116–17).

From an Indigenous perspective, Boal's relationship to Freire's pedagogy of the oppressed is problematic because of the missionary undertone of its

Marxist-inflected emancipatory discourse, which calls into question the seemingly unilateral integration of the Boalian performance paradigm by social scientists. In "Theatre as Suture: Grassroots Performance, Decolonization and Healing," for example, Driskill articulates a critique of the Theatre of the Oppressed methodology within the context of Indigenous communities based on seven years of experience as an activist. While acknowledging that the Theatre of the Oppressed model benefits from "the radical and transformational possibilities in Freire," Driskill argues that "it also inherits a missionary history and approach in which Freire's work is implicated" (159). Highlighting the alphabetic literacy projects which were key to Freire's activism, Driskill states that "while certainly alphabetic literacy is often an important survival skill for the oppressed, the teaching of literacy is also deeply implicated in colonial and missionary projects" (158). In light of the violent history of Canadian residential schools that severed Aboriginal children from their families and uprooted them from their ancestral culture and native land, Driskill contends that "it makes sense for Native People to be critically wary of Freireian work," and stresses: "[M]any of the concepts that Freire asserts in regards to pedagogical approaches—community-specific models that differ from the 'banking model' of education, for instance—are already present in many of our traditional pedagogies" (158–59).

This critique is furthered by the editors of *Rethinking Freire: Globalization and the Environmental Crisis*, who state in the introduction that, according to Third World activists who tested the pedagogy of the oppressed in their work with specific communities, Freire's approach is "based on Western assumptions that undermine indigenous knowledge systems." C.A. Bowers and Frédérique Apffel-Marglin hence suggest that the emancipatory vision associated with such an approach is grounded in "the same assumptions that underlie the planetary citizenship envisioned by the neoliberals promoting the Western model of global development" (vii–viii). Bowers later contends that it is urgent to acknowledge that Freire's emancipatory discourse is "based on earlier metaphorical constructions that did not take into account the fact that the fate of humans is dependent on the viability of natural systems" and that the preservation of biodiversity and "the recovery of the environment and community" are dependent on a nuanced understanding of the function and value of traditions (140–43).

Questioning Freire's conviction that the individual can and should be freed by critical thinking from the weight of tradition, Bowers argues that such a view is linked to conceptions of self-determination that emerged from the Industrial Revolution in Europe (139). He infers that this kind of individualism isolates members of a society by replacing "wisdom refined over generations of collective experience" with consumer-oriented culture and new technologies upon which everyone becomes increasingly dependent (140–41). Bowers contrasts intergenerational knowledge, which is community-based, with the technology-driven hyperconsumerism that promotes a "world monoculture based on the more environmentally destructive characteristics of the Western mind-set" (145–47). Having specified that he intends neither to romanticize traditional knowledge nor to discount critical inquiry, he provides the example of an Indigenous community in British Columbia whose elders "spent two years discussing how the adoption of computers would change the basic fabric of their community," suggesting that while they were engaged in critical reflection, this discussion was framed "within a knowledge system that highlighted traditions of moral reciprocity within the community—with 'community' being understood as including other living systems of their bioregion" (189).

Finally, in "Red Pedagogy: The Un-methodology," Sandy Grande foregrounds the anthropocentric dimension of Marxism and posits that, while "the quest for indigenous sovereignty [is] tied to issues of *land*, Western constructions of democracy are tied to issues of *property*" (243). She points out that what is at stake for revolutionary theorists is the egalitarian distribution of economic power and exchange, and asks: "*How does the 'egalitarian distribution' of colonized lands constitute greater justice for indigenous people?*" (243, italics in original). Grande further remarks that although Marx was a critic of capitalism, he shared many of its deep cultural assumptions, such as a secular faith in progress and modernity, and the belief that traditional knowledge, connection to one's ancestral land, and spirituality based on one's relationship to the natural world were to be dismissed as the worthless relics of a pre-modern era. While Marx emphasized human agency by invoking the power of human beings to change their social condition, an anti-deterministic view which has greatly contributed to the development of revolutionary movements and struggles for self-determination among oppressed and colonized peoples, Grande concurs with Bowers's critique of Freire by stating that Marxism "reinscribes the colonialist logic that conscripts 'nature' to the service of human society" (248).

While it is undeniable that Boal's approach has been as influential in political theatre practice as Freire's has been in radical critical pedagogy, the absence of a discussion of alternative conceptions of performance and the singling out of the Boalian theatrical paradigm by social scientists results in making it a default position which serves as the sole model of critical pedagogical theatre. I was fortunate to meet Boal during a brief but engaging Theatre of Images workshop held at the University of Southern California in 2003, and I was touched by his kindness and generosity, and impressed by his energy and commitment. I am therefore not advocating Grotowski over Boal, but am suggesting that what Grotowski proposed may open up different possibilities for performance practice and research.

BEYOND THE GROTOWSKI/BRECHT CONUNDRUM

In light of these considerations, I would contend that the Grotowski/Brecht conundrum sustains a dichotomous view of these two major theatre innovators obscuring the fact that both men were left-wing artists from countries which were differently entangled in the two world wars that have come to define the twentieth century in European history. While Grotowski's experience of Nazism and Communism in Poland led him to consider alternatives to fascism and totalitarianism which required him to experiment with theatre in very different ways than did Brecht, his vision of artistic practice within the context of occupied Poland was no less political than Brecht's own conception of theatre in Germany. In "Grotowski's Laboratory Theatre: Dissolution and Diaspora," Robert Findlay discusses Grotowski's work as an anti-Stalinist youth activist and founding member of the Political Center of the Academic Left. In a statement published in 1957 in *Gazeta Krakowska*, Grotowski, who was then twenty-four years old, declared: "We want an organization that will teach people to think politically, to understand their interests, to fight for bread and democracy and for justice and truth in everyday life. We must fight for people to live like humans and be masters of their fate. [...] We must fight for people to speak their minds without fear of being harassed" (in Findlay 182). Two years later, Grotowski founded the Theatre of Thirteen Rows in Opole that was later to become the Laboratory Theatre. Findlay goes on to suggest that the official statements made by Grotowski in the sixties and seventies about the allegedly apolitical nature of his work may be retrospectively interpreted as ingenious smoke screens dissimulating the group's intense engagement in the political life of the country.

Consequently, the differences between Grotowski and Brecht lie more in the way they adapted theatre to the historical, cultural, and social context in which they worked than in their political affiliations, which I would contend were not as dissimilar as theatre scholars have tended to portray them. Most significantly, both directors rejected the conventions of psychological realism and shared the conviction that creative practice must provide an alternative to dominant constructions of reality. While their aesthetics and artistic sensibility were as different as their personal histories, Grotowski and Brecht responded to the complex and dangerous circumstances in which they lived by creating possibilities to resist, oppose, and contest a reality which many of their contemporaries resigned themselves to accept as their fate. As someone who grew up in France, a country whose social fabric was torn between resistance and collaboration during the second world war, that is to say, between two radically different political views of life, I am keenly aware that my culture still struggles with the weight of history experienced as destiny. Radical artistic practices from Dada onward have challenged this form of determinism by destabilizing assumptions that support a class-based, patriarchal, and colonialist social order. This form of productive disorientation can be created through different means, and what I am suggesting is that Grotowski's approach offered means that were experienced to be relevant to the political reality of the time by those who witnessed the Laboratory Theatre performances or participated in the company's post-theatrical experiments. I am therefore interested in how such means might be reclaimed by women seeking alternatives not only to the dominance of psychological realism in theatre, but also to the dominant constructions of reality which prevail in their everyday life and are reflected by conventional realist art.

BRIDGING THE PAST AND THE FUTURE

Conversely to the left-wing progressive European avant-garde artists who were his contemporaries, Grotowski dismissed the idea that his theatre produced anything new:

> I do not think that my work in the theatre may be described as a new method. It can be called a method, but it is a very narrow term. Neither do I believe that it is something new. That kind of exploration most often took place outside the theatre, though inside some theatres as well. What I have in mind is a way of life and cognition. It is a very old way. How it is articulated depends on period and society. [...] In this regard I feel much closer to [the painter of the *Trois Frères* cave] than to artists who think that they create the avant-garde of the new theatre. ("*Réponse à Stanislavski*" 7)

By positing that his conception of theatre is linked to a way of cognition that can be traced back to ancient cave paintings, Grotowski rejects the notion of linear progress, the separation of art and life, and the conflation of creativity with originality. When speaking with the women who participated in the Laboratory Theatre's paratheatrical activities and the Theatre of Sources project, it became clear to me that such a way of cognition was particularly central to the exploration Grotowski and his collaborators conducted outside the theatre. My contention is therefore that making the choice to follow a post-theatrical path in Communist Poland instead of capitalizing on the international reputation he had garnered as a director constitutes a political stance whose impact can only be fully measured when taking into account the testimonies of those who experienced this phase of Grotowski's practical research.

For example, when Seyferth speaks about her work as a member of the international group of young people whom Grotowski entrusted with the development of paratheatre and the Theatre of Sources, she passionately upholds the relevance of this work for today's society. During her talk to the work session participants in 2009 in Brzezinka, she explained that her main motivation for continuing this work and transmitting it to others lies in her belief in people's capacity to sense what makes us complete as human beings. She emphasized the centrality of nature in paratheatre and the Theatre of Sources, and suggested that nature's organic life can help human beings to reconnect with their own organicity and discover deeper aspects of themselves. She inferred that what is most valuable about this work is that it can help individuals to discover that they exist beyond the stereotypes that often seem to constrain and define them.

When I interviewed Seyferth after my work session with her in southwestern France in 2010, she addressed the spiritual dimension of her artistic experience in Poland. She stated that the Theatre of Sources focused on archaic techniques linked to different traditions as well as on re-experiencing the possibilities of "doing things together" on another level than the rational. She pointed out that Europeans had once been closer to the spiritual dimension of nature, and said that when she was in India and saw Westerners in ashrams, it always appeared false to her somehow, because it was not their culture. She then observed that when seeking to reconnect with the spiritual dimension of existence it might be more rewarding to focus on one's own cultural legacy.

I asked Seyferth what she thought this legacy might be for someone from Germany like herself, and she pointed to traces of traditional knowledge, whose holders had included the women who knew the particular properties of medicinal herbs and who were often suspected of witchcraft. She suggested that such traces could be found in the rituals people used to practice in relation with seasonal cycles, harvests, and the equinox. Having noted that in Western Europe rituals had gradually been taken over by the Church, she evoked the ritual practices of North American Indigenous peoples and the ritual traditions of India, in which spiritual relationship to nature is still very much alive. Seyferth also referred to the Haitian group Saint Soleil based in Brzezinka during the period of the Theatre of Sources, and explained that being introduced to this group's work had helped her to understand that the traditional ritual practice of Voodoo was very structured and precise, and that its main function was to sustain a relationship with spirits known as *Mystères* (or *Loas*) who visit people by materializing within their bodies during spirit possession ceremonies. She deplored the fact that the capacity to believe, as Haitian people do, in the life of spirits, seems to have been lost by Europeans.

Believing is such a big force, she noted, adding that, of course, it is not very modern, and it is definitely not scientific. She then countered this notion by observing that ritual practices involving a connection to spirits continue to be valued in many cultures today. I mentioned Grotowski's Collège de France discussion of trance in both Haitian Voodoo and the southern Italian dance known as the Tarantella, with which Seyferth said she was familiar. This led her to remark that the kind of investigation Grotowski had conducted within the realm of performance research was not usually carried out by artists but fell within the purview of academic or religious institutions, and she emphasized that Grotowski worked independently from such contexts. She stated that this kind of research had always been very important to him and could be traced back to his childhood—an influence to which he referred in his eighth and ninth Collège de France lectures as *l'héritage de l'enfance*, namely, the inheritance of childhood. She then remarked that whereas Grotowski was able to continue to pursue aspects of the research linked to the Theatre of Sources during the Objective Drama Project at the University of California, Irvine, where he benefited from financial support that enabled him to invite master performance practitioners from various traditions, he later had to abandon this kind of research due to lack of resources rather than by choice, and she suggested that he might have pursued it further in different circumstances.

We then reflected on the transmission processes connected to this kind of non-academic, non-religious research, and Seyferth, acknowledging the recent passing of Molik, asserted the importance of teaching what she feels are the fundamental aspects of this work, even though very few people today are still involved in transmitting exercises such as the *plastiques* or the kind of paratheatrical experiences that take place in nature. She spoke about her experience of teaching once a year in a theatre school in Toulouse, where most students have no knowledge of Grotowski's work. She observed that these students are nevertheless able to relate to what she teaches and that, while it certainly is challenging for them, they each seem to find something of value for themselves. She stressed that the point of this work is to experience a connection with life as a living force, and that such an experience lies beyond what one already knows, and beyond any system or rules.

As evidenced by their testimonies, the spiritual dimension of the work with nature that characterized Grotowski's paratheatrical and Theatre of Sources experiments has deeply impacted the women who experienced this work either as participants or leaders. The modes of transmission developed by those among them who went on to pursue their own creative research privilege an ecosystemic conception of organic life processes, and their teaching supports a performance paradigm in which embodiment, nature, and spirituality are interdependent. Such a perspective values the type of embodied knowledge transmitted through cultural practices that connect the organicity of the human body with the organicity of the natural world. The spiritual dimension of these practices is foregrounded by Indigenous pedagogy, and scholars such as Smith, Wilson, Meyer, and Absolon emphasize the importance of relationality within Indigenous epistemologies. Favel, whose own artistic work is influenced by his early apprenticeship with Grotowski, Mirecka, and Benesz, makes clear that ceremony is a material way of contributing to the balance of human and non-human sources of life which he views as necessarily interconnected. Sustaining this delicate and often precarious equilibrium is also vital to the work of the artists who have shared their creative research with me, and whose teaching fosters experiential ways of knowing grounded in what I have defined as an ecological understanding of performance, in the broader sense of ecology compatible with Indigenous worldviews. In their search for balance, these remarkable women respond to the dominance of anthropocentric conceptions of creative agency by exploring alternative artistic models which open up otherwise unforeseeable possibilities for contemporary performance.

Afterword

In February 2012, American philosopher and cultural ecologist David Abram was a guest speaker at my university and gave an inspiring lecture about the interrelation of embodiment, nature, and spirituality.[1] Abram explained that air as a natural element is associated in many Indigenous, oral cultures with an embodied consciousness or awareness that permeates the human body through breathing and creates a continuity between the inside and the outside. He referred to the Inuit word *sila*, which shares some of the characteristics of the Hindu term *prana* since it refers to air and wind, and conveys the continuous circulation of the life force that animates the world through a never-ending and ever-changing flux. He inferred that in traditionally oral cultures the unseen atmosphere, by virtue of its invisibility, is often experienced as the most sacred dimension of the sensuous cosmos. He noted that, in the southwest desert, for the Hopi and the other Puebloan peoples, the breath is sometimes considered a person's spirit essence, and that the kachinas, or spirit ancestors, regularly take the form of rain-bearing clouds to visit the land of the living. He honored the inexhaustible complexity and coherence of such traditional worldviews, stressing that for many Indigenous epistemologies, air is an invisible but nonetheless palpable mystery, and hence that singing (and indeed speaking) is a way of influencing and being influenced by the invisible, through the resonance of the sounding body; in traditional oral cultures the power of the human voice is linked to its ability to transform the texture of air, which is what speaks *through* us when we speak.

Abram used his voice during his lecture to give a sense of the way in which breath is transformed into sound, and remarked that in his own Jewish tradition, the most sacred word is YHWH, whose pronunciation remains mysterious because of the absence of vowels, which are associated with the *ruach*, or rushing spirit. Abram stated that it was impossible to represent these sacred sounds until the Greeks introduced vowels into the Semitic invention that we now call the alphabet, and suggested that relying on the vocalized alphabet to write things down produced meaning drained out of air, desacralizing the elemental medium in which we're immersed.

Abram spoke with great respect of the traditional Navajo vision of the cosmos, which holds that the spiralling patterns of our fingerprints and of our toes as well as the shape of our ears reflect the patterns of the wind's action on clouds, trees, and water. He added that listening to one's breathing can be a way of hearing the wind within oneself, and that experiencing mind as wind—that is, experiencing mind not as something held only within us, but as an earthly mystery in which we are bodily immersed—can become a profound way of feeling our deep affinity and solidarity with other animals, plants, and landforms. We are one of the wind's dwelling places, he said. He inferred from his analysis of the connections made between breath, air, and wind in traditional knowledge that conscious breathing is almost always linked to the practice of spirituality, and a primary way of bringing oneself into relation and alignment with the surrounding cosmos.[2]

When I spoke with Abram after his talk and mentioned my research on women who worked with Grotowski, he shared with me the story of how he met the Polish director. He said that, having heard that Grotowski was leading a work session in the United States, he had resolved to try to meet him even though participation in this session was restricted to a particular group of university students. Abram recounted finding a broom near the entrance, picking it up and walking in as if he were a care-taker of the workspace. No one had noticed his presence, and he was able to join the group of students inconspicuously. He then discovered that participants had all been instructed to prepare an action which they were to present to Grotowski. When his turn came, he decided to improvise off one of the sleight-of-hand routines that had been part of his repertoire when travelling as an itinerant magician through southeast Asia. Grotowski was clearly intrigued by this unusual performance, which led to what Abram considered to be a significant exchange with the Polish director.

I was reminded of the creative powers of nature by means of a seemingly magic event which occurred during my seventh work session with Mirecka in Brzezinka in the summer of 2012. I had flown in from the west coast of North America and, due to jetlag, I woke up before dawn on the second morning. I decided to get up and have a quiet breakfast while the others were still sleeping. It was very dark and in order to reach the kitchen at the other end of the building, I would first have to pass through the little narrow room which Seyferth said had been Grotowski's and which opened onto the large cavernous workspace. I entered the darkness, groping for the door to the other side. Once in the workspace, I was walking along the wall to avoid stepping with my sandals onto the wooden floor, when a sudden blaze of light struck the bouquet of roses tied to the central post that served as the axis of the circle around which we sat with Mirecka. This silent explosion of brightness, a stunning theatrical effect, caught me by surprise. I told myself that a ray of the rising sun must have shot through the small windows and hit the roses on the post—but what were the chances of that happening just as I crossed the space? I could see the early morning light seeping in, so I waited in hopeful silence, but small miracles like this only happen once, and nature refused to set the roses on fire again. I thought of the small dark room I had just passed through, where Grotowski's spirit might still be dwelling. Was this a magic trick he had devised to re-enchant this place and challenge my propensity to skepticism by instilling in me a renewed sense of mystery? If so, it was quite efficacious, for I did not understand, but I believed.

*   *   *

"*If research doesn't change you as a person, then you haven't done it right.*" (Shawn Wilson, *Research is Ceremony* 135)

Meetings with Remarkable Women has been a journey, perhaps even a rite of passage, which culminates in this book and the companion documentary films as the material outcomes of my research process. Embodied knowledge is a way of knowing gained through experience, and the holders of this knowledge often teach by challenging the new generation to be resourceful and independent. For the artists involved in my project, this was possibly a way of transmitting to me how they knew what they knew, as women in a tradition dominated by men. They taught me about integrity, courage, and determination. They challenged me to keep learning with care and curiosity, passion and humility, and I have attempted to write respectfully and self-reflexively about the knowledge I was entrusted with during this journey, in the hope of contributing to the transmission processes in which we are all engaged together.

Finding one's own way has been a recurring theme in our discussions, but it was through the work we did and the time we spent together that I realized how much it takes to keep doing the impossible, year after year, which to me constitutes a form of creative resistance that defies societal and cultural norms. I am grateful for my encounters with unconventional and provocative artists who embrace without fear or shame such a challenging approach to performance, and, by doing so in their own way, creatively resist definitions, classifications, formulas, slogans, and other tantalizing recipes for success and productivity that often result in dehumanizing ways of being—ways which we seem to be expected to accept as the only available experience in our increasingly fast-paced existence.

Perhaps it is only when faced with the impossible that we can truly understand what is at stake in being alive today in this world, what resources we need to find in ourselves, cultivate, and transmit, what relationships with each other and our natural environment we must develop, grow, and sustain. For these women, finding one's own way does not mean reinventing the wheel but turning around in the forest to remember where they come from, and drawing from their knowledge of the sources of life—in their own body, in the ground, in the air, and in all four directions. As Absolon suggests, research is a journey which entails much travelling for the body, mind, heart, and spirit—the purpose of such travel being to learn how not to get lost, and to find one's way home.

Landmarks are crucial on this journey, and it is therefore necessary to leave traces not only to be able to find one's way, but also to enable other fellow travellers to do so, including those who have yet to begin the journey. Just as the sustainability of world performance traditions hinges upon direct transmission, so does the artisanal craft which is cultivated by holders of embodied knowledge, whose expertise within their artistic territory enables them to travel in the forest of creativity even on moonless nights. Along with their teaching, they transmit enduring notions of competence, rigor, and audacity. Following in their footsteps and trusting that they know the terrain even in the darkest of times has been more than conducting fieldwork, more than writing this book, more than claiming professional legitimacy based on academic expertise—it has been about remembering where I come from in order to become, somehow, someone's daughter.

The women who shared their work with me have been building bridges towards the future, a seemingly impossible task worth engaging in if we are to find our own ways of linking the shores of creative and critical research across practice and theory, disciplinary divides, artistic categories, and gendered conceptions of the human potential.

Notes

NOTES TO CHAPTER 1

1. This was reported to me by Robert Ornellas, who was in the first group of UC Irvine students selected by Grotowski to take part in his Objective Drama Project.
2. This talk was given by Grotowski at the Brooklyn Academy of Music in New York on February 22, 1969. Leszek Kolankiewicz prepared a text based on the transcription of this talk for the Polish journal *Dialog* in which it was published in 1980 under the title "Odpowiedź Stanisławskiemu." A second version of this talk appeared in French under the title "Réponse à Stanislavski" in the *Journal du Théâtre National de Chaillot* (trans. Maria Berwid-Osinska and Monique Borie) in 1983, the publication to which I am referring here. A third version was published in *TDR* (trans. Kris Salata) in 2008.
3. Grotowski's nine Collège de France lectures took place on March 24; June 2, 16, and 23; October 6, 13, and 20, 1997; January 12 and 26, 1998. I resided in Paris at the time and attended each of these lectures.
4. I would like to thank Jaroslaw Fret and Grzegorz Niziolek for granting me the permission to refer to my series of articles on these lectures published in *Didaskalia* in Polish between 2004 and 2007.
5. Grotowski shared his childhood memories of wartime Poland during his eighth and ninth Collège de France lectures.
6. See http://www.grotowski.net/en/encyclopedia/gitis.
7. Over a period of seven months, Grotowski discussed the philosophical systems of Hinduism, Buddhism, Yoga, the Siankara and Ramanudja systems in the philosophy of Upanishad, the philosophy of Advaita-Vedanta, Confucianism, the Taoist philosophies of Lao-Tse, Chuang-se, and Liet-se, Zen-Buddhism, and European analogues (Osinski 23).
8. To read the entire text of Lester B. Pearson's 1957 Nobel Peace Prize acceptance speech, please go to: http://www.nobelprize.org/nobel_prizes/peace/laureates/1957/pearson-acceptance.html.
9. Caroline (Boué) Erhardt is currently the artistic director of Théâtre de l'Ambroisie; Bertrand Quoniam is the artistic director of Compagnie Odysseus.
10. The members of the project documentation team are: Francesco Galli, Maciej Stawinski, Celeste Taliani, and Maciej Zakrzewski; Chiara Crupi joined the team in 2011.
11. I am very grateful to Manulani Aluli Meyer for sharing with me her text "The Context Within: My Journey into Research" prior to its publication in *Indigenous Pathways in Social Research* (Left Coast Press, 2013).

NOTES TO CHAPTER 2

1. This documentary film titled *Training at the "Teatr Laboratorium" in Wroclaw* was directed by Torgeir Wethal in 1972 and produced by the Odin Teatret.
2. *Acting Therapy* documents a work session led by Zygmunt Molik in 1976 in Wroclaw, Poland. It is featured on the Routledge Performance Archive (www.routledgeperformancearchive.com).
3. Jerzy Grotowski, *Vers un théâtre pauvre*, La Cité—L'Age d'Homme, Lausanne, 1971, 15.
4. Jerzy Grotowski, *Ku teatrowi ubogiemu*, "Odra," 1965, nr, 9, 21–27.
5. Jerzy Grotowski, *Ku teatrowi ubogiemu*, Wroclaw, Institut Grotowski, 2007.
6. Gertrude Stein, "Lecture 3," *Narration*, 37.
7. *Moon and Darkness* was filmed during the 1980 International School of Theatre Anthropology session in Bonn and produced by the Odin Teatret. It is available on the Routledge Performance Archive.

NOTES TO CHAPTER 3

1. The documentary film *Dyrygent* was filmed in 2006 in Brzezinka, Poland, and is featured on the Routledge Performance Archive.
2. Zbigniew Cynkutis's manifesto was published under the title "To Be or to Have" in the Fall 1994 issue of *TDR*.
3. I participated in two work sessions led by Maud Robart hosted by Katharina Seyferth at her Centre International de Recherche et de Formation Théâtrale, Las Teouleres, France in 2005 and 2007. Robart invited me to write about my experience of the first session, which I did in my article titled "Viaggio attraverso lo specchio della tradizione" (Journey through the Mirror of Tradition) featured in *Biblioteca Teatrale: La Ricerca di Maud Robart* BT 77 (January–March 2006), the University of Rome "La Sapienza" *Journal of Theatre Studies* edited by Ferruccio Marotti and Cesare Molinari, 121–27. I subsequently invited Robart to take part in my research project, but she declined.

NOTES TO CHAPTER 4

1. It is worth noting that the idea of the fall from God's grace epitomized by the myth of Adam and Eve in the Garden of Eden is not a component of the Jewish faith.
2. This statement by Tadeusz Kudliński is cited on Grotowski.net, along with a description of Grotowski's *Dziady* (http://www.grotowski.net/en/encyclopedia/dziady-forefathers-eve).
3. The text "Holiday [*Swieto*]" is based in part on the 1972 talks Grotowski gave in New York City at Town Hall on December 12 and at New York University on December 13 (*The Grotowski Sourcebook*, 215).

AFTERWORD

1. David Abram gave this lecture on February 15, 2012 at the University of British Columbia's Okanagan Campus, Kelowna, Canada. I am grateful to him for granting me his permission to refer to parts of his lecture.
2. Abram's lecture was based on the two chapters titled "Mind" and "Mood" in his book *Becoming Animal: An Earthly Cosmology* (2010), and the chapter titled "The Forgetting and Remembering of the Air" in his book *The Spell of the Sensuous: Perception and Language in a More-than-Human World* (1996).

References

Abram, David. Lecture. Faculty of Creative and Critical Studies, University of British Columbia's Okanagan Campus, Kelowna. 15 Feb. 2012.
———. *Becoming Animal: An Earthly Cosmology*. New York: Pantheon, 2010.
———. *The Spell of the Sensuous: Perception and Language in a More-than-Human World*. New York: Pantheon, 1996.
Absolon (Minogiizhigokwe), Kathleen E. *Kaandossiwin: How We Come to Know*. Halifax and Winnipeg: Fernwood, 2011.
Allain, Paul. *Routledge Companion to Performance*. London and New York: Routledge, 2006.
Bailleux, Bernadette. Et dedans Et dehors...la voix. Étude comparée du jeu transitionnel du travail de la voix dans la construction de l'identité de comédiens et de psychothérapeutes. Diss. Université Catholique de Louvain. Louvain-la-Neuve: Presses universitaires de Louvain, 2001.
Barba, Eugenio. *The Paper Canoe: A Guide to Theatre Anthropology*. London and New York: Routledge, 1994.
Barba, Eugenio, and Nicola Savarese. *A Dictionary of Theatre Anthropology: The Secret Art of the Performer*. London and New York: Routledge, 2005.
Barbour, Karen. "Beyond Somatophobia: Phenomenology and Movement Research in Dance." *Junctures: The Journal for Thematic Dialogue* 4 (2005): 35–51.
Beckwith, Martha Warren. *The Kumulipo, a Hawaiian Creation Chant*. Honolulu: U of Hawai'i Press, 1972.
Bernhard, Thomas. *Auslöschung: Ein Zerfall*. Frankfurt: Suhrkamp, 1986.
Blair, Rhonda. *The Actor, Image, and Action: Acting and Cognitive Neuroscience*. London and New York: Routledge, 2008.
———. "Reconsidering Stanislavsky: Feeling, Feminism, and the Actor." *Theatre Topics* 12.2 (2002): 177–190.
Boal, Augusto. "The Theatre as Discourse." *The Twentieth-Century Performance Reader*. Ed. Michael Huxley and Noel Witts. London and New York: Routledge, 1996.
Bourdieu, Pierre. *Le Sens pratique*. Paris: Les Éditions de Minuit, 1980.
Bowers, C.A., and Frédérique Apffel-Marglin, eds. *Rethinking Freire: Globalization and the Environmental Crisis*. Mahwah, NJ: Lawrence Erlbaum Associates, 2005.
Brook, Peter, dir. *Meetings with Remarkable Men: Gurdjieff's Search for Hidden Knowledge*. Screenplay Peter Brook and Jeanne de Salzmann. Prod. Stuart Lyons. Enterprise Pictures Ltd. 1979.
———. "Year of Grotowski" keynote address. Théâtre des Bouffes du Nord, Paris. 19 Oct. 2009.
Campo, Giuliano, and Zygmunt Molik. *Zygmunt Molik's Voice and Body Work: The Legacy of Jerzy Grotowski*. London and New York: Routledge, 2010.

Carnicke, Sharon Marie. "The Knebel Technique: Active Analysis in Practice," *Actor Training*. Second edition. Ed. Allison Hodge. New York: Routledge, 2010. 99–116.

———. *Stanislavsky in Focus*. London and New York: Routledge, 1998.

———. "Stanislavsky and Politics: Active Analysis and the American Legacy of Soviet Oppression." *The Politics of American Actor Training*. Ed. Ellen Margolis and Lissa Tyler Renaud. New York: Routledge, 2010. 15–30.

Castaneda, Carlos. *The Teachings of Don Juan: A Yaqui Way of Knowledge* [1969]. Berkeley and Los Angeles: University of California Press, 2008.

Castarède, Marie-France. *La Voix et ses sortilèges* [1987]. Paris: Editions Les Belles Lettres, 2004.

Chaikin, Joseph. *The Presence of the Actor*. New York: Theatre Communications Group, 1972.

Chekhov, Michael. *On the Technique of Acting* [1952]. New York: HarperCollins Publishers, 1991.

Chilisa, Bagele. *Indigenous Research Methodologies*. Thousand Oaks, CA: Sage, 2012.

Clifford, James, and George E. Marcus, eds. *Writing Culture: The Poetics and Politics of Ethnography; A School of American Research Advanced Seminar*. Berkeley: University of California Press, 1986.

Cohen, Robert. *Acting Power*. London and New York: Routledge, 2013.

Conquergood, Dwight. "Performance Studies: Interventions and Radical Research." *TDR* T174 (Summer 2002): 145–156.

Cynkutis, Zbigniew. "To Be or to Have." *TDR* 38.3 (Fall 1994): 50–56.

Denzin, Norman K., Yvonna S. Lincoln, and Linda Tuhiwai Smith, eds. *Handbook of Critical & Indigenous Methodologies*. Thousand Oaks, CA: Sage, 2008.

———. *Performance Ethnography: Critical Pedagogy and the Politics of Culture*. Thousand Oaks, CA: Sage, 2003.

Dolan, Jill. *Utopia in Performance: Finding Hope at the Theater*. Ann Arbor: University of Michigan Press, 2005.

Dostoyevsky, Feodor. *The Brothers Karamazov* [1880]. Trans. David McDuff. England: Penguin Books, 1993.

Driskill, Qwo-Li. "Theatre as Suture: Grassroots Performance, Decolonization and Healing." *Aboriginal Oral Traditions: Theory, Practice, Ethics*. Ed. Renée Hulan and Renate Eigenbrod. Halifax and Winnipeg: Fernwood Publishing, 2008. 155–168.

Dunkelman, Martha Levine. "Donatello's Mary Magdalen: A Model of Courage and Survival." *Woman's Art Journal* 26.2 (Autumn 2005–Winter 2006): 10–13.

Eckhart, John. "Another Sermon on the Eternal Birth." *Late Medieval Mysticism*. Ed. Ray C. Petry. Philadelphia: The Westminster Press, 1957. 186–192.

Favel, Floyd. "Poetry, Remnants and Ruins: Aboriginal Theatre in Canada." *Canadian Theatre Review* 139 (Summer 2009): 31–35.

Findlay, Robert. "Grotowski's Laboratory Theatre: Dissolution and Diaspora." *The Grotowski Sourcebook*. Ed. Richard Schechner and Lisa Wolford. New York: Routledge, 1997. 172–188.

Fiscus, Daniel A. "The Ecosystemic Life Hypothesis I: Introduction and Definitions." *Bulletin of the Ecological Society of America* 82.4 (Oct. 2001): 248–250.

———. "The Ecosystemic Life Hypothesis II: Four Connected Concepts." *Bulletin of the Ecological Society of America* 83.1 (Jan. 2002): 94–96.

———. "The Ecosystemic Life Hypothesis III: The Hypothesis and Its Implications." *Bulletin of the Ecological Society of America* 83.2 (Apr. 2002): 146–149.

Flaszen, Ludwik. *Grotowski & Company*. Holstebro, Malta, Wroclaw: Icarus, 2010.

———. "Grotowski and Silence." *Théâtre en Pologne/Theatre in Poland* 3–4 (2008): 16–22.

Fónagy, Ivan. *La vive voix, essai de psycho-phonétique.* Preface by Roman Jakobson. Paris: Payot, 1991.
Freire, Paulo. *Pedagogy of the Oppressed* [1970]. New revised 20th-anniversary edition. Trans. Myra Bergman Ramos. New York: Continuum, 1993.
Gainor, Ellen J. "Rethinking Feminism, Stanislavsky, and Performance." *Theatre Topics* 12.2 (2002): 163–175.
Gergen, Kenneth J. *Relational Being: Beyond Self and Community.* Oxford: Oxford University Press, 2009.
Ghelderode, Michel de. *Théâtre II. Le Cavalier bizarre. La Balade du Grand Macabre. Trois acteurs, un drame. Christophe Colomb. Les Femmes au tombeau. La Farce des ténébreux.* Paris: Gallimard, 1960.
Gordon, Mel. "Biomechanics." *TDR* 18.3 (Sept. 1974): 73–88.
Grande, Sandy. "Red Pedagogy: The Un-methodology." *Handbook of Critical & Indigenous Methodologies.* Ed. Norman K. Denzin, Yvonna S. Lincoln, and Linda Tuhiwai Smith. Thousand Oaks, CA: Sage, 2008. 233–254.
Grimes, Ronald. "Route to the Mountain: A Prose Meditation on Grotowski as a Pilgrim" and "The Theatre of Sources." *The Grotowski Sourcebook.* Ed. Richard Schechner and Lisa Wolford. New York: Routledge, 1997. 248–251 and 271–280.
Grosz, Elizabeth. *Volatile Bodies: Toward a Corporeal Feminism.* Bloomington: Indiana University Press, 1994.
Grotowski, Jerzy. "C'était une sorte de volcan." Interview. 8, 9, 10 Feb. 1991. Paris. *Gurdjieff.* Dossiers H. Lausanne: L'Age d'Homme, 1993. 98–115.
———. "From the Theatre Company to Art as Vehicle." Trans. Thomas Richards, Michel A. Moos, and Jerzy Grotowski. *At Work with Grotowski on Physical Actions.* New York: Routledge, 1995. 115–135.
———. "Holiday [Swieto]: The Day that is Holy." Trans. Boleslaw Taborski. *TDR* T-58 (June 1973): 113–135. Alternate version published in *The Grotowski Sourcebook.* Ed. Richard Schechner and Lisa Wolford. London and New York: Routledge, 1997. 215–225.
———. "Ce qui fut."*"Jour Saint" et autres textes.* Paris: Gallimard, 1973. 43–72.
———. *Ku teatrowi ubogiemu.* Wroclaw: Institut Grotowski, 2007.
———. "Ku teatrowi ubogiemu." *Odra,* 1965 nr 9, 21–27.
———."La Lignée Organique au Théâtre et dans le Rituel." Collège de France, Paris. 1997–1998 (1997: 24 Mar., 2 June, 16 June, 23 June, 6 Oct., 13 Oct., 20 Oct.; 1998: 12 and 26 Jan.).
———. "Performer." Trans. Thomas Richards. *The Grotowski Sourcebook.* Ed. Richard Schechner and Lisa Wolford. London and New York: Routledge, 1997. 376–380. First published in *Workcenter of Jerzy Grotowski.* Pontedera, Italy, 1988.
———. "Réponse à Stanislavski." Brooklyn Academy Conference, New York, 22 Feb. 1969. "Odpowiedź Stanislawskiemu." *Dialog* 25.5 (1980): 118–119; and *Journal du Théâtre National de Chaillot* 11 (Apr. 1983): 4–7. Published in English (trans. Kris Salata) in *TDR* (Summer 2008): 31–39.
———. *Towards a Poor Theatre.* Preface by Peter Brook. New York: Simon and Schuster, 1968.
———. "Tu es le fils de quelqu'un" [You Are Someone's Son]. Trans. James Slowiak and Jerzy Grotowski. *The Grotowski Sourcebook.* Ed. Richard Schechner and Lisa Wolford. London and New York: Routledge, 1997. 294–305. First published (trans. Jacques Chwat) in *TDR* T115 (Fall 1987): 30–40.
———. *Vers un théâtre pauvre.* Lausanne: La Cité—L'Age d'Homme, 1971.
Gurdjieff, G.I. *Meetings with Remarkable Men* [1963]. Eastford, CT: Martino Fine Books, 2010.
Hastrup, Kirsten. *A Passage to Anthropology: Between Experience and Theory.* London and New York: Routledge, 1995.

Hoffman, Michael J. "Gertrude Stein in the Psychology Laboratory." *American Quarterly* 17.1 (Spring 1965): 127–132.
Ionesco, Eugène. *Les Chaises; L'impromptu de l'Alma; Tueur sans gages.* Paris: Gallimard, 1963.
———. *Journal en Miettes.* Paris: Gallimard, 1967.
———. *Notes et contre-notes.* Paris: Gallimard, 1966.
Jackson, Shannon. *Professing Performance: Theatre in the Academy from Philology to Performativity.* Cambridge: Cambridge University Press, 2004.
James, William. "What is an Emotion?" *Mind* 9.34 (Apr. 1884): 188–205.
Joyce, James. *Ulysses* [1918]. Eastford, CT: Martino Fine Books, 2012.
Kartsaki, Eirini. "Repeat Repeat: Returns of Performance." Doctoral Diss. in Contemporary Performance, Queen Mary, University of London, 2010.
Knebel, Maria. *L'Analyse-action.* Adapted by Anatoli Vassiliev. Trans. Nicolas Struve, Sergueï Vladimirov, and Stéphane Poliakov. Paris: Actes Sud-Papiers, 2006.
Kolankiewicz, Leszek, ed. "On the Road to Active Culture: The Activities of Grotowski's Theatre Laboratory Institute in the Years 1970–1977." Trans. Boleslaw Taborski. Symposium on Active Culture, 4–5 June, Wroclaw, 1978. Unpublished.
Komorowska, Maja, and Barbara Osterloff. *Pejzaż: Rozmowy z Maja Komorowska.* Warszawa: Wydawnictwo Errata, 2004. English translation: Agnieszka Bresler and Jacek Dobrowolski.
Kurten, Martin. "La terminologie de Stanislavski." *Bouffonneries* 20/21: *Le Siècle Stanislavski.* Lectoure: Bouffonneries-Contrastes, 1989. 66–68.
Lassiter, Eric Luke. *The Chicago Guide to Collaborative Ethnography.* Chicago: University of Chicago Press, 2005.
Lerski, George J., ed. *Historical Dictionary of Poland.* Westport, CT: Greenwood, 1996.
Madison, D. Soyini. *Critical Ethnography: Methods, Ethics, and Performance.* Second edition. Thousand Oaks, CA: Sage, 2011.
Magnat, Virginie. "Can Research Become Ceremony? Performance Ethnography and Indigenous Epistemologies." *Canadian Theatre Review* 151 (Summer 2012): 30–36.
———. "Conducting Embodied Research at the Intersection of Performance Studies, Experimental Ethnography, and Indigenous Methodologies." *Anthropologica—Canadian Anthropology Society Journal* 53.2 (2011): 213–227.
———. "Productive Disorientation, or the Ups and Downs of Embodied Research." *Researching amongst Elites: Challenges and Opportunities in Studying Up.* Ed. Luis L.M. Aguiar and Christopher J. Schneider. Farnham, Surrey: Ashgate, 2012. 179–197.
———. "Viaggio attraverso lo specchio della tradizione" [Journey through the Mirror of Tradition]. *Biblioteca Teatrale: La Ricerca di Maud Robart.* University of Rome "La Sapienza," *Journal of Theatre Studies* BT 77 (Jan.–Mar. 2006): 121–127
———. "Wyklady Grotowskiego w Collège de France" [Jerzy Grotowski's First Collège de France lecture]. Trans. Grzegorz Ziolkowski. *Didaskalia* 64 (Dec. 2004): 15–18.
———. "Wyklady Grotowskiego w Collège de France" [Jerzy Grotowski's Second Collège de France lecture]. Trans. Grzegorz Ziolkowski. *Didaskalia* 65–66 (Apr. 2005): 85–90.
———. "Wyklady Grotowskiego w Collège de France" [Jerzy Grotowski's Third Collège de France lecture]. Trans. Grzegorz Ziolkowski. *Didaskalia* 67–68 (July 2005): 90–95.
———. "Wyklady Grotowskiego w Collège de France" [Jerzy Grotowski's Fourth Collège de France lecture]. Trans. Grzegorz Ziolkowski. *Didaskalia* 70 (Dec. 2005): 88–93.

———. "Wyklady Grotowskiego w Collège de France" [Jerzy Grotowski's Fifth Collège de France lecture]. Trans. Grzegorz Ziolkowski. *Didaskalia* 71 (Feb. 2006): 89–94.

———. "Wyklady Grotowskiego w Collège de France" [Jerzy Grotowski's Sixth Collège de France lecture]. Trans. Grzegorz Ziolkowski. *Didaskalia* 73–74 (July 2006): 93–97.

———. "Wyklady Grotowskiego w Collège de France" [Jerzy Grotowski's Seventh Collège de France lecture]. Trans. Grzegorz Ziolkowski. *Didaskalia* 77 (Feb. 2007): 114–120.

McGinn, Bernard, ed. *Meister Eckhart and the Beguine Mystics: Hadewijch of Brabant, Mechthild of Magdeburg, and Marguerite Porete*. New York: Continuum, 1997.

McRobbie, Angela. *The Aftermath of Feminism: Gender, Culture and Social Change*. London: Sage, 2008.

Meyer, Manulani Aluli. "The Context Within: My Journey into Research." *Indigenous Pathways in Social Research*. Ed. D.M. Mertens, B. Chilisa, and F. Cram. Walnut Creek, CA: Left Coast Press, 2013. 249–260.

———. "Indigenous and Authentic: Hawaiian Epistemology and the Triangulation of Meaning." *Handbook of Critical & Indigenous Methodologies*. Ed. Norman K. Denzin, Yvonna S. Lincoln, and Linda Tuhiwai Smith. Thousand Oaks, CA: Sage, 2008. 217–232.

———. "Our Own Liberation: Reflections on Hawaiian Epistemology." *The Contemporary Pacific* (Spring 2001), University of Hawai'i Press. 124–148.

Mickiewicz, Adam. *Forefather's Eve* [1832]. Trans. Charles S. Kraszewski. New York: 208/30 Press, 2010.

———. *Pan Tadeusz* [1834]. Trans. Kenneth R. MacKenzie. New York: Hippocrene Books: 2007.

Mohanty, J.N. "The Other Culture." *Phenomenology of the Cultural Disciplines*. Ed. Mano Daniel and Lester Embree. Dordrecht: Kluwer, 1994. 135–146.

Nicholson, Helen. *Applied Drama: Theatre and Performance Practices*. New York: Palgrave Macmillan, 2005.

Osinski, Zbigniew. *Grotowski and His Laboratory*. Trans. and abridged by Lillian Vallee and Robert Findlay. New York: PAJ Publications, 1986.

Oyewùmí, Oyèronké. *The Invention of Women*. Minneapolis: University of Minnesota Press, 1997.

Pearson, Lester Bowles. Nobel Peace Prize acceptance speech in Oslo, 10 Dec. 1957. *Les Prix Nobel en 1957*. Ed. Göran Liljestrand. Stockholm: Nobel Foundation, 1958.

Pilatova, Jana. *Hnízdo Grotowského—Na Prahu Divadelní Antropologie* [*Grotowski's Nest—On the Threshold of Theatre Anthropology*]. Prague: Světové Divadlo, 2009. English translation: Anna Pilatova.

Pink, Sarah. *Doing Sensory Ethnography*. London: Sage, 2009.

Porete, Marguerite. *The Mirror of Simple Souls*. Trans. Ellen L. Babinsky. Mahwah, NJ: Paulist Press, 1993.

Rasmussen, Iben Nagel. *Den blinde hest: Barbas forestillinger*. Copenhagen: Lindhardt og Ringhof, 1998. English translation: Judy Barba.

———. "Letter to Grotowski." *Memorias de Teatro: Revista del Festival de Teatro de Cali* 6 (Nov. 2009–Apr. 2010): 8.

Ricard, Mathieu. "The Habits of Happiness." TED talk. Feb. 2004.

Richards, Thomas. *At Work with Grotowski on Physical Actions*. London and New York: Routledge, 1995.

Schechner, Richard. *Between Theater and Anthropology*. Philadelphia: University of Pennsylvania Press, 1985.

———. "Exit 30's, Enter 60's." *Public Domain: Essays on the Theatre*. New York: Bobbs-Merrill, 1969.

———. Performance Studies: An Introduction. London: Routledge, 2002.
Schechner, Richard, and Lisa Wolford, eds. *The Grotowski Sourcebook*. London and New York: Routledge, 1997.
Sinisterra, José Sanchis. *Tres dramaturgias: La noche de Molly Bloom (Ulises de J. Joyce); Bartleby, el escribiente (Herman Melville); Carta de la Maga a bebé Rocamadour (Rayuela)*. Madrid: Editorial Fundamentos, 1996.
Slowiak, James, and Jairo Cuesta. *Jerzy Grotowski*. London and New York: Routledge, 2007.
Smith, Linda Tuhiwai. *Decolonizing Methodologies: Research and Indigenous Peoples*. London: Zed Books, 1999.
Stanislavsky, Konstantin. *An Actor Prepares*. Trans. Elizabeth Reynolds Hapgood. London: Methuen, 1986.
———. "The Actor: Work on Oneself." Trans. Jean Benedetti. *TDR* 37 (Spring 1993): 38–43.
———. *Building a Character*. Trans. Elizabeth Reynolds Hapgood. New York: Theatre Arts, 1949.
———. *Creating a Role*. Trans. Elizabeth Reynolds Hapgood. New York: Theatre Arts, 1961.
———. *Ma Vie dans l'Art* [1924]. Trans. Denise Yoccoz. Lausanne: Théâtre des Années Vingt, L'Age d'Homme, 1980.
Stein, Gertrude. "Lecture 3." *Narration*. Chicago: University of Chicago Press, 1935. 37.
Stoller, Paul. *Sensuous Scholarship*. Philadelphia: University of Pennsylvania, 1997.
Storm, Hyemeyohsts. *Seven Arrows* [1972]. New York: Ballantine, 1985.
Taylor, Diana. *The Archive and the Repertoire: Performing Cultural Memory in the Americas*. Durham: Duke University Press, 2003.
Toporkov, Vasily O. *Stanislavski in Rehearsal*. Trans. and introduction Jean Benedetti. London and New York: Routledge, 2004.
Turner, Victor Witter. "Dramatic Ritual/Ritual Drama: Performative and Reflexive Anthropology." *Interculturalism and Performance: Writings from PAJ*. Ed. Bonnie Marranca and Gautam Dasgupta. New York: PAJ, 1991. 99–111.
Viola, Bill. *Reasons for Knocking at an Empty House: Writings 1973–1994*. Ed. Robert Violette and Bill Viola. London: Thames & Hudson, 2005.
Wajda, Andrzej. *Wesele* [*The Wedding*]. Stanisław Wyspiański. Screenplay Andrzej Kijowski. Prod. Film Polski, Zespoly Realizatorow Filmowych. Film, 1972.
Wiles, Timothy. *The Theatre Event*. Chicago: University of Chicago Press, 1980.
Wilson, Shawn. *Research is Ceremony: Indigenous Research Methods*. Halifax and Winnipeg: Fernwood, 2008.
Young, Iris Marion. "Throwing like a Girl: A Phenomenology of Feminine Body Comportment Motility and Spatiality." *Human Studies* 3 (1980): 137–156.

INTERVIEWS

Ahrne, Marianne. Personal interview. 28 Aug. 2010.
Albahaca, Elizabeth. Personal interview. 4 and 6 June 2010; 20 Nov. 2011.
Benesz, Ewa. Personal interview. 26 and 30 Aug. 2010.
Ciechowicz-Chwastniewska, Danuta. Personal interview. 28 Aug. 2010.
Dowlasz, Inka. Personal interview. 30 Aug. 2010.
Favel, Floyd. Personal interview. 28 Jan. 2011.
Komorowska, Maja. Personal interview. 22 June 2010.
Manthey, Elżbieta. Personal interview. 29 Aug. 2010.
Mirecka, Rena. Personal interview. 9 and 10 July 2010.

Pilatova, Jana. Personal interview. 27 Aug. 2010.
Rasmussen, Iben Nagel. Personal interview. 16 Dec. 2011.
Seyferth, Katharina. Personal interview. 30 July 2010.

PERFORMANCES

Ester's Book. Perf. Iben Nagel Rasmussen and Uta Motz. Dir. Iben Nagel Rasmussen. *Meetings with Remarkable Women* Festival. Prod. Virginie Magnat and Grotowski Institute. Wroclaw, Poland. 3 Aug. 2009.
Feast of You Shen. Perf. Ang Gey Pin and Dario Valtancoli. Dir. Ang Gey Pin. *Meetings with Remarkable Women* Festival. Prod. Virginie Magnat and Grotowski Institute. Brzezinka, Poland. 4 Aug. 2009.
I, Rumores Silencio. Perf. and dir. Dora Arreola. *Meetings with Remarkable Women* Festival. Prod. Virginie Magnat and Grotowski Institute. Brzezinka, Poland. 4 Aug. 2009.
One Breath Left. Perf. Ang Gey Pin. Dir. Mario Biagini and Thomas Richards. Prod. Workcenter of Jerzy Grotowski and Thomas Richards. Pontedera, Italy. Dec. 2001.
The Night of Molly Bloom. Dir. Elizabeth Albahaca. Perf. Maria Fernanda Ferro. Prod. Virginie Magnat and Grotowski Institute. Wroclaw, Poland. 5 Aug. 2009.
Rooms. Perf. and dir. Katharina Seyferth. *Meetings with Remarkable Women* Festival. Prod. Virginie Magnat and Grotowski Institute. Wroclaw, Poland. 5 Aug. 2009.

DOCUMENTARY FILMS

Acting Therapy. Perf. Zygmunt Molik and Rena Mirecka. Prod. Cinopsis. Wroclaw, Poland. 1976.
The Body Speaks: Exercises of the Theater Laboratory of Wroclaw [1975]. Perf. Ryszard Cieslak. Creative Arts Television. 2007.
Brzezinka: An Introduction by Katharina Seyferth. Cinematography: Celeste Taliani. Prod. Virginie Magnat. *Meetings with Remarkable Women* Documentary Film Series. Grotowski Institute, Brzezinka, Poland. 2009. (www.routledgeperformancearchive.com).
The Dream: A Paratheatrical Laboratory with Rena Mirecka. Cinematography: Maciej Stawinski in collaboration with Rena Mirecka. Prod. Virginie Magnat. *Meetings with Remarkable Women* Documentary Film Series. Grotowski Institute. Brzezinka, Poland. 2009. (www.routledgeperformancearchive.com).
Dyrygent. Perf. Zygmunt Molik. Dir. Tomasz Mielnik. Brzezinka, Poland. 2006.
Feast of You Shen. Perf. Ang Gey Pin and Dario Valtancoli. Dir. Ang Gey Pin. Cinematography: Maciej Zakrzewski. Prod. Virginie Magnat. *Meetings with Remarkable Women* Documentary Film Series. Grotowski Institute, Brzezinka, Poland. 2009.
Iben Nagel Rasmussen and The Bridge of Winds. Cinematography: Francesco Galli, Celeste Taliani, Chiara Crupi, and Virginie Magnat. Prod. Virginie Magnat. *Meetings with Remarkable Women* Documentary Film Series. Odin Teatret, Holstebro, Denmark. 2011.
In Conversation with Iben Nagel Rasmussen. Cinematography: Francesco Galli, Celeste Taliani, and Chiara Crupi. Prod. Virginie Magnat. *Meetings with Remarkable Women* Documentary Film Series. Odin Teatret. Holstebro, Denmark. 2011.
I, Rumores Silencio. Perf. and dir. Dora Arreola. Cinematography: Francesco Galli and Celeste Taliani. Prod. Virginie Magnat. *Meetings with Remarkable Women* Documentary Film Series. Grotowski Institute. Brzezinka, Poland. 2009.

220 References

Meeting with Ewa Benesz. Cinematography: Celeste Taliani. Prod. Virginie Magnat. *Meetings with Remarkable Women* Documentary Film Series. Sardinia, Italy. 2010 and 2011.

Meeting with Maja Komorowska. Cinematography: Celeste Taliani. Prod. Virginie Magnat. *Meetings with Remarkable Women* Documentary Film Series. Warsaw, Poland. 2010.

Meeting with Stefania Gardecka. Cinematography: Celeste Taliani. Prod. Virginie Magnat. *Meetings with Remarkable Women* Documentary Film Series. Warsaw, Poland. 2010.

Meeting with Stefania Gardecka, Ewa Benesz, Marianne Ahrne, Jana Pilatova, Inka Dowlasz, Danuta Ciechowicz-Chwastniewska, and Elżbieta Manthey. Trans. Dominika Laster. Cinematography: Celeste Taliani. Prod. Virginie Magnat. *Meetings with Remarkable Women* Documentary Film Series. Sardinia, Italy. 2010.

Moon and Darkness. Perf. Iben Nagel Rasmussen. Prod. Odin Teatret. International School of Theatre Anthropology. Bonn, Germany. 1980.

The Night of Molly Bloom. Dir. Elizabeth Albahaca. Perf. Maria Fernanda Ferro. Cinematography: Francesco Galli. Prod. Virginie Magnat. *Meetings with Remarkable Women* Documentary Film Series. Grotowski Institute. Wroclaw, Poland. 2009.

Rooms. Perf. and dir. Katharina Seyferth. Cinematography: Celeste Taliani. Prod. Virginie Magnat. *Meetings with Remarkable Women* Documentary Film Series. Grotowski Institute. Wroclaw, Poland. 2009. (www.routledgeperformancearchive.com).

Towards Organic Presence: On the Edge of Theatre—A Work Session with Katharina Seyferth. Cinematography: Celeste Taliani. Prod. Virginie Magnat. *Meetings with Remarkable Women* Documentary Film Series. Grotowski Institute. Brzezinka, Poland. 2009. (www.routledgeperformancearchive.com).

Training at the "Teatr Laboratorium" in Wroclaw. Dir. Torgeir Wethal. Prod. Odin Teatret. Holstebro, Denmark. 1972.

Work Session with Iben Nagel Rasmussen. Cinematography: Francesco Galli. Prod. Virginie Magnat. *Meetings with Remarkable Women* Documentary Film Series. Wroclaw, Poland. 2009. (www.routledgeperformancearchive.com).

Index

A
Aboriginal
  children, 201
Absolon, Kathleen E., 45–46, 54–56, 123, 206, 210
  Kaandossiwin: How We Come to Know, 45, 54–55
academic, "dominant system—", 29
"academic apartheid," 28
academic "division of labor," 28
academy, the
  and embodied knowledge, 35, 37
  gender privileging in, 2
  mistrust of, by performance practitioners, 28
  and the Other, 30, 34
  practice/theory divide in, 29, 35
accountability, of researchers, 31
action. See also Method of Physical Actions
  associations and, 65, 152, 177
  blasphemous, 188
  and The Body Alphabet, 125–126
  Czuwania (The Vigils), 179
  dramatic, 106
  impulses and, 59, 65, 103, 185
  organic, 136, 141
  paratheatrical, 102
  physical, 58–59
    Grotowski's work with, 60, 61, 64–66
    Stanislavsky's work with, 13–14, 19, 22–23, 60, 66
    and vocal training, 120–122
  and the *plastiques*, 75, 121, 124
  receptive, 66
  ritual, 52, 79, 96, 174
  Stein's research on automatic, habitual, repetitive—, 101

Active Analysis, 1–2, 4
Active Culture, 157, 169–171, 183
activists
  Anti-Stalinist, 203
  cultural, 10
  Indigenous, 29, 53, 201
  Third World, 201
Actor, Image, and Action; Acting and Cognitive Neuroscience, The (Blair), 17
Adorno, Theodor, 189
"Affective, active awareness," trans. of *perezhivanie*, 18
Aftermath of Feminism, The (McRobbie), 8
agency
  alternative forms of, 138, 144
  creative
    anthropocentric conceptions of, 206
    of cultural activists, 10
    women's, 5, 68, 144
  of Mary Magdalene, 90
  spirituality and, 168, 198
  voice and, 128–132
Ahrne, Marianne, 50, 182–185
  photo, 182
Akropolis, 50, 74, 83
Albahaca, Elizabeth, 51, 57, 87–93, 102, 199
  Art as vehicle, 93
  and the Laboratory Theatre, 57, 89–92
  as Mary Magdalene, 89–90
  Night of Molly Bloom, The, 87
  and paratheatre, 170
  photos, 51, 88
  vocal training, 123
alive
  being fully (while performing), 13, 75, 83, 101

feeling (in the training), 104, 113, 122, 126
impulse-based actions, state of being, 58–59
prana (breath), 120
aliveness, 23
Allain, Paul, 199
ancestors
  relationship with (in traditional ritual practices), 42, 113
  voices of (in body memory), 129, 146
Ang, Gey Pin, 138–143
  photos, 140, 142
animal
  moving as, 85
  qualities of organicity, 61
anthropology, 29–30, 36, 45
anti
  -regime, 192, 198
  -Semitism, 186
  -Soviet, 186
  -theatrical prejudice, 24
Apocalypsis cum figuris, 89–91, 169, 188–192, 196
apprenticeship, 39, 50, 54
  of Albahaca, 89
  of Favel, 206
  of Pilatova, 184, 188–189
archetypes, 90–91, 94, 176
Arreola, Dora, 148–152, 164
  photos, 142, 149
Art as presentation, 5, 27, 171
Art as vehicle, 5, 40
  and Albahaca, 89, 93
  and Arreola, 148
  and Molik, 123
  period of, 15, 63, 89, 93, 134, 170
  relation to "Art as presentation," 27, 171
Artaud, Antonin, 3, 47, 83
artificiality, 61, 120, 172
aspiration, 121, 171–173
associations, 63–65
  according to Damasio, 20
  connection to actions, 63–65, 177
  in the creative process, 85
  and 'deep work,' 152
  and embodied experience, 83, 143
  and the flux of impulses, 120, 123, 126–127
  linked to conventional social context, 64
  of ideas and images, in Stanislavsky's System, 22

personal, 13, 52, 82, 86, 121, 134
as terminology, Stanislavsky-Grotowski lineage, 63–65
not borrowed from psychology, 64
and training exercises, 75, 104
and women's agency, 68
authenticity, 102, 157–158
awareness
  active, 18, 102
  and behavior, 20
  and consciousness in the training, 71
  and consciousness linked not to language but to presence, 67
  embodied, 23, 67, 143, 207
  of the performer, 45, 77
  as quality of perception, 53
  and sensual maturity, 146, 160

B
Bailleux, Bernadette, 129–132
  Et dedans Et dehors, la voix, 129
balance, 113–116
  alteration of, 37, 45, 104
  between doing and not doing, 98, 103, 136
  between human and non-human life, 53, 165, 206
  between mind and body, 113–114
  and precarious equilibrium, 11, 45, 113
  search for—, 206
  and space, 150
  in vocal training, 135
Barba, Eugenio
  Dictionary of Theatre Anthropology, 159
  non-Western performance traditions, 37
  Paper Canoe, The, 11, 38, 136, 159, 162
  precarious equilibrium, 45
  pre-expressivity, 105
  "thinking in motion," 38, 159, 162
  vocal improvisation, 132
Barbour, Karen, 35, 52, 158–161
  "Beyond 'Somatophobia': Phenomenology and Movement Research in Dance," 35
Bauls, the, 21, 171, 180
Beckett, Samuel, 86
  Endgame, 86
  Happy Days, 86
Beehives, 197
Beguines, the, 168

belief, 173–177
  capacity for, 205
  and encounter with spirit, 33
  and faith, 177
  faith (hope, and love, per Jill Dolan), 158
  and the impulse-based process, 62
  and organicity, 62
Benedetti, Jean, 2, 64
  on Brecht and Stanislavsky, 2
  on Stanislavsky's Magic If, 64
Benesz, Ewa, 51, 93–97, 182
  and the Laboratory Theatre, 57
  and *Pan Tadeusz*, 93
  photos, 51, 96, 175, 182
  working with natural elements, 95–96
  work session in Sardinia, 94, 173–177
Berliner Ensemble, 199
Between Theater and Anthropology (Schechner), 24
"Beyond 'Somatophobia': Phenomenology and Movement Research in Dance" (Barbour), 35
Biagini, Mario, 93, 123
binary oppositions
  familiar/strange and sameness/different, 44
  femininity/masculinity, 165
bio
  -diversity, 165
  -energetic, 129, 132
  -logic, 162
  -logical determinism, 31
Biomechanics, 19, 60
birth
  and embodied experience, 83
  of impulses, 69
  "shared or double—", in actor-director relationship, 83
Blacking, John, 159
Blair, Rhonda, 16–20, 23
  Actor, Image, and Action; Acting and Cognitive Neuroscience, The, 17
  "Reconsidering Stanislavsky: Feeling, Feminism, and the Actor," 17
blasphemy, and the sacred in *The Constant Prince*, 188
Boal, Augusto, 37, 200–202
  Theatre of the Oppressed, 37, 200–202
Body Alphabet, the, 84, 124–127

body
  -in-life, 65, 113–156
    and actions, 126
    Grotowski's definition of, 65
    and the natural environment, 116–117, 156
    and silence, 152
    and voice, 125, 136
  memory, 144, 152, 167, 188
    Grotowski's definition of, 65
    Komorowska and, 80, 84
    Seyferth and, 154
  -mind, 98, 113, 160–162. *See also* dualism
    dichotomy, 19, 35, 165
    Stanislavsky and, 22
    training the, 104, 138
  -voice connection, 124–127, 134, 136, 152
    Ang and, 139
    and cultural memory, 129–130
    implications of, 127
    Molik and, 123–124
    and organicity, 120, 127
    and place, 146
    and traditional song, 143
    and process, 122
Bourdieu, Pierre, 130, 138
brain
  Damasio on the (embodied consciousness and emotion), 19–20
  plasticity, Ricard on, 138
breath. *See also prana*
  and embodied consciousness, 207
  Indian and Tibetan practices, 73, 118, 120, 137
  and the life of the spine, 69
  and voice, 128, 134, 136
  and The Wind Dance, 108
Brecht, Bertolt
  and Grotowski, 198–204
  Mother Courage, 199
  and Toporkov, 2
Bridge of Winds, The, 50, 105, 108, 112
Brook, Peter, 4, 7, 26
  Meetings with Remarkable Men, 4
Brothers Karamazov, The (Dostoyevsky), 189–190
Brzezinka
  Dyrygent, 48
  Forest of, 154
  Grotowski in, 153, 180
  Laboratory of Creative Research in, 50, 74, 164

Mirecka in, 40, 74, 79, 119
and paratheatre, 57, 91
and relationship to nature, 118
Seyferth in, 97, 102, 153, 178
Theatre of Sources in, 180, 204–205
Buscarino, Maurizio, 90

C
Carnicke, Sharon Marie
  and Knebel, 1, 2, 4
  and Stanislavsky, 2, 15, 17–18, 73
  interest in yoga, 3, 20–21
Cartesian dualism. *See* dualism
Castarède, Marie-France, 129
Catholic
  absolutism, 198
  conception of Mary Magdalene, 90
  Mass, 86
  Poland, 91, 187
center. *See also* energetic center
  of the body, 146
centered, state of being, 146
"Ce qui fut" (Grotowski), 60
ceremony
  per Favel, 40, 206
  and research, per Wilson, 30, 147
Chaikin, Joseph
  actor as salesman, indictment of, 8
  the dominance of psychological realism, 5–6
  and Grotowski, 6
  unanswerable questions to do with being alive, 177
chakras, 120, 137, 180. *See also* energetic center
chanting
  in *The Constant Prince,* 188
  and Hawaiian culture, 145
  Mirecka's use of in teaching, 72, 118, 137, 138
Chekhov, Michael, 63–64
children, connection to, 195
Chilisa, Bagele, 54
Chinese Opera, 38, 138, 199
Christ figure
  in *The Constant Prince,* 85, 188
  of the Simpleton in *Apocalypsis cum figuris,* 174, 176
Church, the, 187, 190, 205
Ciechowicz-Chwastniewska, Danuta, 182–183, 192–195
  photo, 182
Cieslak, Ryszard
  and Albahaca, 92

in *The Body Speaks,* 11
in *The Constant Prince,* 24, 26, 73, 85, 185–188
training demonstration with Odin Teatret actors, 70
and Rasmussen, 105–107
and Seyferth, 97
in *Towards a Poor Theatre,* 141
and training, 84, 89, 121–122
Clifford, James, 24
codification, 38, 138, 159–160
cognition, experiential modes of, 28, 127, 145
cognitive
  and leadership abilities, 161, 163
  control and embodied experience, 30
  neuroscience and performance, 17–19, 37
  patterns, alteration of through productive disorientation, 39
  process of performance, 3
Cohen, Robert, 21–23
Collège de France lectures, Grotowski's
  dates of, 211n3
  discussions
    Apocalypsis cum figuris, 189
    "Art as presentation" and "Art as vehicle," 27, 171
    body-voice connection, 120, 133–134
    Brecht, 199
    emotional memory, 19
    energetic centers, 72, 118
    exercises, value of, 75
    impulse-based process, 60, 64
    organicity, 61, 64, 99
    performance, aesthetic and ritual, 53
    physical/spiritual connection, 66
    physical training and relationship to the body, 121–122
    plastique exercises, 68
    Polish historical, political, and cultural context, 187–188
    practice *versus* "playing a game of ideas," 28
    presence as embodied awareness, 67
    second horizon, 172
    Stanislavsky's Method of Physical Actions, 12
    traditional practices, 8
    Vakhtangov, 14
    working with personal associations, 85–86

colonialism, 43, 114. *See also* post-colonialism
  in anthropology, 30, 36
  Indigenous critique of and resistance to, 114–115, 201
colonization, 202
colonize
  academic forays into performance that—artistic practice, 28
Communism in Poland, 7, 114, 198, 203, 204
communitas, 157
community
  intergenerational knowledge in, 201
  Jewish, in Poland, 186
  -positioned narratives, 31
  and research ethics, 30–34
  and space/place, 147
  theatre, in Poland, 187
competence
  of the artist, 10, 189, 192, 199, 210
  Grotowski on, 10, 26, 92, 121, 172, 189
  notion of, 210
  Pilatova on, 192
conformism, 9, 173, 189
Conquergood, Dwight, 28, 34, 36
conscious experience, 17–18, 23, 101–102
consciousness
  "actor's dual-", 3
  alternative conceptions of presence and, 68
  artisanal-, 27
  double or multiple- (of feminist and Indigenous researchers), 43
  embodiment and, 17, 18, 158, 207
  linked to presence by Mirecka, 71
  non-Western conceptions of, 21
  and repetition, 101, 138
  spirituality dismissed as false, 32
  stream-of-writing, 52, 87
  yoga and, 20
Constant Prince, The (Grotowski), 24, 26, 73, 185, 188
contradiction
  productive- (in Komorowska's Tarudante), 85
  specific to the conditions of the actor's work, 18
  technique of, 15
contradictions, law of, 78
conventions, 30, 36, 40
  gendered, 17, 160, 163

of political resistance, 198
of realism, 5, 12, 65, 203
theatre-, forms of
  alternatives to, 68
  Laboratory Theatre as distinguished from, 181, 187
corporeal
  field and embodied condition, 38
  "— life of the actor," 21
  sensations, separation of intellectual processes and, 17
corporeality, ancient, 167–168
cosmic
  center point, 146
  energies, 72
courage
  to enter into the unknown, 11
  and meaning, connection between, 167
  practice of, and consciousness, 54, 56
  and singing, 141
  in "The Tiger" exercise, 184
craft
  the actor's, per Favel, 41
  artisanal, 210
  of the performer, 11
  being credible in one's, per Grotowski, 10
  commitment to, by Rasmussen, 112
  questioning the alleged limitations of one's, 27
  the researcher's, 55
Craig, Edward Gordon, 15
creative, 10–11, 169
  act, the, 61, 75
  independence
    of Grotowski's women collaborators, 5, 68, 163, 173
  life, sources of, 75
  potential, human, 31
    of actors, 22, 62
    Grotowski's investigation of, 9
    of performance, 19
  power, 62
    per Eckhart, 168
  practice (*see also* practice, creative)
    function of, 166
  research, 25, 28, 31
    of Benesz, 173
    of Mirecka, 43, 72, 78
    of Seyferth, 97, 104
    of Stanislavsky, 3
creativity
  conflation of, with originality, 204

embodied, 144, 198
feminist, 17
intuition and, 30
organicity and, 64
training and, 75, 80
vocal, 126, 128, 132
crisis
  ecological, 114
  as focus of Poor Theatre, 191
  in 1968 Poland, 189
  of representation, 36
  spiritual, 53
Crupi, Chiara, 112
Cuesta, Jairo, 150, 169
cultural
  activists
    artists as, 10
  cultural ancestry, 32, 129
  cultural capital, 105
  cultural constructions
    of artistic lineage, 4
    dominant, 4
    of gender, 6, 16, 160, 165
  cultural continuity, 31, 144
  diversity, 165
  economy, female body in market-driven, 8
  identity
    Polish, 186
    sustained through material practice, 115
  knowledge, stored in action, 36, 162
  memory, 94, 129
  policies, Soviet, 1
  practices
    and experience, 53–54
    Indigenous, 40, 72, 145
    literary and embodied, 35, 206
  process, 16, 35, 36, 38, 40
    embodied and performative aspects of, 35
    kinetic understanding of, 36
    psychophysical involvement in, 38
  production, hegemonic modes of, 9
culture(s). *See also* Active Culture
  ancestral
    and native land, 201
  art
    and spirituality as means of resistance, 9
  consumer, and individualism, 201
  denial and repression of the body in Western, 35
  dominant, 6, 8
  European, roots of, 96
  gendered social organization in Western
    and societies, 162
  Indigenous oral, 207
  Indian, influence on Grotowski, 21
  Judeo-Christian, 161
  Polish, context for Grotowski's work, 186
  practicing, 53
  print, institutionalization of, 34
  of research, 54
  women on the periphery of, 9
curiosity, and second horizon, 27
cybernetic approach to acting, 21–22
Czuwania, 179. *See also* Vigils, The

D

daily behavior, 73
  elimination of, 15, 64, 138
  "extra-", 37, 138
  and impulses, 60, 65
  non-, 179
daily gestures, 64
daily practice, 118
daily training, 75, 105, 143, 183
Damasio, Antonio, 17–20
dance
  communal, 194
  contemporary, 148
  improvisation, 159
  Karen Barbour, 159
  modern, 3
  "— of the beginner," 152
  ritual, 96
  studies, 35, 52
  Tarantella, the, 205
  training, Albahaca's, 89
daughters
  illegitimate, women as, 2–6, 9
  and mothers, lived experience as, 83
  "*Tu es la fille de quelqu'un*," 4, 25–29, 32
de-conditioning, 134, 138, 163
Decroux, Etienne, 89, 171–172
Delsarte, François, 69, 74, 124
democracy, 53, 202–203
Denzin, Norman K., 35–37, 200
Descartes' error, per Damasio, 17
detachment, and creative power, 168
determination
  paratheatre and, 170
  self-
    Industrial Revolution and, 201–202

performance and, 105
determinism, 22, 31, 203. *See also*
    biological determinism
deterministic
    dimension
        of Bourdieu's notion of *habitus*,
            138
    interpretation, of James's scenario, 22
    perspective, non- (on performance), 21
    view
        anti-, Marx's, 202
devices, alternative representational,
    52
dialogical model of cross-cultural
    research, 44
dialogical process, 44
dialogism, 52, 161
Dictionary of Theatre Anthropology
    (Barba and Savarese), 159
Didaskalia, 7
dilettantism, 10–11
director-actor collaboration, 83
disarmament, 12
disbelief, 34, 62
discipline, 74, 80, 122, 165, 184, 191
disorientation, 162
    productive-, 37–39, 138, 203
distillation of signs, 15
diversity
    bio-, 201
    cultural, of the Grotowski diaspora,
        165
    of women's artistic practices, 5, 31
documentation
    of Bridge of Winds group, 108, 112
    collaborative, 50, 52
Dolan, Jill, 158, 162
"dominant system academics," 29
don de soi, 24, 62
Dostoyevsky, Fyodor, 189–191, 198
    The Brothers Karamazov, 189–190
Dowlasz, Inka, 182, 195–196
dream
    Komorowska's, 82
    Rasmussen's, 105
Driskill, Qwo-Li, 144, 201
dualism, 17, 35, 39, 165
duchowe, 66

E
Eckhart, John (Meister), 166, 168–169
ecological
    crisis, 114
    health, 116

ecology, body-voice connection and,
    120
ecosystem
    body-in-life experienced as if it were
        an, 156
    natural, 156, 165
    of one's organism, 136
ecosystemic
    conception of organicity, 116–118, 206
    conception of the actor's organic
        process, 120
    balance between all forms of life,
        165
    "— life hypothesis," (per Fiscus),
        116–117
    performance paradigm, 117–118, 147
Elders
    in the Grotowski diaspora, 40, 115
    Hawaiian, 33–34, 145
embodied
    agency, 68
    and empathetic engagement, in
        research, 20
    awareness, 23
    consciousness, 18, 67
    experience, 25
        in Active Culture, 157
        as fundamental aspect of perfor-
            mance, 61
        in Indigenous conceptions of
            knowledge, 53
        James's conception of, 101
        the performer's, 52
        within the research process,
            30–31, 38
        of singing, 31, 144
        of spirituality, 32, 198
        women's, 132, 160–161
    knowledge of Grotowski-based
        training (the author's), 28
    nature of experience, 18
    reflexive standpoint, 16
    research, 50–56
        characteristics of, 39
        embracing first-person narratives
            in, 161
        process, envisioned by Stoller, 39
    embodied ways of knowing, trusting,
        160–165
embodiment. *See also under* knowledge
    consciousness and, 17–18, 101–102
    emotions and, 19
    ethnography and, 30–31, 35–36
    gendered constraints and, 161

impulses and, 59, 83
nature and, 116, 165, 198, 206, 207
neuroscientific understanding of, 19
relationship to space/place, 75, 94
research and, 25, 30, 39, 43, 50–56
spirituality and, 32–34, 157, 207
voice and, 120, 129, 132–138
emotion. *See also* feeling
 feelings, as distinct from, 20, 162–163
 feminist critique of, in the Method, 17, 19
 and physical action, 22, 60
 in Stanislavsky's System, 13, 16
emotional memory, 19
empathetic
 knowledge, 146
 research, 30, 33, 39
 writing, 25
Endgame (Beckett), 86
energetic
 balance, 47, 113
 center, 70, 72, 73, 75, 118
energy
 blockages of, 70
 chakras and, 72, 79
 and dance, 108
 ecosystemic flow of, 117–118, 123, 156
 exploration of movement and, 106–107
 impulses and, 126
 organicity and, 73, 98, 120
 and performance, 11, 77, 79
 in the *plastique* exercises, 75, 77, 84, 103
 of silence, 152–153
 sound and, 134–137
 in training, 98
Enlightenment, 34–35
environment
 the natural, relationship to, 113–117, 120, 147, 206
 perception of one's, 102, 159
 reaction to one's, 19
environmentalist
 critique of Freire, 200–202
epistemologies
 grounded in process, practice and place, 34
 Indigenous, 30, 37, 55, 114, 206
epistemology, Hawaiian, 145, 163
Erhardt, Caroline (Boué), 47, 211n9
essentialism, strategic, 114
essentialist, 3, 16

essentialized, "woman," 162, 165
Et dedans Et dehors, la voix (Bailleux), 129
Ethical
 researchers (as warriors), 56
 imperative, in research, 34
 principles of creative work in the Grotowski diaspora, 104
 research perspectives guided by Indigenous principles, 53
 responsibility of researchers, 55
ethnographic
 authority, 30
 fieldwork
  alternative conceptions of, 39
  alternative models of, Lassiter, 30
  experience as embodied, Hastrup, 38
  Indigenous critique of, 30
  multi-sited, 11, 25, 30
 politics of representation, 30
 texts, performance of, 36
ethnography
 alternative conceptions of, 30, 36, 39
 feminist, 30–31
 performance, 36–40
  Conquergood, 36
  Denzin, 36–37
  Turner, 35–36
 sensory, 38–39
  Pink, 38
  Stoller, 39
Ewangelie, 86, 89, 93
exaltation, moments of, 15
exercises. *See also plastiques*
 breathing, 72, 118, 120, 137
 Kathakali, 21
 at the Laboratory Theatre, 68, 75, 106
 non-physicality of, 121
 non-verbal, 152, 154
 principles of, 75, 77, 98, 107
 types of, 95, 103, 108, 141, 150, 184
 vocal, 125–126, 133
 yoga-based, 106, 151
"Exit 30's, Enter 60's" (Schechner), 22
experiential
 approach to performance, 16, 31
 knowledge, 34, 35, 54, 163
 modes of cognition, 28, 127, 145
 perspective, of energetic centers, 72
 ways of learning, 50
expressivity, 61, 85, 136
 non-, 103
 pre-, 11, 105

extra-daily behavior. *See under* daily behavior

F
faith, 34, 167, 177, 212n1
  Jill Dolan on
    belief, hope, and love, 158
fascism, 9, 199, 203
Favel, Floyd
  ceremonies and relationship to ancestors, 42
  human and non-human sources of life, 206
  theatre, tradition, and ritual, connection between, 53, 113
  warrior ethic, 55
  on working with Mirecka and Grotowski, 39–43
fear
  addressed in Mirecka's teaching, 41
  and lack of meaning, 167
  linked to experience of fascism and totalitarianism, 9
  overcoming (during training), 11
  and proto-narrative, 19
feeling. *See also* emotion
  custvovat, 18
  in Damasio's theory, 20
  emotion, as distinct from, 20, 162–163
  of longing and loss, 82
  -mind and thinking body, not separated, 144
  perezhivanie, 18
feelings
  in Chekhov's psychological gesture, 63
  of the heart and logic of mind, connection between, 29
feminism, 158–160
  critique of Western—, 162
feminist critique, of Stanislavskian acting techniques, 16–17
Ferro, Maria Fernanda, 87, 92
Fiscus, Daniel A., 116–117
Flaszen, Ludwik, 9, 67, 178
  author's meetings with, 48–49
  research on voice, 127–128
  role of silence, 153
  role of the spectator, 62, 152
flux, 207
  of associations, 64, 143
  of impulses, 65–66, 120–123, 127
  theory of, Heraclitus's, 23

Fónagy, Ivan, 129
forest, 113–117, 120, 147, 167, 206
  of Brzezinka, 97, 102, 118, 153–156
freedom
  of the body, 122
  creative, 9, 72, 105, 150
  cultural and political, 186, 189–190
  and risk-taking, 191
  through relinquishing control, letting go, 11
Freire, Paulo, 37, 200–202

G
Gainor, Ellen, 16–17, 23
Galli, Francesco, 110, 112, 211n10
Gardecka, Stefania, 7, 51, 115, 181–182, 192
Gardecki, Piotr, 4
Garoute, Tiga, 194
gender
  normative behavior, 130, 158–161
  normative roles, 6, 17, 68
  politics, and Stanislavsky, 2
  privileging, 32, 47
  representations of, essentialist, 31
  sex and, conflation of, 162
  -specific training, 26
gendered
  behavior
    as codified performance, 158–160
    de/re-conditioning of, through training, 163
    as enculturated *habitus*, 163
    as semiotically constructed, 159
  constraints, 161
  identity, 159
  socialization process, 159
gestures
  action, as distinct from, 124–125
  daily, 64–65
  and external form, 70
  and impulses, 63, 65, 68, 71
  "psychological —", 63
  vocal ("*geste vocal*"), 129
gift
  of oneself, 24 (See also *don de soi*)
  sacrifice as, 73
  traditional knowledge as, 54
Girardon, Evelyne, 130
given circumstances
  linked to conventional social context, 64
  of a play, 60
  of a role, 22

Grimes, Ronald, 157, 169
  "The Theatre of Sources," 169
Grosz, Elizabeth, 158, 161
Grotowski, Jerzy. *See also* Collège de France lectures
  Abram and, 207–208
  academic constructions of, 3
  Active Culture, 157, 169, 183
  and artificiality, 61
  and associations, 63–65, 86
  and awareness, 53
  Brecht and, 199, 202–204
  and chakras (*See* and energetic centers)
  childhood, 86, 190, 205
  contradictory view on life, 78
  and creative agency, 10
  and creative resistance, 11
  Decroux and, 172
  don de soi, 24
  and embodiment, 34, 52, 67, 121–122
  and energetic centers, 72–73, 118
  Favel and, 39–43, 206
  and impulse-based actions, 58–60
  influence on contemporary performance, 26
  "invisible influence" of his work, 27
  legacy of, 3, 5, 26
  Master Class taught by, at U.C. Irvine, 2, 48
  Molik and, 178
  and the natural world, 153–156, 167
  and organicity, 61–64, 73
  and Polish political climate, 9, 186–188, 192, 198, 203
  post-theatrical work, 32, 42, 169, 170
  research on the body-voice connection, 120
  scholarly texts on, 26
  and silence, 152–153
  Stanislavsky and
    differences in work, 120
    Hinduism and yoga, influence of, 21
    lineage from, 3–4, 12–25, 61–63, 66–68, 159
    Method of Physical Actions, 12–14
  Theatre of Sources, 97, 153, 180–183, 192
  Vakhtangov and, 14, 63
  and voice, 132–138, 144
  works
    Akropolis, 50, 74, 83
    Apocalypsis cum figuris, 89–91, 169, 188–192, 196
    "Ce qui fut," 60
    The Constant Prince, 24, 26, 73, 185, 188
    "Holiday, The Day That is Holy," 8, 166
    "Performer," 53, 66–67, 103, 167–168
    "Réponse à Stanislavski," 7
    Towards a Poor Theatre, 15, 26
    "Tu es le fils de quelqu'un," 4, 9
Grotowski Institute, the, 50, 98, 110, 139
Grotowski Sourcebook, The (Schechner and Wolford), 4, 26, 167
Gurdjieff, G.I., 4

H
habitus, 130, 138, 159–160, 163
Haitian Voodoo, 205
Happy Days (Beckett), 86
harvest, 55–56, 96, 174, 205
Hastrup, Kirsten, 38
head
  and heart, 163, 171
  in research, 39, 78
  -resonator, 132, 135
healing
  Mirecka's teaching as, 41, 43
  properties of knowledge and research, 33, 55
  research process as, 54, 115
  vocal work as, 144
health, 41–42, 137, 160
  ecological, 116
  mental and physical, 114
healthy, being, 41–42. *See also* unhealthy, relationship to the body
heart
  and embodiment, 16
  and head, 163, 171
  logic of mind and the feelings of the, 29
  in research, 29–30, 38–39, 55, 210
  and second horizon, 27
  and *wu wei,* 137
heritage
  of colonialism, 43
  cultural
    of Ang, 139, 164
    of Arreola, 164

intellectual, 158, 161–162
Hinduism, 3, 20–21, 211n7
history
  of Christian religion, 166
  missionary, in Freire's and Boal's work, 201
  personal
    Ahrne's, 183
    Grotowski's and Brecht's, 203
    Polish, 9, 186–187
  theatre
    Brecht in, 199
    Grotowski in, 3, 199
    Stanislavsky in, 1, 199
    women in, 4–6
  violent, of Canadian residential schools, 201
holistic, 20, 116
  approach to acting, 1, 2, 21
  and "wholistic," 55–56
hope
  for the future, linked to well-being of the planet, 114
  Jill Dolan on faith, belief, —, and love, 158
  performance as site of struggle, negotiation, and, 36
  and utopian performatives, 158
human. *See also* non-human
  agency, 38, 202
  behavior, 12, 16
  beings, as partner-witnesses of nature, 116
  body, energetic centers in, 72, 118
  connection to nature, 40, 53, 61, 98, 146, 167
  creative potential, 9, 19, 22, 31
  dynamics of interactions, in research, 39
  experience, 9, 15, 161, 166
  Jill Dolan on being fully, 158
  reactions, 69, 74
  spirit, as burning flame, 91
  voice, 128, 134, 136, 207
hybridity
  artist-scholar, 35, 45, 52
  Benesz's perspective, 173
  Seyferth's approach, 58, 103
  theatrical and para-/post-theatrical, 171
hyperconsumerism, 201

I
identity, production of female, 161

ideology, 200
"I-I," the, 66–68
illustration
imitation
  and redundancy, in dilettantism, 11
  of the text by actors, 71
imagination
  body, and voice, balance between, 113
  desires, and personal experiences, in voice, 143
  the Body Alphabet and, 127
  Magic If and, 64
  precision and, for Albahaca, 89
imitation of power, for Mirecka, 77
immediacy, 23, 52, 101
impossible, the, 209
  Grotowski's propensity for, 6–8, 184, 189
  in Molik's teaching, 75, 135
  and the unknown, 75, 77
improvisation
  dance, 159
  and ethnographic process, 38
  and *études*, 89
  in final phase of Stanislavsky's work, 3
  and the *plastiques*, 70, 77–78
  vocal, 127, 129, 132, 137
  in the Wind Dance, 108
impulse(s), 58–61
  associations and, 68, 72, 83, 120, 126
  -based
    actions, 58
    performance process and women's embodied agency, 68
    process, privileged by Stanislavsky, 14
    process, Stanislavsky-Grotowski lineage, 59
  birth of, in Mirecka's work on the *plastiques,* 69
  gestures and, 64, 68, 71
  intention and, 59–60
  micro-level of, 58
  organicity and, 60–61, 65, 123
  plastiques and, 68, 69, 103
  singing and, 134
  as terminology, Stanislavsky-Grotowski lineage, 58–61
Indigenous
  critique of Augusto Boal and Paulo Freire, 200–202

epistomologies, 37, 55, 114, 206–207
ethics, instilled in the land, 55
knowledge
   ecological, 114–116
   embodied, 144–146, 163
   research methodologies, 3 R's of (respect, reciprocity, relationality), 29
   research principles, 29
     deep listening, 29
     fidelity to what has been learnt, 29
     logic of mind and feelings of the heart, connection between, 29
     non-judgmental consideration, 29
     ritual traditions, in connection with theatre, per Favel, 53
   sovereignty
     cultural, per Meyer, 145
     quest for, per Grande, 202
   spiritual practices, per Abram, 207
individualism, 128, 201
inheritor, legitimate, 27
inner life, 22, 59, 107
   the actor's, 14, 62
   Cieslak's, 73, 121
insider
   'authentic,' 27
   and outsider, simultaneously, 45
   -status, 27
inspiration, 11, 20, 62, 166
instrument
   body as
     in vocal work, 128
     finely tuned (in vocal work), 136
   of knowledge, 165
   sensitive, 80
interconnectedness, 55, 114, 116, 153
interconnections
   between
     body-in-life and natural environment, 116
     inner and outer, in vocal work, 136
     life, breath, sound, and soul or spirit, in vocal work, 128
     Mirecka and Seyferth, 98
     Molik and Mirecka, 123
   transmission of embodied knowledge via network of, 122
intercultural processes, in Favel's work with Mirecka, 40
interdisciplinarity, 25, 37, 44
interrelation
   of body and voice, 120
   of human and non-human life processes, 165, 206
   of impulses, associations, and organicity, 68
   of land and self, 145
   of performance, tradition, and ritual practice, 173
   of spontaneity and precision, in the *plastiques,* 103
intersubjectivity, 16, 30, 52, 161, 167
intuition
   and creativity, 30
   and cultural practices, 162
   Delsarte's, 69
   and physical impulses, 153
   and sensual maturity, 146, 160
   Stanislavsky's, 13, 15, 17–18
Ionesco, Eugène, 199–200
   L'Impromptu de l'Alma, 199

J
James, William, 19, 101
Janik, Karina, 174, 182
Jewish, 95, 186, 207
jo-ha-kyu, 11, 59, 136
journaling, creative, 52
journey
   life as a, 156
   research as, 54, 210
   into the unknown, 152, 167
   vocal process as, 143
   work process as, 177, 187
joy
   and the body, 122
   in early paratheatrical experiments, 91
   linked to freedom gained through training, 72
   and the work with associations, 86

K
Kaandossiwin: How We Come to Know (Absolon), 45, 54–55
Kartsaki, Eirini, 101–103
Kathakali, 21, 38, 138, 160
kinaesthetic, 52
kinetic, 36
Knebel, Maria, 1–4
knowledge
   dominant conceptions of, 30
   ecological, 114, 131
   embodied
     cultural processes, 38
     gained through doing, 28

Indigenous, 114–115, 146
legitimization of, in the academy, 37
in performance, 35, 50, 70, 118
in traditional cultural practices, 32
and traditional songs, 143–144
women's, 5, 160–165
experiential, 34, 35, 54
hegemonic economy of, 34
Indigenous, 53, 114
intergenerational, 201
"practiced," 54
search for, 45
self-, 68, 144, 159
traditional, 40, 43, 115, 144, 202, 205
women's, 30
Komorowska, Maja, 7, 26, 80–87
in *Apocalypsis cum figuris*, 188
body memory, 84–86
in *The Constant Prince*, 48, 85
on dreams, 80, 82
in *Endgame*, 86
in *Ewangelie*, 89
in *Extinction*, 80, 84, 86, 87
in *Happy Days*, 86
Laboratory Theatre, 57
motherhood, 83–84
Pejzaz, 80
photos, 51, 81
on shared space, 147
Kurten, Martin, 17–18, 102
"affective, active awareness," 18

L

Laboratory Theatre
Akropolis, 50, 74, 83
Apocalypsis cum figuris, 89–91, 169, 188–192, 196
birth and parenting at, 83–84
closing of, 79, 92
Constant Prince, The, 189
Ewangelie, 86, 93
members of, 7, 9, 25, 184
non-daily behavior in, 15
and paratheatrical activities, 97, 157, 169 (*See also* Active Culture)
Polish political climate and, 181, 187, 189, 192
spectators and, 24
Theatre of Thirteen Rows and, 57, 147, 186, 203
training
as benchmark in experimental performance practice, 26
specific to the company, 66–70, 75, 83, 92, 103, 124
vocal exercises in the, 133–134, 136
vocal exercises in, 133–134, 136
work ethic of, 7, 115
workspace of, 99, 184
lâcher-prise, 11
language
awareness as consciousness linked not to — but to presence, 67
body-, Molik's Body Alphabet, 125
Cherokee, 144
and "intellectual heritage," 161
Occitan, 130
resonators in different, 133
wooden (*See langue de bois*)
langue
-*de bois* (wooden language), 129
vs. parole, 130
Lassiter, Luke Eric, 30–33
Laster, Dominika, 182–183
left-wing
artists, 203–204
movement, in Venezuela, 87
legacy
Brecht's, 198
colonial, anthropology's, 36
Grotowski's, 164
tree metaphor of, 74, 123
women collaborators, 5, 26
Occitan cultural, 131
Stanislavsky's contested—, 1, 2, 15, 23
life
"normal," readjusting to, after para-theatrical work, 181
real-, 13
"the-", 126
sources of, human and non-human, 206
liminality, 157
limitations
overcoming one's perceived, 26–27, 70, 144, 160, 187
of psychological realism, 5–6, 12, 47
of research methodologies, 33
of the System, 15
L'Impromptu de l'Alma (Ionesco), 199
lineage
identity and, 32
Stanislavsky-Grotowski, 4–5, 12–25, 61, 66, 159
lived experience
creative agency and, 144

and disorientation, 38
embodied, 44, 83, 129
Kiowa people's, of the power of songs, 33
in research, 30–31, 161
and voice, 143
women's, 158
women's, of Grotowski's theatrical and paratheatrical research, 115
liveness (as attentive consciousness), 101
Lucca, Stéphane, 174, 182
Lupa, Krystian, 80, 84–86

M

Madison, Soyini, 16
magic (of theatre), 83, 199–200
Magic If, 64–65
Mann, Thomas, 189
Manthey, Elżbieta, 182–183, 196–198
mantras, 72, 137, 138
Marcello, Daniela, 174, 182–183
Marxist "atheistic philosophy," 1, 37, 200–202
Marxist-inflected emancipatory discourses, 37
   Environmentalist critique of, 201–202
   Indigenous critique of, 200–202
Mary Magdalene, 89–91, 197
masculine conception of the performer, 26
master
   -performer, 67, 112, 148
   -teacher, 43, 79, 146
mastery, per Grotowski, 10
materialist
   paradigm in the academy, 200
   "the Soviet regime's Marxist — expectations," 1
McRobbie, Angela, 8, 160
   Aftermath of Feminism, The, 8
mechanical
   movement, 66, 69, 125–126
   thought processes, 24
medicine wheel, 40, 42
meditation, 152, 180, 197
   and brain plasticity, 138
   and yoga, 20
meetings
   with the other, 11, 77, 137, 194
   with the unknown, 77, 126
Meetings with Remarkable Men (Brook), 4
mentors, 53–54, 92, 145–146, 163

Method, the, 16–18
method acting, 20, 22–23
Method of Physical Actions, the, 1, 2, 4, 13, 14
methodologies
   alternative research, 31
   conventional research, 30, 36, 40
   feminist research, 32
   Indigenous research, 32
   interdisciplinary, 25, 44
methodology, 201
   interdisciplinary, 25
Meyer, Manulani Aluli, 32–34, 43, 53–54, 144–146, 162, 163
Meyerhold, Vsevolod, 15, 19, 60
mind
   in Active Analysis, 1
   associating "man" with the, 165
   bypassing the rational and analytical, 22
   and embodiment, 16
   Freudian model of, 17
   logic of, and the feelings of the heart, 29
   questioning only with the, 28
   and the unknown, 136
mind-body dualism. *See* dualism
Mirecka, Rena, 7, 57, 68–79, 174
   and Benesz, 94
   and chakras, 120
   in *The Constant Prince,* 48
   and ecosystemic organicity, 118, 122
   in *Ewangelie,* 86
   and Favel, 39–43, 114
   photos, 51, 76, 119
   the *plastiques,* 84, 121, 124
   and Seyferth, 97–98, 104
   vocal work, 136–138
mistrust of the academy, by performance practitioners, 28
modernity, 34, 202
Mohanty, J. N., 44
Molik, Zygmunt, 48
   and Albahaca, 90–91
   Body Alphabet, 84, 124–127
   plastique exercises, influence of, 124
montage, 37, 61
   effect, 87, 174
   textual, 127, 189
moral responsibility, of researchers to the community, 31
Moscow Art Theatre, 3, 12, 14–15
mother
   Absolon's, 45

Ahrne's, 183
Grotowski's, 86
Komorowska as, 84
Komorowska's, 82–83
Rasmussen's, 110
-tongue (author's), 45, 130
Mother Courage (Brecht), 199
Motions, the, 102, 155, 193
Mountain Project, the, 97, 178–179, 196–197
multi-sited fieldwork, 11, 25, 30
music
  and energy, 137
  in Mirecka's teaching, 137
  vocal, 129
mutual
  appropriation, per Chilisa, 54, 5631
  communication, per Mohanty, 44, 54
mutually beneficial
  dissemination strategies, 54
  documentation, 52
  relationships, between artists and scholars, 35, 52
  research, for ethnographers and community, 31
mystery, 65, 136, 190, 207–209

N
narratives (academically-positioned), 31
nationalism, 186
natural
  Grotowski's use of the term 'organic' instead of the term, 13
nature
  meditation in, 138
  meeting with, 197
  organicity and, 61, 73, 120, 126
  psychophysical connection to, 40, 116
  relationship to, in Benesz's teaching, 94, 174
  relationship to, in Mirecka's teaching, 118–120
  relationship to, in paratheatre, 98, 102, 177–178, 204
  spiritual connection to, 53, 96, 205
  "woman," association with, 165
Nazism, 203
neoliberalism, 53, 201
neuroscience, 17–19
New Age, 41
Nicholson, Helen, 200
Noh, 11, 38, 138
non
  -doing, 99, 103, 137
  -human life, 53, 118, 146, 156, 167, 206
  -human movement, 120
  -human partners, connection to, 40
  -verbal, 65, 73, 127, 129, 179
normative
  communitas, 157
  gender roles, 6, 68, 161, 163, 173
  vocal behavior, 130
norms, 44
  gender, 163
  social, 7, 209

O
Objective Drama Project, 2, 23, 102, 181, 206
Occitan, 130–131
Odin Teatret, 105–107, 132–133
Open Theatre, 5–6
Opole, Poland, 57, 80, 147
Oppressed
  Freire's pedagogy of the, 200–202
oppression
  gendered, 163
  Soviet, 3
oppressive political regime
  Communist, 7
  Czech, 7
organicity, 61–63, 204, 206
  alternative conception of, 117
  artificiality and, 61, 120
  associations and, 64, 68, 120
  of the body-in-life, 152
  child and, 61
  definition of, 61
  ecosystemic, 116–118
  energetic centers and, 73
  impulse-based process and, 61
  as terminology, Stanislavsky-Grotowski lineage, 61–63
  in training, 118, 123, 135
organic process, 17, 120, 123, 127
  associations and, 63–65, 83, 127
  natural, linked to the ecology of the body-in-life, 53, 116, 118
Ornellas, Robert, 47–48, 182–183
Osinski, Zbigniew, 48
Other, the
  in ethnographic representations, 30
Others
  disenfranchised
    women as, 116

Oyewùmi, Oyèronké, 162, 165

P

Paper Canoe, The (Barba), 11, 38, 136, 159, 162
parareligious, 157
paratheatre, 169, 177–181
　and Active Culture, 169
　Benesz's divergence from, 94
　Dowlasz and, 196
　experiments in, 15, 42, 91
　Holiday: the day that is holy, 170
　influence of North American Indigenous traditions on, 40
　Manthey and, 197
　Molik and, 177–178
　Mountain of Fire, the, 193
　Seyferth and, 102–103
　theatre and, 91, 102–103
　　differences between, 193
　　transition between, 91, 170, 192
　and Theatre of Sources, 169–170, 180–181, 193, 204
　Tree of People, the, 170, 193
　The Vigils, 179
　vocal work in, 136
parole, 129–130
participatory
　theatre
　　based on Boal's Theatre of the Oppressed, 37
participatory
　non-hierarchical, and inclusive model
　　The Bridge of Winds as, 112
　paratheatrical activities, 157, 170, 179
　practice, ethnography as, 39
　research experiments, 32
patriarchal
　class-based
　　and colonialist social order (France), 203
　dimension of Stanislavsky's legacy critiqued by feminists, 3
Pearson, Lester B., 44, 211n8
Pearson College, 43, 44, 46, 130
pedagogy
　Freire's, 37, 200, 202
　Indigenous, 53, 115, 200, 206
　of place, 147
pelvis, in physical and vocal training, 11, 75, 84, 125, 135
perezhivanie, 17–18, 101–102. See conscious experience

performance
　ecological understanding of, 116
　ethnography, 36–40
　experiential approach to, 16, 31
　experts, 25, 28
　models, conventional, 116
　processes
　　embodiment in, 122, 206
　　and ethnography, 38
　　Grotowski's investigation of, 57, 61, 99, 120, 153
　　Mirecka's embodied knowledge of, 118
　　Mirecka's investigation of, 40
　　ritual —, investigation of, 32
　　Stanislavsky's insights into, 16–17, 19, 58
　as research, 28
　studies, 28, 35
　"— turn," the, in the humanities and social sciences, 35
performative
　action, 9
　critical pedagogy, 200
　dimensions of
　　cultural processes, embodied and, 35
　ethnography, 36
　process, of the "I-I," 66
　vs. discursive systems, 35
"Performer" (Grotowski), 53, 66–67, 103, 167–168
phenomenology, 35, 44, 159
physical actions
　Stanislavsky's choice to focus on, 13
physicality, 1, 121, 133
　codified, 160
　"non-", 121
　non-realistic, 84
physical score, 52, 59, 61, 157
　Cieslak's extremely precise in *The Constant Prince,* 73
Pilatova, Jana, 184–192
　photo, 182
pilgrimage, and Active Culture, 157
Pink, Sarah, 38–39, 50
place
　body and, 146
　epistemologies grounded in, 34
　identity and, 32–33, 115
　pedagogy of, 143–148
　relationship to, 33, 94, 102
　workspace as special—, 104

plastique exercises, the, 78, 121–122
  author's experience of, 78
  development of, by Mirecka, 68–69
  Mirecka and, 70–71, 74–75, 77
  Molik and, 124–127
  Seyferth and, 97, 102–103
"Poetry, Remnants and Ruins: Aboriginal Theatre in Canada," 53
Poland
  Catholic, context of, 91
  Communist, 114, 198, 203–204
  Grotowski's childhood in, 9
  Laboratory of Creative Research in, 155
  Laboratory Theatre in, 7, 186 (*see also* Brzezinka)
  Meetings with Remarkable Women in, 80, 97
  Mountain Project in, 178
  Solidarność movement in, 181
  Theatre of Sources in, 180
  uprising in (1968), 158, 185
politics
  creative agency and, 169
  gender, 2, 163
  Polish, 7, 114, 186, 198
  post-theatrical period and, 198–200
  race, 145
  of representation, in ethnography, 30–31
  of Stalinist Russia, 1–2, 7
pontifex, performer as —, or maker of bridges, 103
Poor Theatre, 47, 101, 169. See also *Towards a Poor Theatre*
  features of, 191
  and *via negativa,* 10
Porete, Marguerite, 168
positionality, in research process, 30
  author's —, 43–49
post-colonialism, 25, 36–37
post-theatrical experiments, 116, 183, 203
  in body-voice connection, 120
  in Brzezinka, 57
post-theatrical period
  capacity for belief in, 62
  search for balance in, 150
  voice work during, 127–128, 134
post-theatrical research
  Active Culture as, 169
  crossing and blurring the boundaries delineating theatrical and, 5, 97

lack of knowledge of, because rarely documented, 26
  reconnecting with one's cultural ancestry as key to, 32
potential
  categorizations that limit the human creative, 31
  human creative
    Grotowski's investigation of, 9
  of performance, 37, 177
  in performance space, 162
  Stanislavsky's insights into, 19, 22
  vocal, exploration of, 132
potentialities
  associations and, 65
  fulfilling all of our, 118
potentiality and dialogic space of performance, 162
power of performance, reclaiming the, 68
practice, 9, 75, 166
  artistic, 18, 28, 121, 166, 203
  -based research, 18, 28–31, 35, 37, 117, 127
    on the body-in-life, 117
    on Non-Western performance, 37
    on voice, 127
  creative, function of, 166
  cultural, 15, 32, 53–54, 162, 206
  embodied, 39, 132, 146, 158
  performance-, 121
    body-voice connection and, 120, 136, 160
    experimental, 164
    Grotowski's approach to, 5, 30, 202
    Stanislavsky's approach to, 12, 20
    women's approaches to, 53, 158, 163
  as research in performance, 28
  ritual—, 40, 72, 148, 165, 205
  singing as, 129
  Stanislavsky's conception of, influence of yoga on, 21
practice/theory divide, in the academy, 29
prana, 73, 120, 123, 207
praxis, creative and critical, 35
precarious equilibrium
  as alteration of balance in performance training, 37–38, 138
  as ecological balance between all forms of life, 113–114, 206
  as positionality of the artist-scholar, 45

precision
　Cieslak's, 121
　and freedom, 191
　and silence, 150–152
　of the structure of traditional songs, 144
　technical, of the *plastiques,* 71, 75, 78, 103
　of the Wind Dance, 108
pre-expressivity. *See under* expressivity
pregnancy, 112, 183
　Albahaca's, 90
　Komorowska's, 83
　Manthey's, 197
presence
　as being double, in parable of the "I-I," 67
　as the capacity of being in the moment, 78
　as the interaction between receptive action and active receptivity, 66
　of the performer, as embodied awareness, 67
　and voice, 129
Présences en Regards, 47–48, 90, 104
procession as performance process, 131, 138, 176
processual dimension of performance, 16
propre, 42, 113
protests, in Poland, 185–186, 192, 198
psychological
　gesture, 63
　realism, 13
　　conventions of, 5–6, 203
　　Grotowski and, 64–65
　　limitations of, 47, 59
　　opposition to, 60
　　Stanislavsky and, 1, 3, 14, 61
psychophysical
　connection to nature, 116
　connection to partners, 40
　experimentation with yoga, 3
　fulfillment, through training, 113
　process
　　embodied knowledge in, 38, 158
　　performance as, 22
　　range, in the technique of Active Analysis, 1
　"Putting the Whole Back Together" (Viola), 165–168

Q

qualitative inquiry, 36

Quoniam, Bertrand, 47
quotidian
　behavior, 104
　extra-, 60
　gestures, 63, 65
　reality, 181

R

race
　class, and culture, 45
　critical
　　theory, 36
　　politics, 145
Rasmussen, Iben Nagel, 7, 57–58, 104–112
　and The Bridge of Winds, 105, 108
　Meetings with Remarkable Women, 110
　Odin Teatret, 106–108, 112
　photos, 109, 111
　and vocal training, 132–133
rational
　experience, 205
　thought, 20, 22
reaction, 13, 71, 74, 189
　impulse and, 153, 185
　physical, 69
　spectators', 172, 187, 200
realist
　art
　　conventional constructions in, 204
　theatre, 6, 12, 62, 200
receptivity, 66, 67
reciprocity, and research, 25, 29, 31, 54, 202
"Reconsidering Stanislavsky: Feeling, Feminism, and the Actor" (Blair), 17
reflexive, positionality within research process, 43
relationality
　as balancing process, 146
　empathetic form of, 33
　material or organic, 146
　as principle of Indigenous research, 29, 55, 116, 206
relevance, of research to community, 31
re-living, 18, 22, 65–66
"Réponse à Stanislavski" (Grotowski), 7
research
　cross-cultural, 37, 44–45
　by Grotowski, 4, 26
　paradigms, dominant academic, 28
　process

defined as "sensual scholarship" by Stoller, 39
as defined by Meyer and Absolon, 54
embodied, 39–40, 43, 209
positioning oneself within, 33
relational, 54
topic, researcher's relationship to, 33
researcher
as ethical warrior, 56
as hunter, cook, and care-giver, 55
resistance
the body's, 66, 70, 121
creative practice as, 9, 11, 36, 209
critical sites of, for Indigenous people, 115
political, 203
conventional means of, 198
resulting from opposing tensions within the body, 11, 45
in vocal training, 127, 135–136
resonators. *See* vocal resonators
resources
human, energetic centers *as if* the roots of, 73
natural, 166
personal
internal, 107, 189, 209
responsibility
of artists as social actors, 10
of researchers, 30, 31, 54, 55
restoration of behavior, per Schechner, 160
restored behavior, 24
revolution
-ary theorists, 202
industrial, the, 201
"rehearsal of" (per Boal), 200
rhythm
and chanting, 138, 145
in group work, 95
and *prana*, 73
in the Wind Dance, 108
Ricard, Mathieu, 137, 138
Richards, Thomas, 60, 63, 123
rigor
Grotowski's demand for, 26–28, 89
in Mirecka's teaching, 79
need for, in creative work, 104
of the *plastiques,* 78
and silence, 152
and spirit, 34
rigorous training of gendered socialization (relying on repetition), 160

risk
and artistic freedom, 191
and pleasure, in Damasio's theory, 19
in the training, 106, 185
ritual, 94, 134, 157. *See also under* practice
actions, 52, 96
arts, in Active Culture and Art as vehicle, 157, 170–171
chants, in Afro-Caribbean traditions, 134
cultural, traditional, and — practices, 165
dimension of material practices, 94
performance processes, 32, 53, 145
practice, 173, 176, 188, 205
practices
Hawaiian, 145
traditional, of Indigenous communities in northern Mexico, 145
process, of pilgrimage, 157
space, 174
theatre and, 53, 91, 166
traditions, 53, 186, 205
ritualized
action, in group work, 79, 174
aspect of Mirecka's work, 118
Robart, Maud, 148, 194, 212n3
Rodzinska-Nair, Justyna, 50
ruach, 207

S
sacred
and blasphemous
in *The Constant Prince,* 188
chants, 145
Dziady
relevance in Poland, 186
life as, 73
relationship as, 147
research as, 33
and "*parole,*" 129
space
in the post-theatrical period, 147
in theatre, 53
sacrifice, 24, 62, 73, 79
Saint Soleil, 194, 205
Sanskrit, 120
Saussure, Ferdinand, 129
Schechner, Richard
"Exit 30's, Enter 60's," 22
Grotowski Sourcebook, The, 4, 26, 167
Between Theater and Anthropology, 24

scientific objectivity, 25, 36, 145
scriptocentrism, 34
seasonal, cycles of nature, 94, 174, 205
second horizon, 120, 172–173
self-determination, 105, 201–202
senses
    awakening of, through silence, 153
    knowledge shaped by, 146, 162
    privileging sight over other, in Western culture, 162, 165
    sharpening, in Ang's teaching, 143
sensory
    ethnography, 39
    rapport, experience grounded in, 146
sensuous
    cosmos, 207
    scholarship, 39
Seyferth, Katharina, 7, 57–58, 97–104
    and Gertrude Stein, 101–102
    Meetings with Remarkable Women, 97
    and Mirecka, 97–98
    the Mountain Project, 179
    and organicity, 98
    and paratheatre, 103, 156, 178, 204
    photos, 100, 179
    and the *plastiques*, 121–122
    and ritual practice, 205
    Rooms, 99
    Theatre of Sources, 180–181, 205
shaman, 41
    -ism, 40
shared space, 147, 188
Sheets-Johnstone, Maxine, 159
silence
    "forested"
        of Brzezinka, 153
    in the training and creative work, 121–122, 125, 150–153, 176, 179–180, 194, 199
    in the workspace, 104
silent
    the mind must be, but also present, in the training, 71
    presence, of the second "I" in the "I-I," 67
    witnesses, 15
simplicity, 65, 97, 102, 137, 157
singing, 132–138
    collective, 129
    and creative agency, 128
    and cultural continuity of, for Kiowa people, 31

and experiential cognition, 127
and impulses, 134
to speaking, passage from, 127, 136
Slowiak, James, 150, 169
Smith, Linda Tuhiwai, 114, 206
social sciences, 25, 35–38, 200
solidarity, 33, 187, 208
solitude
    Brzezinka as place of, 153
    what human beings can do with their own (in the Theatre of Sources), 170
somatophobia, 35, 159
song, 127
    spirit as the deepest encounter with (for Kiowa people), 33
    traditional, 31–32, 93, 95, 130–131, 143–144, 146–147, 172
        Greek/Mediterranean, 96, 171
        Greek Orthodox, 171
        Haitian, 194
        Hokkien, 141
        Indian, 180
        Kiowa, 31
        Occitan, 130–131
        Russian Orthodox, 171
        Scandinavian, 133
    vibratory, 123, 134
soul, 2
    and body, bond between, 66
    mind/body/—division, 162
    and voice, 128
sound, 122, 128, 135–137, 145
    ancestral relationship to, 129
source(s)
    of embodied knowledge, 32, 35, 144
    of life, 7, 75, 79, 167, 210
        human and non-human, 206
    of physical actions, 60
    of the sacred, 129
    of vocal vibration, 125
sovereignty
    cultural, 145
    Indigenous, 202
    over one's work, 105
Soviet, 1, 9, 186
    oppression, 3
    totalitarianism, 198
space
    balancing the, 148
    sacred, 53
    taking care of the, 148
    working together to defend and save the, 150

spectator(s)
  participation of
    in Brecht's theatre (according to Ionesco), 200
  positionality of
    in relation to the notion of *don de soi*, 24, 62
  reception of Albahaca's Mary Magdalene by Polish, 91
  as witnesses, 15, 62, 116, 152, 187
spine
  engagement of, 123, 135
  impulses in, 64, 69, 84
  movement of, 11, 75, 103
  as snake, 69, 120
spirit
  -mind, and heart
    included in "wholistic" ways of knowing, 55
  and Active Analysis, 1
  body and, privileging of mind over (in Enlightenment project), 34
  category of
    as distinct from religion (for Hawaiian elders), 34
  and creative agency, 128
  importance of, in research, 33
  and intelligence, 34
spirituality, 143–148
  accessibility of, to all, 168, 198
  and Active Culture, 157
  and connection to nature, 53
  cultural legacy and, 131
  embodiment and, 32, 143, 148
  as a form of false consciousness in academic perspectives, 32
  importance of (for Grotowski's collaborators), 32, 34, 53, 206
  inclusivity of, in Indigenous theoretical frameworks, 32
  Indigenous perspectives on, 114, 145, 147
  Marxist view of, 202
  as means of resistance, 9
  non-religious, 198
  pedagogy of place and, 143–148
spontaneity, 16, 71, 80
  and organicity, 121
  in the *plastiques*, 122
  and precision, 103, 191
  and voice, 129
Spychalski, Teo, 102
stagiaire, 184–185, 188
  definition of, 89

Stanislavsky-Grotowski lineage, the, 4, 12–25, 58–68, 159
  associations in, 63–65
  impulses in, 58–61
  organicity in, 61–63
  physical and spiritual lines in, 66
Stanislavsky in Rehearsal (Toporkov), 2, 23, 64
State, the, 187
Stawinski, Maciej, 79
Stein, Gertrude
  approach to writing, 101–102
  minimalism of, 101
  Tender Buttons: Objects, Food, Rooms, 97
stereotypes, 5–6, 205
stereotypical, 69, 77
Stoller, Paul, 39, 50
stomach, 106, 133, 146, 163
structure
  and artificiality, 120
  bone
    and resonators, 133
  brain
    and meditation, 138
  "hidden — of signs," 15
  "— of rigor," in research, linked to "spirit," 34
  and organicity, as part of actor's process, 62
  of songs, and vibratory quality, 144
  and spontaneity, 121
stylization
  and gendered codification of behavior, 159, 160
  Meyerhold's focus on, 63
stylized
  femininity, 160
  performance traditions, 38, 138, 159
  stage set, in *Akropolis*, 83
suspension of disbelief, 62
System, the, 12, 21, 58
system academics, dominant, 29

T
Tairov, Alexander, 14
Taliani, Celeste, 80, 97, 183
Taylor, Diana, 35
teaching, 53, 68, 117, 120, 152, 163
  Ang's, 139, 141, 143
  Arreola's, 151
  Benesz's, 94–95, 174
  Ciechowicz-Chwastniewska's, 195
  Cieslak's, 70

freedom, Grotowski, 191
gendered behavior, 160
of literacy, Freire, 201
Mirecka's
  balance, search for in, 114, 135
  Eastern philosophies in, 72, 95
  Favel's perspective on, 40
  music in, 137
  organicity in, 98, 118
  "sacrifice" in, 73
Molik's, 48, 78, 123, 126, 128
Rasmussen's, 106–110, 132–133
Seyferth's, 97–98, 102–104, 206
Stanislavsky's, 60, 159
technique
  "affective memory," 17
  archaic, 205
  body-voice integration, 127
  "contradiction," 15
  disorientation, 37
  improvisational, 3
  observation, concentration, and communication, 20
  relaxation, from yoga, 20
  Stanislavskian-derived performance, 16
  stream-of-consciousness, 52
  surrealist montage, 37
  therapeutic, 17
  traditional, 170–171
  value of, 41–42
  vocal, Hawaiian, 145
Tender Buttons: Objects, Food, Rooms (Stein), 97
text
  -based theatre, 37, 47
  in classical theatre, per Mirecka, 71
  organic process informing the, 127, 141
  world-as- (in ethnography), 34
textocentrism, 34
theatre
  conventional, 71
  conventional forms of practice
    alternatives to, 68
    Laboratory Theatre as distinguished from, 181, 187
  Theatre of Sources, 15, 134, 194, 205
    chronology of, 169–170
    nature and, 204, 206
    paratheatre and, 180–181, 193–194, 204
  Theatre of Thirteen Rows, 57, 147, 186, 203
    Komorowska in, 80

theory
  bioenergetic, of voice, 129
  Damasio's, of mind-body dualism, 19
  feminist, 31
  performance, 12, 16, 67
  and practice, division between, 29, 45, 210
  proto-narrative, 19
  psychoanalytic, 17
  race, 36
"The Theatre of Sources" (Grimes), 169
thinking
  in concepts, 38, 159
  in motion, 38, 159, 162
"Throwing Like a Girl" (Young), 159–161
Toporkov, Vasili, 2, 4, 14, 23, 58, 64
"total act," the, 73
totalitarianism, 9, 198–199, 203
Towards a Poor Theatre (Grotowski), 15, 26
tradition
  non-Western, 15, 43
  oral, 18, 26, 35, 131, 162
  performance, 146
    Asian, 67
    male-oriented, 116, 209
    non-Western, 37–38
    ritual, and, 173, 176
    world, 9, 139, 210
  theatre and, performance as point of convergence between, 113
  Western, 166
trans-generational modes of transmission, 123, 141, 145, 162
transmission processes, 122–125
  of body-voice training, influence of the *plastiques* on, 124, 127
  different modes of, after Grotowski's death, 93
  of embodied knowledge, 5, 50
  in the Grotowski diaspora, 25, 58, 68, 152
  of non-academic research, 206
  oral, 145
  patrilineal, 1, 4
  Seyferth on, 58
  of traditional knowledge, performance as vital to, 115
  of traditional songs, 147
  trans-generational, 141
  of vocal training, 123

transnational
  community of artists, 5, 58, 112, 115, 122, 164
  homogeneity, 9
travel
  Grotowski's to India, 21
  as part of the research process, per Absolon, 55, 210
Tree of People, the, 170, 178, 193, 197
"Tu es le fils de quelqu'un" (Grotowski), 4, 9
Turner, Victor, 16, 35, 157

U
unhealthy, relationship to the body, 160
United World College, 43, 112
universality, Indigenous concept of, per Meyer, 145
unknown, the
  exploring, in creative work, 75–79, 98, 104
  nature in the performer's encounter with, 126
  overcoming the fear of, 11
  silence and, 152
  voice and, 128
urgency, 23
utopian performatives, 158

V
Vakhtangov, Yevgeny, 14, 63
via negativa, 10, 166
via positiva, 166
vibratory quality
  of the human voice (*See* vocal vibration)
  of musical instruments, 135–136
Vigils, The, 179–180, 193, 196–197
Viola, Bill, 165–169, 198
  "Putting the Whole Back Together," 165–168
vocalization, 125, 129
vocalizing, 125, 131
vocal
  resonators, 106, 132–135
  vibration
    body-in-life as source of, 125, 136
    kuolo, Hawaiian term for, 145
    and physical action, 122
    and the Voice-Vehicle, 128
    volume as distinct from, 135
    and *wu wei*, 137

voice. *See also* body-voice connection; vocal resonators; vocal vibration
  bioenergetic approach to, 132
  as earliest mode of expression in infancy, 129
  and energetic balance, 113
  as extension of movement, 120
  and the flux of associations, 143
  as metaphor for human relations, 129
  and normative gender behavior, 130
  as vehicle, 128
  vibratory qualities of, 52, 123, 127
  women's, Rasmussen's work with, 134
  working with, in the training, 133, 143

W
Weigel, Helene, 199
well-being, 97, 113, 141
Wethal, Torgeir, 106–107, 133
white privilege, 29
"wholistic," 55, 56
Wilson, Shawn, 29, 147, 206
Wind Dance, the, 108–110, 137
wisdom, 12, 163, 201
  "the place of", 146
witness
  bearing, 62, 116
  don de soi, 62
  partner, nature as, 116
  and performer, 103
  spectator as, 15, 62, 116, 152, 187
witnesses
  human beings as partner-, of nature, 116
working-class, 43
"work on oneself," the, 14, 22, 50, 67–68, 136–138
workspace
  awareness of, 77
  relationship to, in the creative process, 136
  special treatment of, 104, 147
world
  performance traditions, 43
  -sense, 162
Wroclaw
  Beehives in, 197
  Laboratory Theatre in, 50
  Meetings with Remarkable Women in, 97, 139
  performances in public spaces in, 94
  protests in, 185

wu wei, as non-doing, 99, 137

Y

Year of Grotowski, 48, 50
   keynote address by Peter Brook (in Paris), 26
   talks by the author (in Krakow and Paris), 48–49
yoga
   -based exercises, 80, 106, 151
   Benesz's work with, 40, 74
   Grotowski's work with, 21
   Mirecka's work with, 40, 74
   Stanislavsky's work with, 3
Young, Iris, 159–161
   "Throwing Like a Girl," 159–161

Z

Zakrzewski, Maciej, 139
Zeami, Motokiyo, 11